EXPLORING AUTISTIC SEXUALITIES, RELATIONALITY, AND GENDERS

This edited collection of contributions explores non-normative genders, sexualities, and relationality among Autistic people.

Written within an explicitly neuro-affirmative frame, the collection celebrates the diversity and richness of Autistic identity, sexuality, gender, and relationships, exploring areas such as consent, embodiment, ink, kink, sex education, and therapeutic work. All editors and contributors are neurodivergent and members of the communities that the book focuses on, providing an authentic and unique exploration of gender, sexuality, and relationality in Autistic people *by* Autistic/other neurodivergent authors.

The book is primarily intended for postgraduate students and academics across disciplines including sociology, social work, psychology, disability studies, inclusive and special education, and sexual education. Mental health professionals and educators will also find it a useful resource to support their Autistic clients as well as developing their own understanding about how to support Autistic people in a neurodiversity-affirming, kink-affirming, LGBTQ+, and gender-variant way.

Hanna Bertilsdotter Rosqvist is a sociologist and a Professor in Social Work at Södertörn University, Sweden. Her research focuses on research methods and theory development within Neurodiversity Studies. She has published several papers on the theme of gender and sexuality, among Autistic people as well as among non-autistic people. She has edited several books, among them *Neurodiversity Studies: A New Critical Paradigm* (edited by Hanna Bertilsdotter Rosqvist, Nick Chown, and Anna Stenning, 2020).

Anna Day is a neurodivergent principal clinical psychologist and parent to an Autistic young person. Anna has extensive clinical experience in the United

Kingdom's National Health Service (NHS) in a community mental health team and specialist psychological therapies service, and now works for The Adult Autism Practice, Dublin, within a neuro-affirmative approach with adults seeking Autism identification. They have a particular interest in gender, sex, and relationship diversity issues and neuroqueering. Anna and colleagues have published the successful *Adult Autism Assessment Handbook: A Neurodiversity Affirming Approach* (2021) and are working on *The Neurodiversity Affirmative Child Autism Assessment Handbook*.

Meaghan Krazinski is a neurodivergent PhD candidate in Inclusive Special Education at Syracuse University, United States. Her research interests include neurodiversity; neurodivergent college student experiences; inclusive education; Autistic identity, gender, and relationality; and arts-based research methods. She has published work on Autistic understandings of gender, race, and identity in *Hypatia: A Journal of Feminist Philosophy,* and an analysis of Disabled students' experiences with online learning using a queer phenomenological method, as well as a forthcoming co-authored work on neuroqueering, education, and culturally sustaining practices.

ROUTLEDGE RESEARCH IN GENDER AND SOCIETY

For more information about this series, please visit: https://www.routledge.com/Routledge-Research-in-Gender-and-Society/book-series/SE0271

EXPLORING AUTISTIC SEXUALITIES, RELATIONALITY, AND GENDERS

Living Under a Double Rainbow

*Edited by Hanna Bertilsdotter Rosqvist,
Anna Day, and Meaghan Krazinski*

Routledge
Taylor & Francis Group

LONDON AND NEW YORK

Designed cover image: Meaghan Krazinski

First published 2025
by Routledge
4 Park Square, Milton Park, Abingdon, Oxon OX14 4RN

and by Routledge
605 Third Avenue, New York, NY 10158

Routledge is an imprint of the Taylor & Francis Group, an informa business

© 2025 selection and editorial matter, Hanna Bertilsdotter Rosqvist, Anna Day, and Meaghan Krazinski; individual chapters, the contributors

The right of Hanna Bertilsdotter Rosqvist, Anna Day, and Meaghan Krazinski to be identified as the authors of the editorial material, and of the authors for their individual chapters, has been asserted in accordance with sections 77 and 78 of the Copyright, Designs and Patents Act 1988.

British Library Cataloguing-in-Publication Data
A catalogue record for this book is available from the British Library

Library of Congress Cataloging-in-Publication Data
Names: Bertilsdotter Rosqvist, Hanna, 1976- editor. | Day, Anna, editor. | Krazinski, Meaghan, editor.
Title: Exploring autistic sexualities, relationality, and genders : living under a double rainbow / edited by Hanna Bertilsdotter Rosqvist, Anna Day, Meaghan Krazinski.
Description: Abingdon, Oxon ; New York, NY : Routledge, 2025. | Series: Routledge research in gender and society | Includes bibliographical references and index.
Identifiers: LCCN 2024025436 (print) | LCCN 2024025437 (ebook) | ISBN 9781032576121 (hardback) | ISBN 9781032576114 (paperback) | ISBN 9781003440154 (ebook)
Subjects: LCSH: Autistic sexual minorities.
Classification: LCC HV1570.25.S49 .E97 2025 (print) | LCC HV1570.25.S49 (ebook) | DDC 616.85/882--dc23/eng/20240625
LC record available at https://lccn.loc.gov/2024025436
LC ebook record available at https://lccn.loc.gov/2024025437

ISBN: 978-1-032-57612-1 (hbk)
ISBN: 978-1-032-57611-4 (pbk)
ISBN: 978-1-003-44015-4 (ebk)

DOI: 10.4324/9781003440154

Typeset in Sabon
by Taylor & Francis Books

CONTENTS

Conclusion   211

ILLUSTRATIONS

Figure

Tables

CONTRIBUTORS

Editors

Hanna Bertilsdotter Rosqvist is a sociologist and a Professor in Social Work at Södertörn University, Sweden. Her research focuses on research methods and theory development within Neurodiversity Studies. She has published several papers on the theme of gender and sexuality, among Autistic people as well as among non-autistic people. She has edited several books, among them *Neurodiversity Studies: A New Critical Paradigm* (edited by Hanna Bertilsdotter Rosqvist, Nick Chown, and Anna Stenning, 2020).

Anna Day (she/they) is a neurodivergent principal clinical psychologist registered with the UK Health and Care Professionals Council and a parent to an Autistic young person. They have a BSc (Hons) Psychology from Royal Holloway, University of London, PhD Psychology, and Postgraduate Certificate in Teaching and Learning in Higher Education from Keele University. They were a lecturer in social and developmental psychology, then a postdoctoral research fellow prior to returning to Royal Holloway, University of London to complete their DClinPsy training. Anna has extensive clinical experience as a clinical psychologist in the UK's National Health Service in a community mental health team and specialist psychological therapies service and has contributed to shortlisting of DClinPsy applicants for a UK training course for several years. They worked with a neurodevelopmental service for several years cofacilitating postassessment groups for newly identified Autistic adults. They now work as principal clinical psychologist for The Adult Autism Practice, Dublin, working within a neuro-affirmative approach with adults seeking autism identification. They have a particular interest in gender, sex, and relationship diversity issues and neuroqueering. Anna has been an expert member on a Health Research

Authority Research Ethics Committee. Anna and colleagues have published the successful *Adult Autism Assessment Handbook: A Neurodiversity Affirming Approach* (Jessica Kingsley Publishers) and are working on *The Neurodiversity Affirmative Child Autism Assessment Handbook* (Jessica Kingsley Publishers).

Meaghan Krazinski is a neurodivergent PhD candidate in Inclusive Special Education at Syracuse University, United States, where she is completing a certificate of advanced study in women's and gender studies, which informs her work. She holds a Master of Science in special education and a certificate of advanced studies in disability studies. Her research interests include neurodiversity; neurodivergent college student experiences; inclusive education; autistic identity, gender, and relationality; and arts-based research methods. She has presented and published on the topics of neurodivergence and gender, and inclusive education. She has published a review on the book *Sincerely, Your Autistic Child* by Onaiwu et al. (2021), *Disability Studies Quarterly Community Blog*, 2022. She has contributed to the edited collection *Inclusive Pedagogical Practices Amidst a Global Pandemic: Perspectives from Around the Globe*, edited by Lawrence Meda and Jonathan Chitiyo (Springer, 2022). Her forthcoming work, *Classrooms as Healing Spaces*, which investigates the relationships between healing, trauma, and disability labels, is in press with the *Journal of Trauma Studies in Education*. She also has an autoethnographic work on Autistic understandings of gender, race, and identity to be published in *Hypatia: A Journal of Feminist Philosophy*.

Contributors

Mayne Benedetto (Chapter 5) serves as the president of the advisory board at the Portuguese Associação Portuguesa Voz do Autista (APVA) and is currently pursuing a doctorate in medical anthropology at the Institute of Social Sciences (ICS), University of Lisbon. Her doctoral thesis, a collaborative autoethnography, explores the implications of how historical constructs surrounding whiteness and normality impact the experiences of autistic individuals. The overarching aim of her research is to contribute to a more substantive and realistic understanding of autism, ultimately leading to improved support and accommodations beyond the pathology paradigm.

Helene Delilah (Chapter 8) identifies herself as neuroqueer, diagnosed with both autism and AD(H)D, and is passionately interested in sexuality education specifically aimed toward neurodivergence, kink, BDSM and fetishism. She is cowriter (with M. Flodman) of the book *Stora sexboken, för tjejer som har sex med tjejer* (The great book of sex, for girls who have sex with girls; Normal, 2007) in which BDSM is included as one chapter. Since 2004, she has been employed at the Stockholm branch of the Swedish Association for Sexuality Education (RFSU). Delilah is founder and former president of the queer leather club LASH in Stockholm for more than a decade (1995–2008). Through the years, Delilah has held various BDSM- and sex-related workshops mainly for women who have sex with women. She has also been engaged in sex activism leading Sweden to remove fetish and BDSM as clinical diagnoses in 2009, which was followed by the World Health Organization in 2018.

Kim Fernald (Chapter 11), MSW, LICSW, worked serving children, adolescents, and adults therapeutically. Kimberly met clients where they were and took a trauma-informed perspective to honor, support, and serve with compassion. She worked extensively with people with substance use disorders. She became a yoga teacher after studying at Yogaville in Virginia.

Mika Hagerlid (Chapter 6) is a senior lecturer in the Department of Criminology at Malmö University, Sweden. They are engaged in ongoing projects about sexual offenses, sexual harassment, the inclusion of neurodiverse students in higher education, and other subjects. They have previous experience of organizing BDSM clubs and other BDSM events for queer audiences.

David Jackson-Perry (Chapter 9), PhD, is a visiting scholar at Queen's University, Belfast. His research explores autistic experiences of intimacy, sexuality, and authenticity. David has presented widely and published several articles in these areas, as well as chapters in *Neurodiversity Studies: A New Critical Paradigm* (Hanna Bertilsdotter Rosqvist, Nick Chown, and Anna Stenning, eds.; Routledge, 2020) and *Working with Autistic Transgender and Non-Binary People* (Marianthi Kourti, ed.; Jessica Kingsley Publishers, 2021). He was co-initiator and organiser of Intimate Lives? (2018), the first conference to focus specifically on autism, sexuality, gender, and identity in the United Kingdom. David is also a specialist in sexual health and is HIV project manager at Lausanne University Hospital in Switzerland. He has a diagnosis of ADHD.

E Merten (Chapter 11), MSW, LICSW, is a clinical social worker and psychotherapist working with individuals and groups in western Massachusetts. E is passionate about working with clients along the intersections of trauma, attachment, relationships, gender, sexuality, and neurotype. E's work is informed by their own experiences of queerness, non-normative relationship structures, trauma, and ADHD.

Katie Munday (Chapter 4) in a multiply neurodivergent researcher, consultant, and youth work leader demystifying neurodivergent and queer experiences. During their MRes they collected and shared the stories of gender-diverse Autistic adults to co-create recommendations for future research. They have published on healthcare and education inequity for disabled people and gender-diverse people and those who live at these intersections. Currently, they are involved in research on disabled and transgender people's experiences of cancer services – they have shared their findings at the Houses of Parliament; All-Party Parliamentary Group on Cancer. Their research interests include Autistic people's experience of gender and sexuality, cancer service inequity, and Autistic people's experiences of substance use, and substance use services.

Anna Nygren (Chapter 10) is a doctoral student in literary studies at Åbo Akademi and an adjunct lecturer in literary composition at the University of Gothenburg. Anna is also active as a writer, translator, and playwright. Their doctoral thesis examines Monika Fagerholm's novel *Vem dödade bambi?* from a queer perspective. Their research interests also encompass neuroqueerness and ecocritical or posthumanistic approaches to text.

Ariel E. Pliskin (Chapter 11), MSW, LICSW, is an AuDHD psychotherapist, educator, and ordained minister in the Zen Peacemaker Order. Ariel holds certifications in yoga and mindfulness instruction and is an American Association of Sexuality Educators, Counselors and Therapists (AASECT) Certified Sex Therapist (CST) and Certified Sexuality Educator (CSE). Ariel teaches courses on autism at the University of Massachusetts in Amherst and serves as the Relationship and Sex Therapy program manager at Advance Psychotherapy Practice.

Sara Rocha (Chapter 5) is vice president of the European Council of Autistic People and vice chair of the European Disability Forum Women's Committee. She is cofounder and president of Associação Portuguesa Voz do Autista, the first autistic self-advocacy in Portugal. She has an MSc in healthcare management and economics and works as a data manager for the public and primary care department at the University of Cambridge. Sara worked as a consultant and adviser on several international projects on disability data and policy, including on citizen-generated data.

Lydia Stetson (Chapter 12), M.A., is a bisexual/queer adult-discovered/identified AuDHD cis-woman. Lydia has a master of arts in counseling psychology and is also currently pursuing her Ph.D. in clinical psychology. Lydia's interest in sexual and gender health related to Autistic experiences has grown steadily from her undergraduate experience as a sexual assault peer educator through her university's health center, to her work with neurodivergent adults in a community-based program, to her experience as a master's level mental health clinician privileged to build therapeutic relationships with gender, sex, and relationship diversity Autistic youth and adults, and finally (for now) to looking to qualitatively explore the lived experiences of queer Autistic individuals in her doctoral dissertation.

Alex Toft (Chapter 3) was a research fellow, most recently working at Nottingham Trent University in the School of Social Sciences. His research focused on sexuality, gender, disability, spirituality, and identity. During his academic career, he published widely in journals such as *Sexualities, Sociological Research Online*, and *Journal of Bisexuality*. However, the world of academia with its obsession on making huge amounts of money became a stifling and unpleasant place to work. Nowadays, you will find him tending green spaces and caring for plants.

Hanna Vaughn (Chapter 11) (she/her) is a femme neurodivergent social worker specializing in fat and queer liberation. She received an MSW at Boston University. She has presented internationally on the topics of neurodivergence and BDSM, and on anti-fat bias in the kink community.

GLOSSARY

Alexithymia	Alexithymia is a concept that has often been portrayed in clinical terms as a person's "difficulty" in recognizing or processing emotions in conventional ways. However, this book challenges that simplistic view and proposes that alexithymia is a term framed within neurotypical perspectives, encompassing variations in how individuals process, sense, and label emotions. These variations can be considered both strengths and weaknesses, depending on the context and the individual's perception. Alexithymia can arise from experiences such as trauma or be present throughout one's life.
Allistic	Non-autistic person.
Autigender	Gender identity as intertwined with and dependent on Autistic neurology.[1]
Autiqueer	When one's autism greatly affects one's queerness.[2]
BDSM	(bondage and discipline, Dominance and submission, and sadism and masochism) falls under the kink umbrella and refers to practices that involve exchange of power and control between individuals. Examples of these practices may include the act of restraining or being restrained, often using ropes, handcuffs, or other tools to limit physical movement; the consensual use of rules, rewards, and punishments to dictate and the behavior of the submissive partner; the exertion of or submission to control, authority, or power by one individual over another in a consensual and negotiated manner; or deriving pleasure from inflicting or experiencing pain, humiliation, or

	control on another person. To note, BDSM practices occur within the boundaries of consensual and carefully negotiated activities and prioritise the well-being of all involved parties.
Bodymind	A term that refers to the inseparability of the body and the mind as is often presupposed in the histories of Cartesian dualism that influence modern sciences, philosophy, medicine, education, and many other fields. The term "bodymind" is useful in discussing the way one's experience of neurodivergence cannot be relegated to issues of either the body or the mind but rather must always be taken in tandem.[3]
Bottom	In the context of kink and BDSM, bottom is a person who takes on the submissive or receiving role during a scene or an activity. The roles of Top and bottom are not necessarily fixed and can be fluid; individuals may switch roles depending on their agreements.
Camouflaging	Any social survival strategy or approach used to blend into one's surroundings so that differences are less discernible to onlookers. Camouflaging is related to masking.
Cisheteronormativity	A dominant norm that privileges cisgender and heterosexual people and relationships. This system is a product of the colonial systems of power[4] and therefore entwined with other systems of power such as race, class, and language.
Cisnormativity	The expectation that all people are cissexual or cisgender: "The expectation that all people are cissexual, that those assigned male at birth always grow up to be men and those assigned female at birth always grow up to be women."[5]
Co-regulation	The ability to regulate emotions and stress-related behaviors with the support and direction of a connecting individual.[6]
Dominant	Dominant, or Dom, refers to a person who takes on a controlling or authoritative role in a consensual power exchange dynamic. A dominant partner typically directs and is responsible for making decisions within the negotiated boundaries of the BDSM relationship, while prioritising the safety and well-being of all parties involved.
Double empathy problem	A concept put forth by Milton (2012) intervening in deficit discourse around Autistic empathy. The double empathy problem refers to the disconnect in

	understanding and reciprocity between autistic and allistic individuals and therefore shifting empathy as a construct that is of a fixed capacity located within the individual to a coconstructed phenomenon.[7]
Embodiment	A state or practice of being fully present and connected to one's own body, emotions, and experiences. These can be transformative or healing, often strengthening relationships or self-knowledge. As Prentis Hemphill[8] notes, embodiment involves paying attention to habits, both personally and collectively. This often reveals interconnectedness of physical and emotional well-being and the importance of understanding and processing trauma, oppression, and relational dynamics via the body.
Excess	An intervention in normativity that works by embracing complexity and following that which is typically discarded or suppressed. A challenge to the narrowing of normative frameworks by a shift of focus and value away from the center and into interconnected threads with an emphasis on the materiality and infinity of an additive practice.[9]
Fetishism	An intense sexual or erotic interest on a specific object, body part, behavior, or scenario that goes beyond conventional sexual stimuli. A fetish involves a heightened focus. People with fetishes may find specific objects or actions play a significant role in their fantasies and desires.
Focused interest	Autistic interests as a matter of how much we focus on them (or they focus us).[10]
Fusing	Where a self merges with that of others.[11]
Gender, sexuality, and relationship diversities (GSRD)	Whilst many will be familiar with LGBTQIA+ (lesbian, gay, bisexual, transgender, queer or questioning, intersex, asexual, and more), this does not include other relationship diversities such as those in polyamorous relationships or people involved in BDSM/kink power exchange relationships.[12] We use GSRD to encompass all forms of gender and relationship diversities. However, where researchers used LGBTQIA+ in their work, we have kept to their original terminology. There has been critique about using "diverse" euphemistically for other identity markers such as race and neurodivergence (and rightfully so). Here, we have made an editorial decision to allow GSRD as an adjective precisely because it is such a broad umbrella (i.e., to notice the diversity within diversity).

Heteronormativity, heteronormative logic, or heterosexual matrix	The belief that all bodies with male anatomies, regardless of gender identity, desire female bodies as well as the opposite; all bodies with female anatomies, regardless of gender identity, desire male bodies. [13] Note: This idea is entwined with other colonial systems (e.g., racism, patriarchy, etc.) and erases the existence of trans bodies, intersex bodies, or any body that does not conform to the systems of binary gender.
Identification	A term used instead of "diagnosis" when working within a neuro-affirmative approach. Within a deficit-based, medical model, practitioners will be accustomed to referring to "assessment" and "diagnosis." These terms not only are based within a medical model but are also embedded with implicit power dynamics (e.g., a "diagnosis" is the gift of the practitioner to give). Within a neuro-affirmative way of working, the process is one of collaborative exploration of Autistic identity between the clinical and individual in which both parties work together exploring whether being autistic aligns as an explanation for the person's way of being in the world.
Identity-first language	A clear standard regarding language use is lacking in autism research and practice but has been an issue of debate for some years. Distinctions have been made between terminology that places person before identifier, termed "person-first language" (PFL) – for example, "person with autism" – and terminology that places identifier before person, termed "identity-first language" (IFL) – for example "Autistic person," "Autistic people," "Autistic community," or "Autistic sexualities." We acknowledge that different language use also mirrors different cultural contexts. When working or communicating with Autistic people, our guidance is to follow the individual's preferences. However, our default is to use Autistic unless the person requests otherwise to reflect that being Autistic is our neurology; it is not something we have. The editors choose to capitalise Autistic to indicate its validity as a cultural and political identity of which one is a member of within a larger community. However, throughout the book individual authors have made their own choices around capitalization.

Kink   Sexual practices, fantasies, or preferences that are con-
                         sidered unconventional by mainstream sexual norms.
                         Kinks can encompass a range of interests and can
                         involve elements such as role-playing, BDSM, fetishism,
                         or other forms of alternative sexual expression. Kink, if
                         practised in accordance with the community's ethics, is
                         consensual and should involve communication, trust,
                         and mutual agreement among all parties involved.

Masking   The conscious or unconscious suppression of natural
                         responses and adoption of alternatives across a range of
                         domains including social interaction, sensory experi-
                         ence, cognition, movement, and behavior.[14]

Monotropism   The tendency for our interests to pull us in more
                         strongly than most (non-autistic) people. It rests on a
                         model of the mind as an "interest system": we are all
                         interested in many things, and our interests help direct
                         our attention. Different interests are salient at different
                         times. In a monotropic mind, fewer interests tend to be
                         aroused at any time, and they attract more of our pro-
                         cessing resources, making it harder to deal with things
                         outside of our current attention tunnel.[15]

Neuroconventional   The norms and conventions of neurotypicality includ-
                         ing but not limited to gestures, communications, sig-
                         nals, symbols, and performances that uphold grammars
                         that reinforce neurotypical power.[16]

Neuronormativity   There are different definitions of neuronormativity. Here
                         are four commonly referred to definitions: 1. "The set of
                         social, political, cultural, and personal norms that privi-
                         lege a neurotypical way of thinking, feeling, behaving,
                         and communicating as superior to the others,"[17] where
                         "being neurotypical is the only regular, natural, and
                         valid way to think, feel, behave, and communicate."[18]
                         2. A concept related to neurotypical majority, but they
                         are definitely not the same.[19] 3. Barriers, norms, values,
                         ideas, and so forth generated by the hegemony of
                         "neurotypicality" and "neuro-ableism."[20] 4. A tyr-
                         annical perspective that pathologizes neurodivergent
                         communication styles, perspectives, and knowledge,
                         presuming neurotypical to be the objective default.

Neurotypical gaze   The neurotypical gaze objectifies, fetishizes, or erases
                         neurodivergence and works to naturalise neuroconven-
                         tional ideas about love and relationships and, by this,
                         "misses or altogether discounts the non-normative ways
                         in which neurodivergent people connect with others."

A neurotypical gaze includes a neurotypical pleasure of looking at autism. A "fixing" of autism as a socially undesirable subject position. A primary inward focus "far more interested in examining and preserving the boundaries of normalcy than in gaining insight into autistic subjectivity and interiority."[21]

Safer spaces   Deriving from the idea of safe spaces that are necessary for marginalised groups to explore identity, feelings of pride, and be free of societal harms. Roestone Collective[22] points out that despite the phrase "safe space" originating with the facilitation of protective spaces for free expression among women's and LGBTQ+ groups, overuse of the term can obscure that the cultivation of such a space is "deeply relational" work in which the messiness of naming problems and harms is essential to creating safer spaces and possibilities for future ones. "Safer spaces" signifies a commitment to a praxis that acknowledges the labor involved with maintaining these spaces as they evolve.

Scene   A specific period of time during which people engage in consensual kink or fetish activities with certain predetermined terms. Meaning, before engaging in a scene, participants communicate to discuss their desires, limits, and preferences or establish safe words to halt the scene. After a scene, it is common for individuals to engage in aftercare, which provides emotional and physical support to each other to help process the experience and ensure a positive and nurturing conclusion to the encounter.

Scripting   Creating a detailed script of various permutations of a situation a person is likely to encounter to prepare for any eventuality.

Stimming   An activity that produces sensory input that allows autistic people to regulate otherwise overwhelming input and experiences.[23]

Submissive   In the context of BDSM, a person who willingly and consensually takes on the more passive or surrendering role in a power exchange dynamic. Submissives often find pleasure in following the lead of a dominant partner or in obeying their commands. They often report enjoyment in the ensuing sense of vulnerability or surrender. The submissive partner often relinquishes control within carefully negotiated limits and boundaries and under the terms of mutual consent. The submissive

	has the power to stop or alter the course of activities at any time through the use of a safe word or other agreed-upon signals.
S/switch	A person who enjoys taking on both Dominant and submissive roles during sexual or BDSM activities.
Top	The person who takes the active role in sexual stimuli (as opposed to the bottom). Related to the term "Dominant" and in some cases may be the same. Generally Top refers to a more limited role in a particular act, rather than an ongoing role of dominance that extends beyond a specific sexual exchange.
Unmasking	Autistic persons taking control of their mask and being more authentically themselves. This occurs by choice, after a long process of learning about themselves introspectively, spending time among other autistic people and learning from sharing relatable experiences through outrospection and therapizing themselves in various ways.[24]
Vanilla	"Vanilla sex" refers to conventional or mainstream sexual activities that typically do not involve elements of BDSM, kink, or alternative sexual practices. These sexual behaviors align with societal (neuro)norms and expectations. Vanilla sex is often the only kind of sex privileged under cisheteronorms.

Notes

1 LGBTQIA+ Wiki. (13 November 2023). *Autigender*. https://lgbtqia.wiki/wiki/Autigender

2 LGBTQIA+ Wiki. (11 October 2023). *Autiqueer*. https://lgbtqia.wiki/wiki/Autiqueer

3 See Price, M. (2015). The bodymind problem and the possibilities of pain. *Hypatia*, 30(1), 268–284.

4 Lugones, M. (2007). Heterosexualism and the colonial/modern gender system. *Hypatia*, 22(1), 186–219.

5 Bauer, G.R., Hammond, R., Travers, R., Kaay, M., Hohenadel, K.M., & Boyce, M. (2009). "I don't think this is theoretical; this is our lives": How erasure impacts health care for transgender people. *Journal of the Association of Nurses in AIDS Care*, 20(5), 348–361.

6 Spectrum Gaming. (2022). The importance of coregulation and selfcare. *Co-regulation*. https://www.barrierstoeducation.co.uk/coregulation

7 Milton, D.E. (2012). On the ontological status of autism: The "double empathy problem." *Disability & Society*, 27(6), 883–887.

8 Prentis. (6 April 2022). Transcript: Prentis Hemphill on choosing belonging [Encore] /281. *For the Wild*. https://forthewild.world/podcast-transcripts/prentis-hemphill-on-choosing-belonging-encore-281

9 Ehret, L.R. (2023). After the unspecial education: Poétigogies from the interstices (Doctoral dissertation, McGill University [Canada]).

10 Murray, F. (30 November 2018). Me and monotropism: A unified theory of autism. Psychologist. https://www.bps.org.uk/psychologist/me-and-monotropism-unified-theory-autism

11 Shore, S. (2003). Beyond the wall: Personal experiences with autism and Asperger syndrome (2nd ed.) Autism Asperger Publishing).

12 Davies, D. (26 May 2023). Gender, sex, and relationship therapy: An emergent new psychotherapeutic approach. https://pinktherapy.org/gender-sex-and-relationship-therapy-an-emergent-new-psychotherapeutic-approach/

13 Butler, J. (1990). Gender trouble: Feminism and the subversion of identity. Routledge.

14 Pearson, A., & Rose, K. (2021). A conceptual analysis of autistic masking: Understanding the narrative of stigma and the illusion of choice. *Autism in Adulthood*, 3(1), 52–60.

15 Murray, F. (30 November 2018). Me and monotropism: A unified theory of autism. Psychologist. https://www.bps.org.uk/psychologist/me-and-monotropism-unified-theory-autism

16 McDermott, C. (2022). Theorising the neurotypical gaze: Autistic love and relationships in the Bridge (Bron/Broen 2011–2018). *Medical Humanities*, 48(1), 5.

17 Herrán Salcedo, B. (10 April 2021). Autista construyendo. Neurotypical people are not trash. https://neuroclastic.com/neurotypical-people-are-not-trash/

18 Herrán Salcedo, B. (10 April 2021). Autista construyendo. Neurotypical people are not trash. https://neuroclastic.com/neurotypical-people-are-not-trash/

19 Herrán Salcedo, B. (10 April 2021). Autista construyendo. Neurotypical people are not trash. https://neuroclastic.com/neurotypical-people-are-not-trash/

20 Huijg, D.D. (2020). Neuronormativity in theorising agency: An argument for a critical neurodiversity approach. In Neurodiversity Studies (pp. 213–217). Routledge.

21 McDermott, C. (2022). Theorising the neurotypical gaze: Autistic love and relationships in the Bridge (Bron/Broen 2011–2018). *Medical Humanities*, 48(1), 4.

22 Roestone Collective. (2014). Safe space: Towards a reconceptualization. Antipode, 46(5), 1346–1365.

23 Kapp, S.K., Steward, R., Crane, L., Elliott, D., Elphick, C., Pellicano, E., & Russell, G. (2019). "People should be allowed to do what they like": Autistic adults' views and experiences of stimming. *Autism*, 23(7), 1782–1792.

24 Pearson, A., & Rose, K. (2021). A conceptual analysis of autistic masking: Understanding the narrative of stigma and the illusion of choice. *Autism in Adulthood*, 3(1), 52–60.

INTRODUCTION

1

INTRODUCTION

Hanna Bertilsdotter Rosqvist, Anna Day and Meaghan Krazinski

Rainbows show us the beauty and variance within light. Our approach in this book is to combine different perspectives, moving from a focus on one aspect of identity (e.g., either being Autistic, or gender identity/sexuality, relationality) to explore the colors of our intertwining identities that each contribute to our unique way of being in the world. Focusing on only one aspect of identity means that we miss the beauty of the threads contributing to our lived experiences, how they entangle with each other, and the uniqueness of each person. By exploring what it means to live under a double rainbow, we invite readers to immerse themselves in the colors and multidimensional aspects of Autistic identity as it relates to diverse genders, sexualities, and relationality, exploring how each contribute to Autistic people's embodied experiences.

This edited collection is written from the perspectives of researchers, clinicians, and Autistic people. We are an international, multidisciplinary team of Autistic and otherwise neurodivergent people uniting with a shared passion for exploring, celebrating, and promoting understanding of Autistic neurology and the richness and diversity of our experiences. By coming together and drawing on our professional and/or lived experiences, we seek to counterbalance the narratives of deficit and stigma that many Autistic people encounter in relation to their Autistic identity and gender, sexuality, and relationality diversities. We explore the variance of the construction and/or experience of gender identity, sexuality, and relationality in Autistic people *by* Autistic people as we reflect on these issues as they are lived and written about within research, clinical practice, fiction, and education.

Collectively, we work within a neurodiversity-affirming frame rather than aspiring to neuronormativity and its sibling, cisheteronormativity. We understand diversity to be the fundamental nature of neurology, gender, and sexuality across humankind. Being neurodivergent is a naturally occurring brain

DOI: 10.4324/9781003440154-2

difference that leads to a different way of experiencing the world and is not a "disorder" or "condition". It is fundamental to everything about that person, who moves through the world and experiences it as a neurodivergent person. Building off the social model of disability, we see the challenges that can be associated with being neurodivergent as primarily arising from living in a world that does not always recognise or meet our needs. Any difficulties arise from the mismatch between our neurology and an environment designed by and dictated by the perceived neuromajority (i.e., neurotypical people). The challenge is not being Autistic but in our environment. This includes challenges presented by societal pressures and norms around gender, relationships, and sexuality. Autistic functioning (or flourishing) is driven by the relationship between the individual and their environment. As Beardon (2017) has written,

Autistic person + environment = outcome.

Naming ourselves, Telling our stories differently

Knowledge of Autistic experience is typically constructed by neurotypical people rather than Autistic people. Drawing on neuroqueer theory (Walker, 2021), our work "not only is grounded in non-neuro-normative perspectives but also refuses to assume that the default reader or viewer is neurotypical" (Gray-Hammond, 2022). In this book, we seek to ground our work in our own bodies and neurodivergent embodied theorizing. We assume that the default reader or viewer is neurodivergent or a neurotypical ally to our community.

This has different important implications. One of them is to deliberately *cite differently*. We draw on Ahmed's (2017) citation policy[1] (*Living a Feminist Life*) and seek not to repeat rhetoric of deficit or to directly cite researchers whose work is both rejected by and has caused harm to the Autistic community. Similarly, Limburg has suggested that when she writes,

this is my account, written under my name, and I'm not going to describe myself in someone else's terms; that is the very opposite of what I want to do.
(Limburg, 2022, p. 5)

We think about the possibilities of not describing ourselves "in someone else's terms". Throughout, we deliberately reference Autistic writers, researchers, and bloggers where possible, recognising that all sources of knowledge are valid. As Gray-Hammond puts it,

We all have something to say, but we don't all have the privilege of a platform from which to say it.
(Gray-Hammond, 2022, p. 52)

Employing a politics of citation creates space for developing a terminology that better mirrors our embodied experience. We hope our book will work as a safer reading space, where what we read makes us feel excited and affirmed as well as loved and desired. We focus on *where it is we are going*, not where the field has been, adopting Walker's (2021) position of radical positivity, meaning that

> our ultimate focus is always on creating something good: the more free and empowered and beautifully weird self we want to be, the better future we want for the world, the creative and constructive solution to any problem at hand. . . . Our primary focus is always on what we are fighting for, the positive alternatives we're working to create, rather than what we're fighting against.
>
> *(Walker, 2023, personal communication, Discord)*

We are mindful of our use of language, acknowledging that even if we seek to ground our work in our neurodivergent-embodied theorizing, we may be pulled toward assuming that the default reader or viewer is a person well acquainted with academic ways of writing. We have aimed to make our language and main concept use accessible for a broader neurodivergent readership as part of a wider goal of importing community theorizing into academia in order to transform the autism and sexuality/gender/relationality research field. See the Glossary explaining key terms and language use.

BRIEF NOTE ON LANGUAGE

We have used **identity-first language (IFL)** and capitalized Autistic when writing as editors to reflect not only that being Autistic is essential to our selfhood and identity but also that we hold pride in Autistic culture and understand the political nature of claiming this identity. We have chosen to let each contributor decide for themselves their language use according to their own language and cultural preferences.

Gender, Sexuality, and Relationships Diversities (GSRD): We use GSRD to encompass all forms of gender and relationship diversities (see www.pinktherapy.com) when we are writing as editors. Where researchers used LGBTQIA+ in their work, we have kept to their original terminology.

Neuroqueer theory

Neuroqueer theory and neuroqueering have origins in the work of multiple scholars, including Walker (2021) and Yergeau (2018). Neuroqueer theory is a queer theory–informed understanding of the culturally constructed and situated nature of neurotypicality, which also allows us to better understand the meaning of neurodivergence. Neuroqueerness is fluid.

> To claim an identity of neuroqueer is not necessarily to identify with a gender, dis/ability label, or sexual orientation but rather to challenge the existence of these categorizations in the first place.
>
> *(Kleekamp, 2021, p. 411)*

Walker (2021) describes neuroqueer as a *verb*: a practice of queering (defying, disrupting, liberating oneself from) neuronormativity and heteronormativity. It is also an *adjective*: describing those things that are associated with the practices or result from those practices—for example, neuroqueer theory, neuroqueer perspectives, neuroqueer, embodiments, and so forth. Within Walker's (2021) approach, neuroqueering engages

> in practices intended to undo or subvert one's one cultural conditioning and one's ingrained habits of neuro-normative and heteronormative performance, with the aim of reclaiming one's capacity to give more full expression to one's uniquely weird potentials and inclinations.
>
> *(Walker, 2021, p. 162)*

Neuroqueer is choosing to "actively engage with one's potential for neurodivergence and queerness, and the intersections and synergies of those potentials" (Walker, 2021, p. 175). Importantly, we do not need to be either queer or neurodivergent to neuroqueer. Anyone has the potential to neuroqueer regardless of neurotype. From the approach of Walker, neuroqueering refers to "the act or process of challenging, subverting, defying, and/or creatively fucking with neuronormativity".[2] Central here is to "decenter the neurotypical perspective and the neurotypical gaze", which means producing "work which not only is grounded in non-neuronormative perspectives, but also refuses to assume that the default reader or viewer is neurotypical".[3]

Much as in queer communities, an evolution of this term is underway within neurodivergent communities. Like queerness, neuroqueer can operate as both a theoretical lens to examine what already exists, or how someone identifies, as well as a motion away from normativity and into experiences that have yet to come. In this book, we use neuroqueer in different ways, allowing it to travel and do different things in different contexts. If a member of the communities to which we belong finds a particularly use liberatory, we understand that to be in alignment with broader aims of upending the clutches of neuronormativity.

Autistic sexualities from a distance: The problem of deficit-based framings of Autistic sexuality

In working on this book, we have explored many different theories and previous research accounts of Autistic sexualities, relationality, and genders alongside working with our own experiences as data. We have sought to minimize repeating rhetoric of deficit and to avoid citing researchers whose work is both rejected by and has caused harm to the Autistic community. However, to situate the book from where we are going and against that which we are pushing back, we need to do some "back storying".

In the following sections, we map out deficit-based framings of Autistic sexuality in research, or what we refer to as *Autistic sexualities from a distance*. In this section, we echo the language used by the researchers. These framings have a significant rooting in public consciousness as evidenced by the recent popularity of the show *Love on the Spectrum* in which seeing Autistic people as capable (or even desiring of) intimacy harnessed the attention of many neurotypical audiences. Despite claiming to center Autistic kinds of intimacy, the show largely portrays cisheteronormative Autistic people seeking to access neurotypical privileges associated with seeking a relationship. These assumptions will be contrasted in the next section of the chapter, to framings of Autistic sexuality more in line with a neurodiversity-affirmative approach to Autistic experience, led by Autistic people themselves, which we refer to as *a rainbow of Autistic sexualities*.

A deficit-based framing of Autistic sexuality is illustrated by Schöttle et al. (2017) who write,

> Like nonaffected adults, individuals with autism spectrum disorders (ASDs) show the entire range of sexual behaviours. However, due to the core symptoms of the disorder spectrum, including deficits in social skills, sensory hypo- and hypersensitivities, and repetitive behaviours, some ASD individuals might develop quantitatively above-average or nonnormative sexual behaviours and interests.

Within a deficit-based framing, there are multiple tensions in how researchers describe sexual experience and expression in Autistic people. Turner et al. (2021, abstract) explains that while Autistic people "show the whole range of sexual fantasies and sexual behaviour just like their non-affected counterparts", simultaneously, we are viewed as showing "some peculiarities concerning sexual experiences and sexual behaviour". Looking at Autistic sexualities from a distance, the following problems arise:

1. Neuronormative comparison
2. Some peculiarities
3. The right amount of "muchness"
4. Theory-practice gap
5. The problem of cisheteronormativity

Neuronormative comparison

Central in definitions of autism is both what has been referred to as social and cognitive expressions or "external manifestations" (Murray et al., 2023) and looking at autism from the outside (from a neurotypical gaze). This neuronormative comparison between Autistic people and our non-autistic, neuro-typical (sometimes also referred to as "healthy control group"; cf Ashmawi et al., 2022) is central to how Autistic people's experiences are conceptualised. Deficit-based framings locate us as failing in neurotypicality at a macro level and as failing to perform neurotypical sexualities at a more micro level.

Some peculiarities

Research has focused on Autistic sexual practices as mainly comprising a bundle of "some peculiarities" since the early days of the autism and sexuality research field. This includes, for example, "violating norms" of couple-oriented *sociosexualities* exercised in private homely spaces, such as masturbation (Van Bourgondiera et al., 1997), particularly in public (Van Son-Schoones & Van Bilsen, 1995). In line with this, Autistic people (foremost men) have been represented by researchers as "hypersexual" and engaged in "paraphilic fanta-sies and behavior" (Schöttle et al., 2017; see also Turner et al., 2021; Fernandes et al., 2016; Van Son-Schoones & Van Bilsen, 1995), and as having non-socio-sexual objects of desires (Gatzia & Arnaud, 2022; see also Simner et al., 2019). These constructions pathologize Autistic sexuality, stressing "restricted, repeti-tive patterns of behaviour, interests, or activities" as part of the "diagnostic criteria" for autism. Unquestioningly reifying these Autistic sexualities *from a distance* perspective, our sexual practices have been associated with "stereo-typed sexual interests; sensory fascinations with a sexual connotation; para-philia" (Hellemans et al., 2010; see also Kellaher, 2015) or what Kellaher (2015) refers to as "deviant arousal sexual behaviours".

The right amount of "muchness"

From assumptions of a right amount of "muchness", Autistic people either are described as having an "obsessive preoccupation with sex" (Van Son-Schoones & Van Bilsen, 1995; see also Gougeon, 2010; Hellemans et al., 2010) or as being asexual/less interested in sex than non-autistic people. In line with this, Qualls et al. (2018) reported that Autistic people had "fewer sexual experiences" than non-autistic people. The fact that these inherent contradictions exist in much of the literature should lead scholars to question their validity; however, these stereotypes often still circulate unquestioned. Such literature describes us as lurching between being either *too* interested or not interested *enough* in sex (based on arbitrary neuronormative assumptions). Clearly, this is nonsensical regardless of neurotype – the "right" amount of "muchness" will vary according to the individual concerned. Everyone has different levels of interest in sex. There is no right amount of muchness, and yet this is what the predominant narrative around Autistic sexuality would have us believe.

Much of extant research locates Autistic sexuality within a double-bind – as lurching on a "see-saw" between "too much" interest to "too little", the right amount of "muchness". Either we have problematized sexual attractions and expression (regarding fantasies or objects or being *too* sexual), or we are disinterested in sex and disconnected from relationships. Our sexual expressions are pathologized *because* we are Autistic. At the same time, great variances in sexual interest, preference, and expression within the non-autistic community is not subject to such problematic framing. How can we ever achieve the right amount of "muchness" when it comes to our sexual expression when viewed from a neurotypical gaze when this standpoint problematises Autistic identity itself and ignores the great diversity of sexual expression and identity that occur across all neurotypes? The answer is, of course, we should not and do not seek to constrain our Autistic expression to neuronormative notions of the right degree of "muchness" whether that be related to our sexuality and sexual expression or how we exist in the world.

Theory-practice gap

The theory-practice gap is what Gougeon (2010) refers to as difficulties among Autistic people "in translating knowledge into practice", or what earlier researchers described as difficulties in "realising sex education" (Van Son-Schoones & Van Bilsen, 1995). This theory-practice gap has been associated with notions of Autistic social and communication differences, where some researchers have represented Autistic people as "not being able to have intimate relationships" (Gougeon, 2010), with Autistic youths' sexual difficulties being described as a consequence of them being "painfully aware" that they are "being different from their peers" (Van Son-Schoones & Van Bilsen, 1995). For example, Ronis et al. (2021) interviewed self-identifying asexual Autistic people, arguing that among them some at least have "some sexual attraction to others", and "some participants linked their asexual identity more with a lack of desire or perceived skill to engage in interpersonal relations than a lack of sexual attraction" (Ronis et al., 2021; see also Turner et al., 2021; Weir et al., 2021).

The problem of cisheteronormativity

From a perspective stressing Autistic people's cisheteronormative failures a gender distinction is commonly made where Autistic people assigned female at birth are pictured as having more sexual and romantic experiences than Autistic people assigned male at birth (Pecora et al., 2019; Holmes et al., 2020). Autistic people assigned female at birth are also less likely to have experienced "reprimands" for expressing sexuality deemed as "sexually inappropriate conduct" (Holmes et al., 2020). In contrast to neurotypical people assigned female at birth, however, Autistic people assigned female at birth are represented as having less sexual desire, fewer sexual behaviors, and less sexual awareness (Bush, 2019; Pecora et al., 2019). The cognitive dissonance caused by neuro-norms here is strong as these phenomena (sexual experiences and access to exposure to experiences) are assumed to be "privilege" of AFAB Autistic people, while a separate conversation around the statistics of genderized sexual violence seeks to protect this group from these experiences. Once we shift to the voices of Autistic people, we realize that these overlap. Access to neuronormative sexual experiences are not much of a privilege after all if they do not affirm the proclivities of one's bodymind. Higher rates of gender variance and sexual minority orientations among Autistic people has been interpreted by Rudolph et al. (2018) as uncertain self-identification and/or a defiance of traditional ways of categorizing sexual identity. Comparisons of these types, between neurotypes and genders, which are rife in the literature around autism, essentialize and reinforce gender binaries. This not only obfuscates nonbinary and trans Autistic identities and bodies but also downplays the central role with which gender nonconformity is often inextricably connected to the Autistic experience.

Much of the research around Autistic sexual expression/identity mirrors the deficit-based narratives that dominate conceptualizations of Autistic experience instead taking up the nuance and diversities of our identities. The literature approaches Autistic sexual expression as problematic and "atypical", and appears to wrestle with the concept of Autistic people as gendered and sexual beings. Our preferences, expression, and sexual experiences are subject to scrutiny that neurotypical people would undoubtedly find as abhorrent as do the Autistic community. There is an apparent discomfort in the mere notion that Autistic people have sexual desires, fantasies, and practices just as any non-autistic person, but because autism has so long been viewed through a deficit-based lens, so is our sexual expression. For example, masturbation in neurotypical adolescents is typically seen as a usual part of sexual development and exploration and remains a private activity. But for Autistic adolescents, we often see it becoming problematized, and what *should* still be a private matter for the individual becomes framed within a problematized lens of "supporting private time" and out of the private domain. This may be because some research focuses particularly on those with a co-occurring intellectual disability, and historically people with intellectual disabilities have been intensely surveilled around sexual expression and falsely constructed as lacking sexual agency (Gill, 2015). We do not dispute that there is a need for some Autistic people to be supported in safe sexual practices – for example, around when (or how to safely) engage in sexual practices. However, this should be within an approach that does not problematize sexual experimentation and isolate the individual further. Rather, support should enable the individual to *safely* meet *their* sexual needs, not being driven by an agenda that sees any sexual behavior as problematic simply because the individual is Autistic, or the behavior is outside of the cishetero norm.

Reading the research, it is often hard to see how Autistic people might ever engage in sexual practices, let alone seek out and enjoy sex aligned with our sexual preferences. Meanwhile, Autistic people who truly are asexual are viewed as a "problem" to solve (Kim, 2011). In other words, the deficit-based framings of Autistic sexuality means that the richness, diversity, and sexual pleasures of our community are typically misunderstood. There is a flourishing GSRD Autistic community, even though the literature suggests otherwise. Here we are, thriving, enjoying sex with partners who relate to and understand our sensory and sexual needs and preferences. There are many ways to be in the world and equally as many ways in which to explore and express our sexual needs and preferences. Viewing our sexualities from a neurotypical gaze means missing out on learning about respecting one's own and others' sensory and sexual needs, and how to navigate this with our partner(s). Fortunately, researchers are challenging these problematic conceptualisations of Autistic people as lacking sexual knowledge, experience, or interest in relationships (e.g., Kellaher, 2015; see also Ronis et al., 2021; Bush et al., 2021; Fernandes et al., 2016), while acknowledging that sexuality *is* important for Autistic people, challenging the negative societal perceptions about the sexuality of autistic people (Byers et al., 2013; Kellaher, 2015), as well as the importance of self-reported sexuality research among Autistic people (Bush, 2019).

A rainbow of Autistic sexualities

Experience and expression of sexuality and gender may differ in the Autistic population compared with neurotypical people (Sala et al., 2020; George & Stokes, 2018). This includes more sexual minority orientations or gender non-conforming experiences (in particular among Autistic people assigned female at birth: Dewinter et al., 2017; May et al., 2017; Hillier et al., 2020; George & Stokes, 2018; Rudolph et al., 2018; Bejerot & Eriksson, 2014; Sala et al., 2020; Qualls et al., 2018; Hartman et al., 2023; George & Stokes, 2018; Warrier et al. 2020; Weir et al. 2021; Cooper et al. 2018; Dewinter et al. 2017; Janssen et al. 2016; Strang et al. 2018). This illustrates how being Autistic can have an impact on both sexuality and gender/experiences of gender (Cain & Velasco, 2021; Sala et al., 2020). However, Hartman et al. (2023) point out that there has been little research focusing on having multiple identities – for example, being Autistic and different gender identities. Among few studies focusing on multiple identities among Autistic people (Hillier et al., 2020), the participants variously described not feeling they fit in the LGBTQIA+ community because of their Autistic communities or vice versa, not fitting in the Autistic community because of their sexuality and/or gender identity or finding that having multiple identities positive as they had additional group with whom to identify. Similarly, Miller et al. (2020) explored how Autistic people make meaning and express multiple social identities, such as using context to prioritise which identity is more salient, when identities intermingle, and the value of connection to both one's own identity and having others around us who both value and possess similar identities. In other words, research suggests much variability in the experience and expression of multiple identities. We may be "unmasked" (cf Pearson & Rose, 2021) with regard to Autistic identity in one context (e.g., work or in family contexts) but not "out" with regard to sexuality/gender/relationality or vice versa. For some people, discovery of Autistic identity fosters an exploration of the self that allows identification and recognition of queerness, whereas for others, it is identifying as gay/trans/nonbinary/kinky and so forth that leads to identification of Autistic identity. There are many paths that we tread in our exploration of ourselves, recognition and expression of queerness and Autistic identity.

These paths demonstrate how Autistic ways of being are both inherently entwined with gender and sexuality and, simultaneously, may queer rigid identity categories of sexualities regardless of label.[4] Other gender identities such as *autigender, gendervague,* and *neurogender* have emerged to demonstrate the unique ways in which neurodivergent people may experience gender itself (Brown, 2020). However, there has been relatively little exploration of the overlaps between Autistic and perceived non-normative gender identity (Hillier et al., 2020), and even less literature that probes this further by exploring relationship structure and sexual practices.

Current clinical and research literature typically ignores the multiple identities and experiences that Autistic people have whereas a comprehensive approach considers multiple identities (Hartman et al., 2023), recognizing that we do not have a single identity or community but are multifaceted. Minority stress theory posits that minority groups can have increased likelihood of experiencing negative physical and mental health outcomes from cumulative experiences of stigma and discrimination (Chiang et al., 2017; McConnell et al., 2018). Gillespie-Lynch and Botha (2021) point out that we must understand differences *within* the Autistic community to support all Autistic people experience the dignity that they deserve.

Like many Autistic people, we prefer direct communication and are not hesitant to "say the thing" that others are unwilling to say. This is a communication style that has got many of us "in trouble". For example, One of Us (cf Francis and Hey, 2009) has been referred to as an "Anarchist" for pushing back against accepted narratives. Neuroconventional communication styles, therefore, continues to contribute to the oppression of Autistic people who seek frank conversations around sexuality, gender, and relationship. We see this silencing as part of neuronormative oppression of Autistic knowledge around sexuality. It prevents us from being valued for our epistemological contributions on these topics and from raising important questions about human sexuality itself. In this sense, we hope that readers will appreciate the honesty with which the authors in this book tackle these topics and relinquish any "squeamishness" as part of a practice of a neuroaffirmative approach to sexuality, gender, and relationality. An intention of this book is asking the reader to decouple "non-normative" from "harmful" and to thereby be able to enact greater care for Autistic people by becoming more incisive with our understandings of sexuality. Furthermore, it is important to underscore the stakes of these discussions as more than mere increased self-expression, as Autistic people of color more easily face carceral implications of the pathologization of their sexuality.

The content in the book in general seeks to support and nurture a pleasure approach on autism. We want to explore, learn from each other, are curious in "not what a neurodivergent body is, but what a neurodivergent body can do" (Bertilsdotter Rosqvist et al., in press; cf Gatens, 1994; Grosz, 1994), aiming at what Jackson-Perry in his chapter refers to as a "flourishing intimate autistic life". This is in contrast to research on Autistic sexualities from a distance in which Autistic sexualities are commonly associated with a sorted box of risks (cf Bertilsdotter Rosqvist, 2014). However, while this book intentionally focuses on celebrating Autistic sexuality and does not repeat deficit-based narratives around either our sexuality *or* "vulnerability", it would however be unethical, irresponsible, and misleading not to include discussion of consent. We do so in an intermission after this introductory chapter.

Introducing the chapter contents

A key aim of this book is to focus specifically on the connections between gender, sexuality, relationality, and Autistic identity, including contributors from a wide range of perspectives. Our aim is to provide an exploration of Autistic sexuality *by* Autistic people, reflecting the rich diversity of our sexual preferences, gender identities, and practices as *we live it*, not filtered through deficit-based, cis-, hetero-, or neuronormative lenses. This is a celebration of sex, gender, and relationality, of how we "do" and view sex in all its various forms and practices (solo, with perhaps multiple partners, within different relationship structures, e.g., power exchange relationships within the kink/BDSM scene), and of our diverse gender identities. In terms of structure, the book is divided into four sections: **Beginnings; Evolving understandings: Naming the nameless so it can be thought; Unlearning, relearning; Conclusion.**

Beginnings

In the opening chapters, we explore Autistic sexualities in all their diversities from queer approaches, recontextualizing traditionally pathologized topics around sexual, romantic, and gendered proclivities of Autistic people by using neuroqueer and neurodiversity-affirming frameworks to reveal new understandings about these phenomena. In Chapter 3, **Alex Toft** explores the intersection of autism and LGBT+ in relation to the lived experiences of young Autistic LGBT+ people, focusing on how they understand the intersection, how it works in everyday life and the language used to express this. In Chapter 4, **Katie Munday** discusses shifting research paradigms around being trans and Autistic and asks how we can neuroqueer research to center Autistic and gender diverse voices within research. In Chapter 5, **Sara Rocha** and **Mayne Benedetto** document what they frame as neuroaffirming ways of looking at experiences of sexuality and relationships for Autistic women and nonbinary people.

Evolving understandings: Naming the nameless so it can be thought

The second part of the book moves to exploring our understanding of our bodies, embodiment, and how we might communicate about these. Contributors explore how the "unthought known" (Bollas, 1987; 2018: when we have a sense of knowing something, yet are unable to identify or articulate what that is) might be named within the constraints of language and how our embodiment serve as a conduit for communication. In Chapter 6, **Mika Hagerlid** explores an autiqueer love for BDSM, with emphasis on reclaiming and remarking BDSM practices. In Chapter 7, **Anna Day** and **Meaghan Krazinski** reflect on exploration of unmasking and gender identity as a process of "becoming" and the liberation that moving away from neuronormative assumptions can provide in exploring and revealing both queer and Autistic identity. They also examine unmasking and becoming as these concepts relate to embodiment and relationality.

Unlearning, relearning

The third part of the book moves to examination of unlearning and relearning about Autistic sexuality, gender, and relationality. In Chapter 8, **Helene Delilah** and **Hanna Bertilsdotter Rosqvist** explores BDSM/kink and fetishism and Autistic people, illustrating how various BDSM practices and lifestyles can be associated with experiences of calm achieved by meeting sensory needs (e.g., either intense sensory input or sensory deprivation) but also how clarity in negotiation and communication within power exchange relationship can create security and trust. In Chapter 9, **David Jackson-Perry** examines intimate Autistic relationships, disrupting discourses around deficits. In Chapter 10, **Hanna Bertilsdotter Rosqvist** and **Anna Nygren** present a beautiful and powerful examination of how neurodivergent sexualities are rethought or retold through text-sharing practices, and discussion of representations and expressions of Autistic love and sexual acts in fiction. In Chapter 11, **Ariel Pliskin, Kim Fernald, Hanna Vaughn, and E Merten** explore what Autistic sex education should look like from a neuroaffirmative perspective, integrating the neurodiversity paradigm with research, "sex-positive peace-making" (Pliskin, 2020), and practices of mindfulness. In Chapter 12, **Lydia Stetson** explores possibilities of a neuroaffirmative working alliance between GSRD Autistic people and their healthcare providers.

Conclusion

In the concluding Chapter 13, **Hanna Bertilsdotter Rosqvist, Anna Day,** and **Meaghan Krazinski** celebrate the riot of rainbows explored within the wider book to present clinical and practice learning points in working with queer clients and students, reflect on our multiple comings out as editors as a mirror to declaration of identities across different contexts, and discuss practice recommendations for neuroaffirmative sexual education practice.

Notes on editors and privileges

The editors of this book are aware of their privilege in writing this book. Collectively, we hold many marginalised identities, yet we acknowledge that there are many other Autistic people who hold multiple identities who did not have the opportunity to contribute to this book. We have aspired to not speak for those belonging to communities/having identities that we do not share as editors while recognizing our privilege in writing this book and the voices are those that are absent from the text.

Hanna Bertilsdotter Rosqvist (she/her) is a white neurodivergent senior researcher in sociology and social work. She is a Swedish citizen, cis-gendered woman, a Bisexual BDSM practitioner with a past as an activist within both the BDSM queer women community in Stockholm (Sweden) as well as the Bisexual movement in Sweden.

Anna Day (she/they) is a white neurodivergent principal clinical psychologist working with Autistic adults. This book has formed part of their "unmasking" and provoked internal reflection and exploration of their gender identity.

Meaghan Krazinski (she/they) is a white multiply neurodivergent doctoral candidate in special education with areas of advanced study in both disability studies and women's and gender studies. Meaghan is a late-diagnosed Autistic woman who identifies as a woman mostly as a political category. She is an American citizen and former special education teacher and raised by a single mother with English as a first language. Meaghan is also an intimate partner violence survivor which informs how she approaches this work.

Notes

1 "My citation policy has given me more room to attend to those feminists who came before. Citation is feminist memory. Citation is how we acknowledge our debt to those who came before; those who helped us find our way, when the way was obscured because we deviated from the paths we were told to follow" (Ahmed, 2017, pp. 15–16).
2 Gray-Hammond, D. (2022). Neuroqueering the future: An interview with Dr. Nick Walker, author of *Neuroqueer Heresies*. https://neuroclastic.com/neuroqueering-the-future-an-interview-with-dr-nick-walker-author-of-neuroqueer-heresies/. January 26, 2022. Downloaded 06-02-2023.
3 Gray-Hammond, D. (2022). Neuroqueering the future: An interview with Dr. Nick Walker, author of *Neuroqueer Heresies*. https://neuroclastic.com/neuroqueering-the-future-an-interview-with-dr-nick-walker-author-of-neuroqueer-heresies/. January 26, 2022. Downloaded 06-02-2023.
4 As Rachael Groner (2012) writes, "Much as an autistic person is often illegible to the . . . neurotypical (often abbreviated as nt) world, autistic sexuality is illegible to heteronormativity. In a sense, autistic sexuality is always and necessarily queer, even if the people involved are not gay, lesbian, bisexual, or transgender in identity or practice" (p. 265).

References

Ahmed, S. (2017). *Living a feminist life*. Duke University Press.

Ashmawi, N. S., Hammoda, M. A., & Hammoda, M. (2022). Early prediction and eva-luation of risk of autism spectrum disorders. *Cureus*, 14(3).

Beardon, L. (2017). *Autism in adults*. Sheldon Press.

Bejerot, S., & Eriksson, J. M. (2014). Sexuality and gender role in autism spectrum dis-order: A case control study. *PloS ONE*, 9(1), e87961. https://doi.org/10.1371/journal.pone.0087961.

Bertilsdotter Rosqvist, H. (2014). Becoming an "autistic couple": Narratives of sexuality and couplehood within the Swedish autistic self-advocacy movement. *Sexuality and Disability*, 32(3), 351–363. doi:10.1007/s11195-013-9336-2.

Bertilsdotter Rosqvist, H., Chevalier, C., & Nygren, A. (In press). Authoring bodies: doing collective somatic knowing as a neuroqueer feminist phenomenology method. In H. Bertilsdotter Rosqvist & D. Jackson-Perry (Eds.), *The Palgrave handbook of research methods and ethics in neurodiversity studies*. Palgrave.

Bollas, C. (1987). *The shadow of the object: Psychoanalysis of the unthought known*. Free Association Press.

Bollas, C. (2018). *The shadow of the object: Psychoanalysis of the unthought known* (30th anniversary ed.). Routledge.

Brown, L. X. Z. (2020, May 16). Gendervague: At the intersection of autistic and trans. *Experiences (repost)*. https://www.autistichoya.com/2020/05/gendervague-at. intersection-of-autistic.html. Downloaded 22 February 2023.

Bush, H. H. (2019). Dimensions of sexuality among young women, with and without autism, with predominantly sexual minority identities. *Sexuality and Disability*, 37(2), 275–292. doi:10.1007/S11195-018-9532-1.

Bush, H. H., Williams, L. W., & Mendes, E. (2021). Brief report: Asexuality and young women on the autism spectrum. *Journal of Autism and Developmental Disorders*, 51(2), 725–733. doi:10.1007/s10803-020-04565-6.

Byers, E .S., Nichols, S., & Voyer, S. D. (2013). Challenging stereotypes: Sexual function-ing of single adults with high functioning autism spectrum disorder. *Journal of Autism and Developmental Disorders*, 43(11), 2617–2627. doi:10.1007/s10803-013-1813-z.

Cain, L. K., & Velasco, J. C. (2021). Stranded at the intersection of gender, sexuality, and autism: Gray's story. *Disability and Society*, 36(3), 358–375. https://doi.org/10.1080/09687599.2020.1755233.

Chiang, S.-Y., Fleming, T., Lucassen, M., Fenaughty, J., Clark, T., & Denny, S. (2017). Mental health status of double minority adolescents: Findings from national cross sectional health surveys. *Journal of Immigrant and Minority Health*, 19(3), 499–510. https://doi.org/10.1007/s10903-016-0530-z.

Cooper, K., Smith, L. G. E., & Russell, A. J. (2018). Gender identity in autism: Sex differences in social affiliation with gender groups. *Journal of Autism and Develop-mental Disorders*, 48(12), 3995–4006. doi:10.1007/s10803-018-3590-1.

Dewinter, J., De Graaf, H., & Begeer, S. (2017). Sexual orientation, gender identity, and romantic relationships in adolescents and adults with autism spectrum disorder. *Journal of Autism and Developmental Disorders*, 47(9), 2927–2934. doi:10.1007/s10803-10017-3199-3199.

Fernandes, L. C., Gillberg, C. I., Cederlund, M., Hagberg, B., Gillberg, C., & Billstedt, E. (2016). Aspects of sexuality in adolescents and adults diagnosed with autism spec-trum disorders in childhood. *Journal of Autism and Developmental Disorders*, 46(9), 3155–3165. doi:10.1007/s10803-017-3199-9.

Francis, B., & Hey, V. (2009). Talking back to power: Snowballs in hell and the impera-tive of insisting on structural explanations. *Gender and Education*, 21(2), 225–232. doi:10.1080/09540250802680081.

Gatens, M. (1994). The dangers of a woman-centred philosophy. In The polity reader in Gender Studies (pp. 93–107). Polity Press.

Gatzia, D. E., & Arnaud, S. (2022). Loving objects: Can autism explain objectophilia? *Archives of Sexual Behavior*, 51(4), 2117–2133. doi:10.1007/s10508-021-02281-5.

George, R., & Stokes, M. A. (2018). Gender identity and sexual orientation in autism spectrum disorder. *Autism*, 22(8), 970–982. doi:10.1177/1362361317714587.

Gill, M. (2015). *Already doing it: Intellectual disability and sexual agency*. University of Minnesota Press.

Gillespie-Lynch, K., & Botha, M. (2021). Come as you are: Examining autistic identity development and the neurodiversity movement through an intersectional lens. *Human Development*, 66, 93–112. doi:10.13140/RG.2.2.33966.02881.

Gougeon, N. A. (2010). Sexuality and autism: A critical review of selected literature using a social-relational model of disability. *American Journal of Sexuality Education*, 5(4), 328–361. https://doi.org/10.1080/15546128.2010.527237.

Gray-Hammond, D. (2022). Neuroqueering the future: An interview with Dr. Nick Walker author of *Neuroqueer Heresies*. https://neuroclastic.com/neuroqueering-the-future-an-.interview-with-dr-nick-walker-author-of-neuroqueer-heresies/. Downloaded 6 February 2023.

Groner, R. (2012). Sex as "Spock." In *Sex and disability* (pp. 263–282). Duke University Press.

Grosz, E. (1994). *Volatile bodies: Toward a corporeal feminism*. Indiana University Press.

Hartman, D., O'Donnell-Killen, T., Doyle, J. K., Kavanagh, M., Day, A., & Azevedo, J. (2023). *The adult autism assessment handbook: A neurodiversity affirmative approach*. Jessica Kingsley.

Hellemans, H., Roeyers, H., Leplae, W., Dewaele, T., & Deboutte, D. (2010). Sexual behavior in male adolescents and young adults with autism spectrum disorder and borderline/mild mental retardation. *Sexuality and Disability*, 28(2), 93–104. doi:10.1007/s11195-009-9145-9.

Hillier, A., Gallop, N., Mendes, E., Tellez, D., Buckingham, A., Nizami, A., & Otoole, D. (2020). LGBTQ+ and autism spectrum disorder: Experiences and challenges. *International Journal of Transgender Health*, 21(1), 98–110. https://doi.org/10.1080/15532739.2019.1594484.

Holmes, L., Shattuck, P. T., Nilssen, A. R., Strassberg, D. S., & Himle, M. B. (2020). Sexual and reproductive health service utilization and sexuality for teens on the autism spectrum. *Journal of Developmental and Behavioral Pediatrics: JDBP*, 41(9), 667–679. doi:10.1097/DBP.0000000000000838.

Janssen, A., Huang, H., & Duncan, C. (2016). Gender variance among youth with autism spectrum disorders: A retrospective chart review. *Transgender Health*, 1(1), 63–68. https://doi.org/10.1089/trgh.2015.0007.

Kellaher, D. C. (2015). Sexual behavior and autism spectrum disorders: An update and discussion. *Current Psychiatry Reports*, 17(4), 562. https://doi.org/10.1007/s11920-015-0562-4.

Kim, E. (2011). Asexuality in disability narratives. *Sexualities*, 14(4), 479–493. https://doi-org.libezproxy2.syr.edu/10.1177/1363460711406463.

Kleekamp, M. C. (2021). Neuroqueer. In *Encyclopedia of queer studies in education* (pp. 410–416). Brill.

Limburg, J. (2022). *Letters to my weird sisters: On autism, feminism and motherhood*. Atlantic Books.

May, T., Pang, K. C., & Williams, K. (2017). Brief report: Sexual attraction and relationships in adolescents with autism. *Journal of Autism and Developmental Disorders*, 47(6), 1910–1916. doi:10.1007/s10803-017-3092-6.

McConnell, E. A., Janulis, P., Phillips, G., Truong, R., & Birkett, M. (2018). Multiple minority stress and LGBT community resilience among sexual minority men. *Psychology of Sexual Orientation and Gender Diversity*, 5(1), 1–12. https://doi.org/10.1037/sgd0000265.

Miller, R. A., Nachman, B. R., & Wynn, R. D. (2020). "I feel like they are all interconnected": Understanding the identity management narratives of autistic LGBTQ college students. *College Student Affairs Journal*, 38(1), 1–15. https://files.eric.ed.gov/fulltext/EJ1255491.pdf.

Murray, D., Milton, D., Green, J., & Bervoets, J. (2023). The human spectrum: A phenomenological enquiry within neurodiversity. *Psychopathology*, 56(3), 220–230. doi:10.1159/000526213.

Pearson, A., & Rose, K. (2021). A conceptual analysis of autistic masking: Understanding the narrative of stigma and the illusion of choice. *Autism in Adulthood*, 3(1), 52–60. doi:10.1089/aut.2020.0043.

Pecora, L. A., Hancock, G. I., Mesibov, G. B., & Stokes, M. A. (2019). Characterising the sexuality and sexual experiences of autistic females. *Journal of Autism and Developmental Disorders*, 49(12), 4834–4846. doi:10.1007/s10803-019-04204-9.

Pliskin, E. (2020). Contributions to positive sexuality from the Zen Peacemakers. *Journal of Positive Sexuality*, 6(1), 24–32. doi:10.51681/1.612.

Qualls, L. R., Hartmann, K., & Paulson, J. F. (2018). Broad autism phenotypic traits and the relationship to sexual orientation and sexual behavior. *Journal of Autism and Developmental Disorders*, 48(12), 3974–3983. doi:10.1007/s10803-018-3556-3.

Ronis, S. T., Byers, E. S., Brotto, L. A., & Nichols, S. (2021). Beyond the label: Asexual identity among individuals on the high-functioning autism spectrum. *Archives of Sexual Behavior*, 50(8), 3831–3842. doi:10.1007/s10508-021-01969-y.

Rudolph, C. E. S., Lundin, A., Åhs, J. W., Dalman, C., & Kosidou, K. (2018). Brief report: Sexual orientation in individuals with autistic traits: Population based study of 47,000 adults in Stockholm County. *Journal of Autism and Developmental Disorders*, 48(2), 619–624. doi:10.1007/s10803-017-3369-9.

Sala, G., Pecora, L., Hooley, M., & Stokes, M. A. (2020). As diverse as the spectrum itself: Trends in sexuality, gender and autism. *Current Developmental Disorders Reports*, 7(2), 59–68. doi:10.1007/s40474-020-00190-1.

Schöttle, D., Briken, P., Tüscher, O., & Turner, D. (2017). Sexuality in autism: Hypersexual and paraphilic behavior in women and men with high-functioning autism spectrum disorder. *Dialogues in Clinical Neuroscience*, 19(4), 381–393. doi:10.31887/DCNS.2017.19.4/dschoettle.

Simner, J., Hughes, J. E. A., & Sagiv, N. (2019). Objectum sexuality: A sexual orientation linked with autism and synaesthesia. *Scientific Reports*, 9(1), 19874 doi:10.1038/s41598-019-56449-0.

Strang, J. F., Powers, M. D., Knauss, M., Sibarium, E., Leibowitz, S. F., Kenworthy, L., Sadikova, E., Wyss, S., Willing, L., Caplan, R., Pervez, N., Nowak, J., Gohari, D., Gomez-Lobo, V., Call, D., & Anthony, L. G. (2018). "They thought it was an obsession": Trajectories and perspectives of autistic transgender and gender-diverse adolescents. *Journal of Autism and Developmental Disorders*, 48(12), 4039–4055. doi:10.1007/s10803-018-3723-6.

Turner, D., Schöttle, D., & Briken, P. (2021). Sexuality in people with autism spectrum disorder and its importance for forensic psychiatry and psychotherapy (Sexualität bei Menschen mit Autismus-Spektrum-Störung und ihre Bedeutung für die forensische Psychiatrie und Psychotherapie). *Forensische Psychiatrie, Psychologie, Kriminologie*, 15(1), 54–61. doi:10.1007/s11757-020-00637-6.

Van Bourgondiera, M. E., Reichle, N. C., & Palmer, A. (1997). Sexual behavior in adults with autism. *Journal of Autism and Developmental Disorders*, 27(2), 113–125. doi:10.1023/a:1025883622452.

Van Son-Schoones, N., & Van Bilsen, P. (1995). Sexuality and autism: A pilot-study of parents, health care workers and autistic persons. *International Journal of Adolescent Medicine and Health*, 8(2), 87–101.

Walker, N. (2021). *Neuroqueer heresies: Notes on the neurodiversity paradigm, autistic empowerment, and postnormal possibilities*. Autonomous Press.

Warrier, V., Greenberg, D. M., Weir, E., Buckingham, C., Smith, P., Lai, M.-C., Allison, C., & Baron-Cohen, S. (2020). Elevated rates of autism, other neurodevelopmental and psychiatric diagnoses, and autistic traits in transgender and gender-diverse individuals. *Nature Communications*, 11(1), 3959. doi:10.1038/s41467-020-17794-1.

Weir, E., Allison, C., & Baron-Cohen, S. (2021). The sexual health, orientation, and activity of autistic adolescents and adults. *Autism Research*, 14(11), 2342–2354. doi:10.1002/aur.2604.

Yergeau, M. (2018). *Authoring autism: On rhetoric and neurological queerness*. Duke University Press.

2

INTERMISSION ON CONSENT

Anna Day and Meaghan Krazinski

Although this book intentionally focuses on celebrating Autistic sexuality and does not repeat deficit-based narratives around either our sexuality or "vulnerability", it would be unethical, irresponsible, and misleading to not acknowledge that higher rates of childhood sexual abuse are reported by Autistic people, as well as higher rates of sexual and physical violence, emotional and domestic abuse, and victimization compared to non-autistic people (Stewart et al., 2022). Nine of the 22 studies included in Dike et al.'s (2022) systemic review of sexual violence toward Autistic people reported elevated rates of sexual violence inflicted on Autistic people compared to non-autistic peers, particularly in adulthood.

As Hartman et al. (2023) point out, the responsibility for sexual abuse and sexual violence is entirely with the perpetrator, and it is a damaging narrative to simply frame Autistic people as more "vulnerable" to sexual violence and only focus on risk factors located within the victim. This shifts the focus away from the abuser's responsibility for their actions and wider systems that should protect individuals in ways that respond to their way of being, and instead locates the "responsibility" for staying safe onto the victim. We adopt the same stance as Hartman et al. (2023) of not condoning a position of focusing on narratives around deficit and "vulnerability" of Autistic people being abused in any way, as the responsibility lies all with the perpetrator.

As we wrote this book, we realised that as much as we wish to celebrate and explore the richness of Autistic sexuality, genders, and relationalities, we could not do so without acknowledging that exploring our sexuality may reflecting on sexual experiences and realising, or now being able to name to ourselves, that they were not consensual. Reading the material presented in the book may be both joyful in examining the rainbow of Autistic sexuality, but we hold space also that it may be painful, facilitating the naming of that which was previously unidentifiable ("This is all the stuff out there, but fuck, it's been inside me and

DOI: 10.4324/9781003440154-3

it's just messed me up" (Lewis, 2022, p. 13)) or too unsayable ("One *will* not, *can*not be this person, because when one was, life was not bearable; and yet, if not-me enters consciousness, one *is* that person" (Stern, 2009, p. 176, italics from the original). We do not always have words to identify or articulate our sexuality and experiences – and this extends to nonconsensual acts. What we seek to clarify, however, is that just because we are finding the words, it does not mean we have consented. Lack of consent, unfortunately, is all too often fully realized in retrospect, particularly for those whose history includes restrictions on the forms of embodiment that is most natural to them. We hold the space here to acknowledge not only that consent is ongoing but that higher standards of consent can be rewritten by reflecting on past experiences. This is a practice in which we suggest Autistic people, with their attenuation to navigating a variety of embodied and sensory experiences as part of everyday existence, may possess an epistemic privilege. That is to say, Autistic people can offer unique insight into contextual nuances that bear on each exchange, while holding those involved to a higher standard of regard for another.

We are mindful that engaging with the material presented in this book may be triggering for some readers and that frank and open discussion of sex might lead to reflection on previous sexual violence (any sexual activity that happened without consent including rape, sexual assault, sexual abuse, and sexual harassment) both historic and more recent. If this is the case, you are not alone. Some of the writing team have been through this process and offer our hands gently as you read.[1] We wish to acknowledge explicitly that exploration of Autistic (or indeed any) sexuality cannot ignore sexual violence, assault, and rape. We remind you that **all responsibility for sexual violence lies solely with the perpetrator.**

Although legislation and legal definitions differ according to different countries, we present here the legal definition of consent in England and Wales as stated in Section 74 of the Sexual Offences Act (2003),[2,3] which states that someone consents to sexual activity if they

- agree by *choice* and
- have both the *freedom* and *capacity* to make that choice.
- There must be a lack of consent by the complainant and a lack of reasonable belief in the consent by the offender.

A full discussion of these criteria is beyond the scope of this book, but we highlight that sexual experiences are more nuanced than the legal definition sets out and encourage further reading around this area.[4,5]

> Please note this does not constitute legal advice around issues of consent, and we encourage you to reach out to sexual violence support organisations in your country for advice, support, and guidance.

What differentiates sex or affection from sexual assault? In *Creating Consent Culture*, Baczynski and Scott (2022) define sexual assault very straightforwardly: "Any unwanted sex act against a person or people against another person. Examples include but are not limited to: non-consensual kissing, groping, or fondling; attempted rape; forcing someone to perform a sexual act; and rape" (p. 213). In other words, the difference is not so much the act as the presence of consent.

We provide a basic explanation of what consent is and what it is not (see also "Consent Is Everything" website[6]). Consent is *an ongoing process of discussing boundaries and what we are comfortable with doing with our bodies.*[7] Consent is not feeling pressured, manipulated, or coerced in any way into any form of sexual activity (even if you have engaged in that activity with that specific partner previously). Consent is not "going along" with what the other person(s) wants, if you are not sure that you are comfortable to do so. Consent is not feeling unable to say no or indicate no. It is not the other person exerting pressure (however subtly) for the other person to do things with their body that they are not sure they wish to do (be it in vanilla sex, kink scenarios, etc.). Consent is not having one's boundaries slowly pushed so that acts one would usually not consent to become gradually normalised by the other person. Consent is not receiving explicit content via social media or chat apps without prior agreement. Consent cannot be given if the person is intoxicated or under the influence of drugs, asleep, unconscious, or if there are unequal power dynamics. There are specific laws around consent in particular scenarios (e.g., position of trust; when someone is "suffering a mental disorder" as set out in the Sexual Offence Act, 2003[8,9]). Furthermore, consent is not just related to sex of course but bodymind autonomy more broadly, which impacts relations of all sorts. We hope that the discussions in this book help readers to think about the need not only for consent in the most commonly discussed sense (verbal, 1:1, directly before a particular act, etc.) but the need for building a consent culture (see Baczynski & Scott, 2022) from the ground up and creating the conditions under which the negotiations of consent become easeful, normalized, and even joyful. Baczynski and Scott (2022) note that the default culture in media and broader society has not been one of consent culture but instead is far too often one of rape culture (i.e., that of coercion). They ask us to "birth a new normal" by starting a cultural shift toward centering consent (p. 35). We think Autistic people are uniquely equipped to add to this conversation (we are very good at interrupting "old normals"). We hope that the topics in this book can help us to draw on the resources of the Autistic community to find new ways to create environment where consent is baked into interactions at every level of embodiment and for all.

The following is summarised from www.rainn.org[10] and https://rapecrisis.org.uk/:[11]

- Consent should be freely and clearly communicated – this is sometimes described as an "enthusiastic yes".
- Enthusiastic consent means looking for a "yes", rather than the absence of a "no" (e.g., verbal or nonverbal cues, highlighting that although nonverbal

cues might represent consent, verbal confirmation or the nonspeaking equivalent should also be sought). Consent means regularly checking in with each other that all partners are in agreement with whatever activity is taking place.

- Consent does not need to be communicated verbally but is an affirmative expression of consent to engage in a *specific* act (e.g., consenting to penetrative vaginal sex does not mean the person has also consented to penetrative anal sex; consenting to penetrative vaginal sex with a condom does not mean the person has consented to penetration without a condom) at a *specific* time (e.g., just because the person consented one occasion, it does not mean they consent on a different occasion).
- Consent also involves withdrawal of consent at any time you feel uncomfortable, whether that is via verbal or nonverbal communication. For example, someone might have initially agreed to anal sex but does not feel OK with it and wishes to stop. They can withdraw consent and the partner should stop. It is assault if they do not.
- Physiological responses like an erection, lubrication, arousal, or orgasm are involuntary, meaning your body might react one way *even when you are not consenting to the activity*. These involuntary physical responses *do* not mean there was consent.

Consent and BDSM/kink

Some chapters discuss BDSM/kink. There is much to learn about the explicitly negotiated consent that is the "single universal characteristic in BDSM sexual interactions and is considered a fundamental tenet in the BDSM community" (Klement, Sagarin, & Lee, 2017, cited in Goerlich, 2021). Consent is a central underpinning of ethical BDSM practice (Shabaz & Chirinos, 2017). Holt (2016) outlines consent within the kink community, as

> defining terms, negotiations of play, individuals freely choosing to engage in play and creating their roles, communicating needs, wants, and desires to partners and open dialogues with self and community, the notion of responsibility and transparency among community members, and safety and ensuring protection from harm.
>
> *(p. 922)*

Here, we offer two frameworks surrounding consent in the BDSM/kink community:

- Risk-Aware Consensual Kink (RACK)[12]
- The 4Cs Framework

RACK involves a conscious assessment of the balance between the level of risk in behavior being undertaken versus the level of trust in the partner. Valid consent is on the basis of foreknowledge of the risks involved and practitioners being aware of how to mitigate risks of certain practices. This means that the "reality of many of BDSM activities is that the level of risk and consideration for bodily practices is heightened compared to other activities that a person may ordinarily consent to" (Oddie, 2020, p. 113). For example, any "breath play" without *prior agreement and discussion of risks and clear consent* is not kink but assault (e.g., in the UK Section 70(1) DA Act 2021 inserted Section 75A into Part 5 of the Serious Crime Act 2015 (SCA 2015) creating an offense of nonfatal strangulation[13]). *All* participants in the activity must be fully aware of all the risks and consent to all those risks.

Within the RACK framework, consent involves negotiating, communicating, taking responsibility, ensuring safety, and so forth. RACK "also gives importance to distinguishing shared fantasy from shared reality. If you lack awareness of the reality, you won't know for what you are giving consent. Hence, you have to gain clarity on the same beforehand".[14]

The 4Cs Framework put forth by Williams et al. (2014) acknowledges that consent is not only carefully *before* but continues *during* and through reflection *after* the act, acknowledging the role of what they call *deep consent*. This calls on BDSM/kink practitioners to engage with consent fully and in each new situation that arises. The 4Cs outlines three levels of consent: (1) surface consent "yes means yes", "no means no"; (2) scene consent (discussing and negotiating the scene in detail, and at any point or during, any partner can withdraw consent using a safe word/sign; and (3) deep consent (the partner may not be in a mental state to use the safe word[15]).

Communication (which includes feeling able to speak up in a discussion of risk) is central to achieving deep consent, as are Caring and Caution. Caring points practitioners to a larger commitment to each other *and* to values around BDSM/kink. Caution involves risk awareness and safety and highlights the centrality of ensuring that no harm is done.

Consent and chapter content

All chapter contributors have been asked to acknowledge the centrality of consent if referencing any sexual activity as we wish this thread to run throughout the book as the authors consider different aspects of Autistic sexual expression and relationalities. Contributors were also asked to reflect in greater detail on consent where, as editors, we felt it was particularly necessary to clarify their conceptualisation of consent (e.g., in vanilla sex vs. BDSM/kink; recommendations for sex education). In Chapter 5, Roche and Benedetto explain how considering Autistic people's sensory and emotional experiences is crucial to consent, describing how neuronormative communication expectations around consent may mean that when an Autistic person does not explicitly give consent (or conversely, not explicitly say no), this may be misinterpreted leading to nonconsensual encounters (Pliskin et al. elaborate in their chapter that conceptualising consent violations as mere miscommunication fails to address the underlying power dynamics of gendered violence). Roche and Benedetto also explain the potential consequences of sensory differences (e.g., a participant reported being "stealthed" – condom removed from penis without knowledge – and not being aware of this because of their sensory differences). In Chapter 6, Hagerlid describes BDSM practices and the need for explicit communication, risk awareness, and informed consent exploring how BDSM provides an empowering context that meets (and cherishes) their need for explicit communication. Hagerlid also highlights that prior to any scene, there should be a discussion on what acts are consented to, those that are not consented to, and safe words/signs. In addition, Hagerlid suggests that the types of emotions one wishes to experience also form part of the consent process. In Chapter 7, Day and Krazinski reference consent as a central process in two mediums to explore embodiment – ink and kink – both in which one person explicitly consents to another "doing" something to their body. In Chapter 8, Delilah and Bertilsdotter Rosqvist explore kink, including in relation to sensory needs, overload, and clear direct communication. They provide multiple practical suggestions of "checklists" of different issues to consider prior to a scene, all of which can be used to negotiate consent (e.g., considering *who* will be involved; *what* is expected to happen before, during, and after; *what* are the individual's hard and soft boundaries; *when* the session will take place and end; *where* it will take place; *why* – the purpose of the session, e.g., power play, rope play; *how* – how all those involved take care of each other, e.g., safe system, risk assessment). In Chapter 9, Jackson-Perry reports that some participants had experienced sexual assault/abuse and also described situations in which they had felt they had to "go along" with the other person's wishes even if they did not wish to. He highlights how consent is often missing from formal sex education although, of course, this should form the cornerstone of any such program. In Chapter 11, Pliskin et al. discuss "bearing witness to others", including discussing sexual desires and boundaries ahead of sexual activities to aid people to understand each other, clarify intentions, and enhance pleasure. They suggest this might include checklists of activities each partner would like to include. Whereas Pliskin et al. frame this as "bearing witness to others", such practices make discussion of consent explicit and structured and offer a means by which to negotiate sexual boundaries.

Even though this book is not specifically about consent, we have sought to center consent throughout, reflecting as Hagerlid writes,

> Consent is a gift of the kind that can never be taken or demanded, only voluntarily given. As such, consent is an act of trust that should always be treated with great care.

> **Suggested links to websites offering further discussion of consent, and information for survivors of sexual violence (including reporting choices and how to access support):**www. https://rapecrisis.org.uk/www.rainn.org/ www.rcne.com/https://www.thesurvivorstrust.org/ https://www.sarsas.org.uk/https://www.nsvrc.org/ https://www.creatingconsentculture.com/resourceshttps://www.healthline.com/health/sexual-assault-resource-guide https://www.projectrespect.ca/

Notes

1 One of Us dedicates this chapter to RW, a police Sexual Offences Investigation Trained Officer (SOIT) for enabling the unsayable to be said.
2 https://www.cps.gov.uk/crime-info/sexual-offences
3 https://www.legislation.gov.uk/ukpga/2003/42/contents
4 For example, Laker, J.A., & Boas, E.M. (In press). *Advancing sexual consent and agential practices in higher education: Towards a new community of Practice.* Routledge.
5 https://www.nhs.uk/aboutNHSChoices/professionals/healthandcareprofessionals/child-sexual-exploitation/Documents/Consent-information-leaflet.pdf
6 http://www.consentiseverything.com/
7 https://care.ucr.edu/education/what-is-consent
8 https://www.cps.gov.uk/crime-info/sexual-offences
9 https://www.legislation.gov.uk/ukpga/2003/42/contents
10 https://www.rainn.org/articles/what-is-consent
11 https://247sexualabusesupport.org.uk/faqs/#what-is-consent
12 Prior to RACK, SSC (Safe, Sane, and Consensual) was the prominent framework. RACK has recently been adopted more widely, and we choose to amplify here, as an alternative to the ableism that is embedded in the framings suggested by Faccio, Casini, and Cipolletta (2014). We would rather frame consent as primarily a question of access than one of fixed ability.
13 https://www.cps.gov.uk/legal-guidance/non-fatal-strangulation-or-non-fatal-suffocation
14 https://www.tickle.life/blog/defining-kink-bdsm-ssc-rack-and-4cs/
15 https://www.tickle.life/blog/defining-kink-bdsm-ssc-rack-and-4cs/

References

Baczynski, M., & Scott, E. (2022). *Creating consent culture: A handbook for educators.* Jessica Kingsley.

Dike, J. E., DeLucia, E. A., Semones, O., Andrzejewski, T., & McDonnell, C. G. (2022). A systematic review of sexual violence among autistic individuals. *Review Journal of Autism and Developmental Disorders*, 1–19. https://doi.org/10.1007/s40489-022-00310-0.

Faccio, E., Casini, C., & Cipolletta, S. (2014). Forbidden games: The construction of sexuality and sexual pleasure by BDSM "players." *Culture, Health & Sexuality*, 16(7), 752–764. https://doi.org/10.1080/13691058.2014.909531.

Goerlich, S. (2021). *The leather couch: Clinical practice with kinky clients.* Routledge.

Hartman, D., O'Donnell-Killen, T., Doyle, J. K., Kavanagh, M., Day, A., & Azevedo, J. (2023). *The adult autism assessment handbook: A neurodiversity affirmative approach.* Jessica Kingsley.

Holt, K. (2016). Blacklisted: Boundaries, violations and retaliatory behavior in the BDSM community. *Deviant Behaviour*, 37(8), 917–930.

Klement, K. R., Sagarin, B. J., & Lee, E. M. (2017). Participating in a culture of consent may be associated with lower rape-supportive beliefs. *Journal of Sex Research*, 14(1), 130–134.

Lewis, G. L. (2022). Queering the Black feminist psychoanalytic. In J. C. Czyzselska (Ed.), *Queering psychotherapy*. Karnac.

Oddie, M. (2020). BDSM and women's gendered embodiment: Other-than-sex pleasure, pain, and power. PhD thesis, Queen's University Kingston.

Shahbaz, C., & Chirinos, P. (2017). *Becoming a kink aware therapist*. Routledge.

Stern, D. B. (2009). Partners in thought: A clinical process theory of narrative. *Psychoanalytic Quarterly*, 78, 701–731.

Stewart, G. R., Corbett, A., Ballard, C., Creese, B., Aarsland, D., Hampshire, A., Charlton, R. A., & Francesca Happé, F. (2022). Traumatic life experiences and post traumatic stress symptoms in middle-aged and older adults with and without autistic traits. *International Journal of Geriatric Psychology*, 37(2), 1–10. https://doi.org/10. 1002/gps.5669.

Williams, D., Thomas, J., Prior, E., & Christensen, M. C. (2014). From "SSC" and "RACK" to the "4Cs": Introducing a new framework for negotiating BDSM participation. *Electronic Journal of Human Sexuality*, 17(5), 1–10.

PART I
Beginnings

3

BEING YOUNG, AUTISTIC, AND LGBT+

Connections, Influences, and Identity Negotiations

Alex Toft

Introduction

Previous research has suggested that the exploration of intersection of being autistic and LGBT+ disrupts popular conceptions of both and highlights prevailing phobia and exclusion (Jack, 2012; Jackson-Perry, 2020; Toft, 2023a, 2023b). In this chapter, this phenomenon is explored in relation to the lived experiences of young autistic LGBT+ people, focusing on how they understand the intersection, how it works in everyday life, and the language used to express this experience.

After an important note on authorship, there is a brief overview of the research landscape in which the chapter resides, highlighting contemporary research on autism and LGBT+ lives. Although it has been detailed elsewhere (Toft, Ward, & Anon, 2022), a concise overview of the methodology of the project and the approach is included. The main body of the chapter is divided into the three areas. First, there is an exploration of how the participants understood their identities on a personal level; second, this then shifts to look at how this works in everyday life, the negotiations and strategies used, the joys and the challenges encountered. Finally, there is a consideration of the language used to explain the intersection and the potential importance of the autigender/ autisexual labels. The chapter concludes by offering thoughts on the implications of this research.

A note on authorship

The data used in this chapter are taken from a collaborative project by the Young Disabled LGBT+ Researchers Group.[1] Although we have previously written entirely collaboratively (Toft, Ward, & Anon, 2022), this chapter has

DOI: 10.4324/9781003440154-5

been written by Toft and then the group have offered suggestions. Most notably perhaps, the group wanted each findings section to begin with an overview of its content and to then present stories that then would link to previous research. The section then concludes with a discussion on the implications of the findings and why they might be challenging for researchers. Put simply, the structure of the chapter has been guided by the group who found the approach outlined most useful and easy to read. This also relates to the layout of the findings (constructed from the themes), which were worded and phrased by the group.

Research landscape

Research exploring the intersection of being autistic and LGBT+ is an emerging area. In 2020, Lewis et al. noted that they had only found three qualitative studies to report during their literature review. The authors also noted that research has tended to also focus on health and gender (not sexuality). However, there has been a recent surge in research in this area that most likely stems from the move toward neurodiversity studies, away from medicalised deficit-driven research, which is often harmful and dehumanising (Kapp, 2019). Although it is true that there has been a slight bias toward exploring gender and autism, some recent research has tended to focus on marginalised sexual and gender identities in general (see Hillier et al., 2020; McAuliffe et al., 2022). It is important to note, however, that there remains a fixation on "what is missing" in the makeup of autistic people, and this receives the most research interest in relation to sexuality and gender. Research on asexuality (see Attanasio et al., 2022; Brotto & Yule, 2017; Ronis et al., 2021), for example, continues to receive exaggerated attention, as research looks for answers as to why more autistic people might be asexual with the presumption that there is something wrong or deficient about their sexuality. Asexuality in this regard is incorrectly conflated with "nonsexuality" whereas in reality, asexuality is a valid queer identity that has been adopted by disabled and autistic people to describe their intimate lives (Cuthbert, 2017).

Research focusing on the intersection of autism and LGBT+ lives has been mostly concerned with broadly working to understand how identity is supported or even reconciled. In the main, this has resulted in an exploration of the importance of community (Hillier et al., 2020; Herrick & Datti, 2022; McAuliffe et al., 2022; Womack et al., 2022). Echoing the rhetoric of Plummer (1995), these articles have argued that finding others like you is beneficial in making sense of yourself and helping to solidify this identity. As McAuliffe et al. (2002) note,

> Participants emphasized that acceptance from others was key to self-acceptance: "while we need to accept ourselves, for ourselves, I think it is important for most of us to be accepted by other people and community is a huge part of that" (Marianne). Community spaces were vital for feeling "safe and accepted" (Mia).

(p. 6)

For much of the emerging research, community is central to supporting autistic LGBT+ people. Womack et al. (2022) suggest that the sense of belonging and being able to connect with others also has a positive effect on mental health. This, in turn, provides assurance and comfort, and supports people to embrace identity. Both McAuliffe et al. (2022) and Womack et al. (2022) highlight the importance of online communities as accessible places to learn about identity.

Research has also explored sex education and the importance of providing information about LGBT+ lives for autistic young people. Herrick and Datti (2022) have called for educators to be mindful of the intricacies of intimate relationships in the lives of autistic young people. However, they also note that as autistic people are more likely to be a sexual minority (as supported by literature such as Dewinter et al. 2015 and Dewinter et al. 2017), it is important to take a broad and inclusive approach to sexual and gender identities.

Hillier et al. (2020) and Lewis et al. (2020) have both conducted more exploratory work, focusing broadly on identity and lived experiences in which the voices of the participants are central. Hillier et al.'s (2020) work is important in laying the groundwork for more intersectional work, as they convincingly make a case that studying negotiations or challenges by focusing solely on autism is unhelpful:

> Only considering their challenges through the lens of autism, somehow separate from their other identities, results in unhelpful and even harmful approaches.
>
> *(p. 106)*

The research also highlights common misunderstandings about autism, which can have serious implications. The infantilisation of autistic people and the suggestions of confusion regarding sexual and gender identity is likely the most prevalent misconception. As both Hillier et al. (2020) and Lewis et al. (2020) note, such a dismissal can result in feeling misunderstood and lead to isolation. Hillier et al. (2020) conclude that being autistic does not appear to have an effect on understanding LGBT+, but it might have some effect on their gender identity. However, this emerging research continues to frame autistic LGBT+ persons as having a "dual identity" (Herrick & Datti, 2022; Hillier et al., 2020; McAuliffe et al., 2022), particularly with regard to how people engage with one community while having two marginalised identities. Although this is useful, it does not present the intersectional approach claimed, which in essence should seek to understand the challenges of an autistic LGBT+ person wholly. Furthermore, this approach tends to conflate autistic identity and sexual/gender identity, when in everyday life, autism as neurodivergence is often more central to a person's makeup.

Emerging work has explored the relationship between autism and gender/sexuality but from a position of difference rather than deficiency, aiming to produce a more nuanced understanding of the relationship and challenges involved. As Jackson-Perry (2020) succinctly states,

Autistic failure to conform to imagined sexual and gender realities may well create social and epistemic unease. This failure exacerbates the crisis of gender – and of sexuality – noted by Butler. However, to confuse failure with deficit is to do it an injustice. Failure, here, is the mark of survival that makes self-recognition possible, albeit at a price.

(p. 226)

As Jackson-Perry (2020) notes, such an understanding is exciting in terms of how this can "question both what we think we know about autism and what we may be able to know about sexuality and gender through autism" (p. 226). It is this tussle that this chapter aims to address using the lived experiences of young people who are autistic and LGBT+.

Findings

Data analysis revealed three major areas where the participants explored the intersection of autism and LGBT+ in their lives. First, in "Understanding identity and intersections", there is an exploration of personal thoughts on identity and intersections, considering how autism and LGBT+ work in their lives. Second, the chapter looks at how the participants experienced everyday social life and the perceptions of others in terms of being autistic and LGBT+. Third, in "Connection/results/influences", the chapter examines the stories that revealed struggles and debates over the language the participants used to describe how autism and LGBT+ identities work together in their lives. In this section, the chapter will explore how important language can be. This importance is also reflected in the participants' use of the labels *autigender* and/or *autisexual* to describe themselves. The experiences of the participants suggest that social norms do not play an integral part in identity formation. Ultimately, such expectations are not prioritised and are not a central tenet in the construction of sexuality and gender identity. The participants highlight the complex negotiations and language creations they need to enact to explain their lived experiences.

Understanding identity and intersections

This section focuses on how the participants understood the intersection of being autistic and LGBT+. The section proposes that the participants used the term *queer* to describe their identities as this resonated more accurately with their experiences of being autistic and LGBT+. Furthermore, the participants proposed reasons, based on their lived experience, as to why being LGBT+ is likely more prevalent for those who are autistic.

I suppose it [queer] means out of step with the normal. Not what is expected. I generally think of it in the case of when I think about what I'm thinking and what other people are thinking of me. I don't think they line up. I don't know if they ever have so yeah.

(Wyn)

This quotation from Wyn summarises the overall ethos of the majority of the participants. The word *queer* was embraced as a catch-all term to describe both sexual and gender identity while also being closely aligned to the participants' experiences of being autistic. In terms of sexuality and gender, it represented not being constrained by traditional understandings of gender and sexuality, with an emphasis on "openness and flexibility".

For many of the participants, however, queer was being used as a response to challenges in that the broadness of the term *queer* gave the participants the language to describe their lives more accurately or more authentically. It offered potential freedom due to the flexibility that many felt represented their identities. In essence, it was a more authentic representation of who they are:

The reason I call myself queer I mean I guess it's more practically inclusive. So includes anyone who falls outside of the norm in regard to sexuality and gender. So I like that it's the possible combinations that has word spanned sources. It also fits my way of saying I'm not just going to try and conform to society; I'm going to make society fit to me if possible.

(Simon)

Most telling is Simon's closing comment here, his specific rejection of what he is supposed to be and how he fits within society. This was discussed by all participants to some extent. Put simply, the participants felt that as autistic LGBT+ people, they were less likely to subscribe to social conventions and cues, particularly in relation to aspects of life that are socially constructed such as gender and sexuality. Glade, during their interview conducted over instant messaging, highlighted this:

I don't take things for granted or accept that we've "always done it like this." I like to know WHY. I wasn't able to have religion because there wasn't enough explanation WHY. I don't do monogamy because no one could tell me WHY I must.

(Glade; emphases original)

Glade then reflected on this further during their diary:

I am secure enough in myself to explore, manipulate and subvert all aspects of gender. Gender is mine and there are no rules.

(Glade)

The participants' gender and sexuality not aligning with expected social norms is an important finding here. The participants argued that their feelings toward gender and sexuality did not match what is socially expected of them. In short, such social norms or cues were not regarded as priorities; they did not feel obliged to enact them. These stories resonate with the work of Liliana Valvano, who highlighted how autistic people find the concept of gender difficult:

> Generally, a lot of autistic people explain that they just don't get gender. It doesn't make sense. It doesn't feel like it's built for or applies to us. And so therefore we often feel like we kind of exist outside of gender and instead we do what feels right socially and physically for our bodies and our minds, which often does not fit a cisnormative standard of gender.
>
> (*Valvano & Shelton, 2021, p. 157*)

Valvano is arguing that society's notions of gender are more likely to be questioned by autistic people. Yet, what might be more accurate and represented in the stories of the participants is that gender is indeed understood, but it is questioned by autistic people. Indeed, many of the participants of the current research proudly displayed an unwillingness to accept what gender means (or perhaps more accurately what dominant assertions of gender mean). As previously noted, research has sought to explain what it is about being autistic that allows for this. The dominant medicalisation has sought to ascribe something being wrong with autistic people and pursued this from a position of deficit. The participants in this research suggest that this focus cannot succeed and the focus should be on the constructs of sexuality and gender themselves.

The participants suggest it is their unwillingness to accept normative social constructs that often results in them falling within the LGBT+ umbrella. Parker, during an interview, explained this clearly:

> *It's like a lot of people are LGBT and autistic 'cause you know they don't exist within this like confines and they don't really understand that there is a complaint, so they just kind of do what they feel is right, don't pay attention to a societal cue which is to be straight.*
>
> (*Parker*)

This resonates with the work of Kourti and MacLeod (2019) who highlighted how autistic individuals resisted gendered roles and subverted sociocultural expectations. In the quotation above, Parker is highlighting how being autistic means they are not being confined by societal cues or expectations. As a result, they do not follow things that others would see as being expected of them. Ben, also during an interview, explained how they only knew about such expectations as a result of being disciplined (in school) for crossing them:

I think the best thing about being autistic is the freedom from social norms, that others can feel trapped by. I acknowledge that they are there, but some of them I only know they are there because I have crossed them.

(Ben)

This has been expressed previously by Jack (2012) in an important theoretical piece. Jack's language is medicalised and not neuroaffirmative, but their thoughts are useful here. Jack (2012) proposed that current models of sexuality and gender do not take neurodivergence into account and should in fact by labeled as neurotypical models:

> Incorporating autistic perspectives helps to further denaturalize sex and gender not only as fluid concepts but as resources for rhetorical acts of self-fashioning. Paying attention to individuals with neurological conditions, in particular, helps to denaturalize models of gender that might, in some cases, be better termed neurotypical models, since they sometimes presume an innate ability to decode and model an appropriate gender identity or, to the contrary, celebrate conscious acts of resistance to normalizing models.
>
> (Jack, 2012, p. 14)

Research in this area, as noted previously, is more developed in terms of gender identity. Emerging research suggests that an autistic response to the dissonance between neurotypical gender and neurodivergent understandings has been to abandon such exhausting work and to no longer pick a side. As Davidson and Tamas (2016) express,

> First-hand autistic accounts highlight the draining and relentless emotional labour that doing gender "typically" requires, and many on the spectrum respond by explicitly rejecting or simply neglecting its confounding demands, identifying with neither side of the m/f divide in attempts to give up the ghost of gender.
>
> (p. 59)

Such rhetoric suggests freedom from restrictions. However, freedom was often not the starting point. The participants argued that understanding themselves was preceded by thoughts of being broken or not being normal, aligning with Coleman-Fountain's (2020) work on misfit identities. Bailey, during their interview, explained how they felt they were "evil" because they did not fit with her parents' expectations of sexuality (in this case). Bailey's parents had told her that being attracted to other girls was a "symptom" of being autistic.

The participants' stories suggest that they did not accept the social formulations of sexuality and gender identity. The stories of the participants of the current research suggest that the problem lies with the rigidity of preserving dominant forms of sexuality and gender identity combined with the refusal to accept the experiences of autistic people. Second, the medicalisation of both autism and LGBT+ is entrenched within wider societies understanding of both. The alignment of both autism and LGBT+ identities with illness means that research will continue to look for ways to fix people who are autistic and LGBT+.

Everyday negotiations

This section explores the participants' experiences of everyday life, paying particular attention to the perceptions of others and how these are negotiated. The focus here is on how identity is negotiated in light of the misperceptions of others.

The participants felt that autism made them who they were, and although challenges existed, it was generally society not being set up for those who are neurodivergent that caused most problems. Glade, for example, summarises this:

> *Neurodivergency is not something that is going to leave me, and I don't believe I would want it to. I have struggles because of it but I'm also me because of it, and I love me.*
>
> *(Glade; they/them)*

Overall, the participants noted challenges and negotiations related to sensory life (touch, sound, stims) and social life (communication, trust, eye contact, facial expressions, knowing what to do/what is expected of them in certain social situations). Both areas of negotiation could lead to exhaustion and a sense of being overwhelmed. During everyday life, the participants did not often experience consideration of these aspects of life and were expected to mask being autistic. It is clear, however, that a good deal of outdated thinking about autism and, in turn, LGBT+ had a negative impact on the participants' lives. Infantilisation is perhaps the most prevalent misperception experienced by the participants, and there is emerging research to support this (Toft et al., 2020; Whittaker, 2022). Participants reported how they "are still getting painted as children, when we are adults" (Luna) and how :they [parents] don't listen to anything I say; they just think of me as a child" (Albert).

For the participants, misperceptions often revealed themselves when they told people that they were autistic. Simon highlighted this when having a discussion with his friend:

> *If I tell him I'm queer or trans, they're like, Oh I thought you might be. And if I tell them I'm autistic, they are like, What really? You don't seem autistic. That's what people's perception seems to be.*
>
> *(Simon)*

Simon's friend did not think that he seemed autistic. This reveals the preconceptions that they had about what autism should look/be like. As Parker stated during an interview, autism is only for "boys who are unsociable and good at maths".

This often resulted in masking (hiding behaviors that might be perceived as autistic) (see Pearson & Rose, 2023) and also a reluctance in talking about autism. Deckard, during an interview, highlighted this:

> One of my friends who is also autistic and LGBT, when I met her in person for the first time, we first met online, I hadn't told her that I was autistic because I couldn't say that I'm autistic. . . . I was worried that I didn't like come across as autistic and that autistic people who I told would question it.
> (Deckard)

This lack of understanding and space for neurodivergent persons is perhaps most acutely observed when exploring the LGBT+ community. This was noted by Parker in their discussion of "weird queers". Parker here is trying to reclaim it as a weapon against the homogenisation of the LGBT+ community and what an LGBT+ identity can be. First, Parker argued that there was resistance to welcoming neurodivergent people into LGBT+ communities:

> I think a lot of people in the LGBT community don't want to acknowledge that a lot of queer people are also neurodivergent because that damages the image of queer people.
> (Parker)

Parker is clear that there is something at play here in terms of what an LGBT+ person should look/be like. Parker continued this by presenting a story of their experience with an ex-associate who identified as an ally:

> [Name], like, identifies as an ally and she has this friend [name], he is like a very high femme gay man and I'm I was like, oh yeah you like the queers when they're pretty and normal. She didn't like you because you were a weird queer. Even though she like classes herself as an ally, she can't handle it when people don't fall into our perceptions of what a gay person is.
> (Parker)

The stories of misperceptions of autism and what is considered the "right kind of queer" highlight at least two things. First, the initial problem faced by autistic LGBT+ persons is the view that they are not capable of understanding their own sexual or gender identity (Santinele Martino, 2017; Toft et al., 2020). As a result, they are labeled as nonsexual and not having any sort of sexual or gender identity. This is complicated by others' misperceptions about what autism is or what an autistic person "looks" like. Second, the LGBT+ community was noted as not being welcoming and there is gatekeeping surrounding what an LGBT+ person should be. The idea of an LGBT+ community has been problematised and highlighted as not being inclusive (Formby, 2017), and this has filtered through to young people's perceptions about who is welcome

(Parmenter et al., 2021; Toft et al., 2020). Coleman-Fountain (2020) has referred to this with regard to misfit identities, noting that how standing out sheds light on people's access to normality. For the participants in the current research, this was expressed as a fear of "weird queers".

Connection/results/influences

Having explored private and social reflections about the relationship between autism and LGBT+, this section moves to explore how the use of language to describe this relationship was important. The participants considered words and phrases such as "connection", "as a result of", and "influenced by" to explore the relationship. The findings have much to say about the emergence of the terms *autisexual* or *autigender*, and there will be an exploration of their meaning and potential importance here.

None of the participants felt that being LGBT+ was "as a result" of being autistic. Such language was seen as being problematic because it implied that being LGBT+ was a symptom of an illness and that being autistic was itself an illness. A number of participants were also cautious about talking about a connection between the two. Connection for them implied that they were joined and worked together in harmony, which they did not agree with. Luna's experiences are per-haps most pertinent here, as they spoke about influence rather than connection:

> *Not connected for me, but they are . . . like oil and water in a container. They are both in a container but they are not mixing but they are still influencing each other, the oil is not displacing the water but it is influencing what the water does. But they can't mix.*
>
> *(Luna)*

Most of the other participants were happy with the word *connection* but were cautious about its use. Connected appeared to refer to influencing each other and linked in some way but could also infer that they were dependent on one another and were the sole influencing factor. As Deckard stated,

> *I think I would probably use the word "connected" as well. I don't see it as a result, but it depends on how that's perceived because it is not my autism alone has resulted in my gender.*
>
> *(Deckard)*

Deckard is clear to point out that connection can imply that there are no external factors outside of being autistic that have an impact on gender/sexuality.

This discussion has important implications for the emerging terms *autigender* and *autisexual*, which refers to the way that autism can influence how gender or sexuality are experienced – for example, gender and sexuality are experienced "through" autism. As Liliana Valvano states:

We can start by recognizing that being autistic is quite literally one's entire neurology, it's how one's entire brain works. Given that, an autistic person's perception of everything is going to be through the lens of an autistic mind. So, an autistic person's perception and experience of gender is also going to be conflated with autistic cognition and perception.

(Valvano & Shelton, 2021, p. 156)

This can have practical/visible outlets such as dress – for example, dressing for comfort rather than gendered purposes (Valvano & Shelton, 2021) – and this was certainly true for the participants in the current research. Ben explained their sensory needs for clothing but did not pander to gendered norms:

My main outfits that I wear are dungarees that are tight on the legs, or leggings. Or a T-shirt that clings, and dungaree dress, wear a lot of dungarees. They are my comfort. That is the outfit that I wear.

(Ben; they/them)

Also important and in line with the focus of this chapter is that this understanding of autigender and autisexual does much to distance autistic people from deficiency-focused narratives. It helps to frame being autistic as a way of being. However, as noted, there needs to be a recognition that autism is not the sole influence; it is, in fact, the lens, as demonstrated by Kai:

I have used that word [autisexual] before; it's useful to describe things to people. Like autisexual, my sexuality is influenced by being autistic because it's me, it's part of me and how I see things, it's nothing better or worse.

(Kai; she)

Kai highlights their use of autisexual to describe their sexuality to others, suggesting that it is a useful way of showing their connection while moving away from making judgments about deficiency.

Conclusion

This chapter has explored the relationship between being autistic and LGBT+ by examining personal and societal negotiations that occur in everyday life. It has proposed a way of understanding that is based on neurodivergency rather than deficiency and suggested the importance of the use of autigender/autisexual to better understand the relationship between autism and LGBT+ identities. Indeed, the use of LGBT+ itself appears too reductive, and this research clearly highlighted the importance of the word *queer* in their lives. Using emerging frameworks and challenging dominant thinking about autism, the chapter concludes by proposing that the focus should be on better understanding the perpetuation of dominant modes of being in terms of gender and sexuality. The ability to sidestep observance of social norms and cues reveals how young autistic LGBT+ persons shape their own identities. The emerging use of autigender and autisexual, alongside Jack's (2012) proposition of challenging neurotypical models of sexuality and gender, and the life stories of the participants of the current research project appear to be important in providing a more nuanced understanding of the intersection in everyday life.

For practitioners, it is important to listen to and to value the experiences and thoughts of the young autistic people with regard to their LGBT+ identities. It is often the case that autistic young people do not prioritise following social conventions/norms regarding sexuality and gender identity. This is something to be celebrated rather than something to try to constrain.

It may be important to be mindful of the environment in which you are working. The stories reported here suggest that most everyday challenges for young autistic people revolve around sensory experiences. Put simply, society in general is not set up for autistic people.

Young autistic LGBT+ people are sexual beings. Contrary to popular beliefs, they are not all asexual, although some do identify in this way as a valid sexual orientation. Many do desire intimate relationships, as is often the case with neurotypical folks.

This chapter has highlighted how the language that we have to discuss sexuality and gender is inadequate. Practitioners need to be mindful of this and should be led by young people in creating new stories and language. The stories highlighted in this chapter have particularly noted the usefulness of the term *queer*, as it allows for greater flexibility and personal agency. However, a more progressive approach would be to acknowledge that existing language is largely irrelevant. For autistic people and communities working together, this is largely unproblematic, but difficulties arise in engagement with neurotypical people trying to gain understanding. The stories in this chapter suggest that flexibility and creativity are important. At the very least, practitioners should be aware of the potentially important ways of thinking represented by the terms *autigender* and *autisexual*.

Practitioners need to be aware that the stories in this chapter are not new. They are not radical or uncommon. These stories have been told for many years but continue to be ignored, most likely as a result of continued medicalisation of autistic identities. There are online communities and activists who have been working tirelessly to redress the balance by allowing autistic people to be experts on their own lives.

Note

1 Referred to as the "group" throughout.

Acknowledgments

I would like to thank the Young Disabled LGBT+ Researchers Group for their help in producing this chapter. Although they did not take part in the writing process this time, their input regarding the structure of the chapter and its layout was very important in working to produce a clear and logical piece of work.

References

Attanasio, M., Masedu, F., Quattrini, F., Pino, M.C., Vagnetti, R., Valenti, M., & Mazza, M. (2021). Are autism spectrum disorder and asexuality connected? *Archives of Sexual Behavior*, 1–25. http://dx.doi.org/10.1007/s10508-021-02177-4.

Bertilsdotter Rosqvist, H., Chown, N., & Stenning, A. (Eds.). (2020). *Neurodiversity studies: A new critical paradigm*. Routledge.

Bertilsdotter Rosqvist, H., & Jackson-Perry, D. (2021). Not doing it properly? (Re)producing and resisting knowledge through narratives of autistic sexualities. *Sexuality and Disability*, 39(2), 327–344. http://dx.doi.org/10.1007/s11195-020-09624-5.

Botha, M., & Cage, E. (2022). "Autism research is in crisis": A mixed method study of researcher's constructions of autistic people and autism research. Epub ahead of print, 14 July 2022.https://doi.org/10.31219/osf.io/w4389.

Botha, M., Dibb, B., & Frost, D. M. (2022). "Autism is me": An investigation of how autistic individuals make sense of autism and stigma. *Disability & Society*, 37(3), 427–453. http://dx.doi.org/10.1080/09687599.2020.1822782.

Braun, V., & Clarke, V. (2006). Using thematic analysis in psychology. *Qualitative Research in Psychology*, 3(2), 77–101. http://dx.doi.org/10.1191/1478088706qp063oa.

Brotto, L. A., & Yule, M. (2017). Asexuality: Sexual orientation, paraphilia, sexual dysfunction, or none of the above? *Archives of Sexual Behavior*, 46(3), 619–627. http://dx.doi.org/10.1007/s10508-016-0802-7.

Chapman, R. (2019). Autism as a form of life: Wittgenstein and the psychological coherence of autism. *Metaphilosophy*, 50(4), 421–440. http://dx.doi.org/10.1111/meta.12366.

Coleman-Fountain, E. (2020). Lived difference: Ordinariness and misfitting in the lives of disabled and LGBT youth. In A. Toft & A. Franklin (Eds.), *Young, disabled and LGBT+: Voices, identities and intersections* (pp. 93–105). Routledge.

Cuthbert, K. (2017). You have to be normal to be abnormal: An empirically grounded exploration of the intersection of asexuality and disability. *Sociology*, 51(2), 241–257. http://dx.doi.org/10.1177/0038038515587639.

Davidson, J., & Tamas, S. (2016). Autism and the ghost of gender. *Emotion, Space and Society* (19), 59–65.

Dewinter, J., De Graaf, H., & Begeer, S. (2017). Sexual orientation, gender identity, and romantic relationships in adolescents and adults with autism spectrum disorder. *Journal of Autism and Developmental Disorders*, 47(9), 2927–2934. doi:10.1007/s10803-017-3199-9.

Dewinter, J., Vermeiren, R., Vanwesenbeeck I., Lobbestael, J., & Nieuwenhuizen, C. (2015). Sexuality in adolescent boys with autism spectrum disorder: Self-reported behaviours and attitudes. *Journal of Autism and Developmental Disorders*, 45(3), 731–741. doi:10.1007/s10803-014-2226-3.

Dinishak, J. (2016). The deficit view and its critics. *Disability Studies Quarterly*, 36(4).

Evans, B. (2013). How autism became autism: The radical transformation of a central concept of child development in Britain. *History of the Human Sciences*, 26(3), 3–31. http://dx.doi.org/10.1177/0952695113484320.

Formby, E. (2017). *Exploring LGBT spaces and communities: Contrasting identities, belongings and wellbeing*. Routledge.

Gillespie-Lynch, K., Kapp, S. K., Brooks, P. J., Pickens, J., & Schwartzman, B. (2017). Whose expertise is it? Evidence for autistic adults as critical autism experts. *Frontiers in Psychology*, 8, 438. http://dx.doi.org/10.3389/fpsyg.2017.00438.

Herrick, S. J., & Datti, P. A. (2022). Autism spectrum disorder and sexual minority identity: Sex education implications. *American Journal of Sexuality Education*, 17(2), 257–276. http://dx.doi.org/10.1080/15546128.2021.2002225.

Hillier, A., Gallop, N., Mendes, E., Tellez, D., Buckingham, A., Nizami, A., & O'Toole, D. (2020). LGBTQ+ and autism spectrum disorder: Experiences and challenges. *International Journal of Transgender Health*, 21(1), 98–110. http://dx.doi.org/10.1080/15532739.2019.1594484.

Jack, J. (2012). Gender copia: Feminist rhetorical perspectives on an autistic concept of sex/gender. *Women's Studies in Communication*, 35(1), 1–17. http://dx.doi.org/10.1080/07491409.2012.667519.

Jackson-Perry, D. (2020). The autistic art of failure? Unknowing imperfect systems of sexuality and gender. *Scandinavian Journal of Disability Research*, 22(1). http://dx.doi.org/10.16993/sjdr.634.

Kapp, S. (2019). How social deficit models exacerbate the medical model: Autism as case in point. *Autism Policy & Practice*, 2(1), 3–28.

Kourti, M., & MacLeod, A. (2019). "I don't feel like a gender, I feel like myself": Autistic individuals raised as girls exploring gender identity. *Autism in Adulthood*, 1(1), 52–59. http://dx.doi.org/10.1089/aut.2018.0001.

Lewis, L. F., Ward, C., Jarvis, N., & Cawley, E. (2020). "Straight sex is complicated enough!": The lived experiences of autistics who are gay, lesbian, bisexual, asexual, or other sexual orientations. *Journal of Autism and Developmental Disorders*, 51(7), 2324–2337. http://dx.doi.org/10.1007/s10803-020-04696-w.

McAuliffe, C., Walsh, R. J., & Cage, E. (2022). "My whole life has been a process of finding labels that fit": A thematic analysis of autistic LGBTQIA+ identity and inclusion in the LGBTQIA+ community. *Autism in Adulthood*. https://doi.org/10.1089/aut.2021.0074.

Milton, D. (2012). On the ontological status of autism: The "double empathy problem." *Disability and Society*, 27(6), 883–887.

Milton, D. (2017). *A mismatch of salience*. Pavilion.

Parmenter, J. G., Galliher, R. V., & Maughan, A. D. (2021). LGBTQ+ emerging adults perceptions of discrimination and exclusion within the LGBTQ+ community. *Psychology & Sexuality*, 12(4), 289–304.

Parsloe, S. M. (2015). Discourses of disability, narratives of community: Reclaiming an autistic identity online. *Journal of Applied Communication Research*, 43(3), 336–356. http://dx.doi.org/10.1080/00909882.2015.1052829.

Pearson, A., & Rose, K. (2023). *Autistic masking: Understanding identity management and the role of stigma*. Pavilion.

Plummer, K. (1995). *Telling sexual stories: Power, change and social worlds*. Routledge.

Reichow, B., Barton, E. E., Boyd, B. A., & Hume, K. (2012). Early intensive behavioral intervention (EIBI) for increasing functional behaviors and skills in young children with autism spectrum disorders (ASD). *Cochrane Collaboration*.

Ronis, S. T., Byers, E. S., Brotto, L. A., & Nichols, S. (2021). Beyond the label: Asexual identity among individuals on the high-functioning autism spectrum. *Archives of Sexual Behavior*, 50(8), 3831–3842. http://dx.doi.org/10.1007/s10508-021-01969-y.

Santinele Martino, A. (2017). Cripping sexualities: An analytic review of theoretical and empirical writing on the intersection of disabilities and sexualities. *Sociology Compass*, 11(5), e12471. http://dx.doi.org/10.1111/soc4.12471.

Strydom, A., Bosco, A., Vickerstaff, V., Hunter, R., & Hassiotis, A. (2020). Clinical and cost effectiveness of staff training in the delivery of Positive Behaviour Support (PBS) for adults with intellectual disabilities, autism spectrum disorder and challenging behaviour-randomised trial. *BMC Psychiatry*, 20(1), 1–13. http://dx.doi.org/10.1186/s12888-020-02577-1.

Toft, A. (2023a). Telling disabled and autistic sexuality stories: Reflecting upon the current research landscape and possible future developments. *Sexes*, 4(1), 102–117. http://dx.doi.org/10.3390/sexes4010010.

Toft, A., (2023b). "These made-up things mean nothing to me": Exploring the intersection of autism and bisexuality in the lives of young people. *Journal of Bisexuality*, 23(3), 1–21. http://dx.doi.org/10.1080/15299716.2023.2214134.

Toft, A., Franklin, A., & Langley, E. (2020). "You're not sure that you are gay yet": The perpetuation of the "phase" in the lives of young disabled LGBT+ people. *Sexualities*, 23(4), 516–529. http://dx.doi.org/10.1177/1363460719842135.

Toft, A., Ward, B., & Anon. (2022). A young disabled LGBT+ researchers group: Working collaboratively to explore the lives of young autistic LGBT+ persons. *Sociological Research Online*, 27(4), 1104–1112. http://dx.doi.org/10.1177/13607804221125233.

Valvano, L., & Shelton, J. (2021.) Existing outside of gender: Autism and gender identity: A conversation with Liliana Valvano. In J. Shelton and G. P. Mallon, *Social work practice with transgender and gender expansive youth* (pp. 153–159). Routledge.

Womack, R., Pope, N. D., & Gibbs, C. (2022). Autism, queer identity, and applied behavior analysis: A case study in multiple minority identity development. *Research Square.*

4

SHIFTING PARADIGMS IN GENDER-DIVERSE AUTISTIC RESEARCH

Katie Munday

Introduction

The experiences of transgender and gender-diverse Autistic people is part of a growing area of academic interest, perhaps due to an increase in formal identification of autism (Brugha et al., 2018) and a growth in openly gender-diverse people across Europe and the United States (Herman et al., 2017; Rider et al., 2018). Due to the infancy of research on this intersection, much of the work is focused on co-occurrence, finding a considerable amount of gender-diverse participants who are also Autistic (Brown, 2016; Walsh et al., 2018). Transgender identities have been estimated to be twice as common in Autistic individuals, with one study finding 50% of their Autistic respondents identified as transgender or nonbinary (Bush, 2016; George & Stokes, 2016). Unfortunately, the overuse of neuronormative and cisgender perspectives within such work creates the measure to which Autistic people are seen as "successful" in doing or understanding gender, framing Autistic gender identity as a manifestation of Autistic insufficiency (Davidson & Tamas, 2016). This hierarchy of normative success supports a pathology paradigm that understands gender-diverse Autistic embodiment as an *impairment, disorder,* or *burden.* In this chapter, I suggest how we can shift away from the pathology paradigm and medical model within transgender and gender-diverse Autistic research toward the neurodiversity paradigm and neuroqueer practices, which understand differences (and their potential associated support needs) as neutral *with* the potential to be liberatory (Walker, 2021; Walker & Raymaker, 2021).

Euro-colonial society exhibits a narrow and inflexible definition of gender in which there are only male and female assigned to people based on their external genitalia at birth (Bailar, 2023). The gender binary was created to gain power and control and has been enforced and *re*inforced across institutions to keep the

DOI: 10.4324/9781003440154-6

status quo (Bailar, 2023). This framework may explain the continued focus on gender dysphoria as a marker for transness in Autistic people. Not only does this focus disregard trans joy, but it also upholds trans-medicalist views, which imply that *all* transgender people experience gender dysphoria – an intense unease due to the mismatch of our assigned sex and gender (NHS, 2022). These standards of trans normativity rely on conformity to a medical model of transition which emphasises a "born in the wrong body" discourse (McBee, 2012). Through this lens, gender-diverse people are held to sociocultural standards of femininity and masculinity, which polices the way we talk, dress, behave, and express ourselves, creating a hierarchy of legitimacy that demands medical transition to "prove" trans identity (Conell, 2010; Johnson, 2016). Many people who exist outside of the gender binary – in their relationship to their body and the type of gender-affirming care they do (or do not) need – are often left out of gender-diverse Autistic research altogether (Serano, 2007).

Furthermore, research that weds trans embodiment to a medical model of transition may be creating additional marginalisation for low-income gender-diverse people, especially those of the global majority (Johnson, 2016). Adhering to a medical model of transgender experience disproportionately affects transgender people of the global majority as well as people who do not experience gender dysphoria or cannot access formal identification due to systemic racism, misogyny, and transphobia (Budge & Pankey, 2016; Son et al., 2020; Wallisch et al., 2023). The 2010 National Center of Transgender Equality and the National Gay and Lesbian Task Force survey of over 6,000 gender-diverse adults living across the United States found that Black trans people and trans people of color were considerably less likely to have health insurance compared to white community members (Grant et al., 2011).

Shifting research paradigms

The neurodiversity paradigm challenges the pathology paradigm's medicalization of autism, exposing this framework as a cultural value judgment (Walker, 2021). Thankfully, the neurodiversity paradigm has begun to permeate academic research, which has seen a modest rise in studies conducted by trans Autistic researchers (Kourti, 2021; Kourti & MacLeod, 2019; Purkis & Lawson, 2021; Sparrow, 2020). Consequently, the intent of academic research has begun to change from one determining "prevalence rates" to one fighting stigma, improving access to healthcare, and advocating for Autistic and trans rights (Gratton, 2020). Similarly, research by allies of gender-diverse Autistic people has created more inclusive recommendations for practice in gender-identity healthcare and education by reflecting on participant experiences and feedback (Bruce et al., 2023; Lehmann et al., 2020; Miller, 2019; Strang et al., 2018). This reframing of gender-diverse Autistic experiences is starting to improve cultural awareness and responsiveness of practitioners, creating professional allies who are aware of the ongoing violence we experience (Gratton, 2020).

These changes ensure that those of us who sit *outside* typical ideas of being Autistic (white, young, male) and transgender (white, thin, and stereotypically *masculine* or *feminine*) – those of us who challenge normativity – can be included in research. Pushing aside the medical model of disability and trans normativity allows us to adopt a neuroqueer framework (Walker, 2021). Neuroqueer appreciates that Autistic people – those who are neurologically and culturally queer – are more likely to queer our gender expression; however, more broadly it is an intentional subversion of norms that anyone can engage with no matter how one identifies (Walker, 2021). Neuroqueering, as with all queering, does not have a set of guidelines and should be as flexible as needed for the researcher and the information they interpret. So, how could one neuroqueer their research?

1. Understand and appreciate that neurodivergence and queerness may be intertwined and inseparable for some people.
2. Appreciate that Autistic, and otherwise neurodivergent people, can queer our performance of gender (and other elements of our identities) through our neurodivergent embodiment and expression. What is queer to us may sit outside the realms of trans-normativity.[1]
3. Make a safe space for participants to lean into the things that make them unique. For example, one participant in Munday (2022) spoke at length about their 3,000+ zine collection; this participant was comfortable enough to talk about their passion with no fear of judgment for talking "off-topic".
4. Engage in research that queers whose voices get the most attention, including community-led research and engagement outside of academic institutions.
5. Support queer neurodivergent colleagues, research team members, students, and so forth. We are the future of transformation within the academy.
6. Create transformative work that goes against academic norms. Research that centers queerness cannot follow the usual conventions of editorial introductions as queerness cannot and should not be defined, as it is a continuous state of becoming (Edelman, 1994). This leaves space for creativity and better accessibility.
7. Produce work that foregrounds neuroqueer experiences, views, and perspectives. Gender-diverse Autistic people are an important part of human diversity. Uplifting our voices can help subvert cultural conditioning to enable a new transformative era of research.

These ideas can support research that facilitates the creation of spaces and communities in which engagement with critical thinking and experimentation with queer neurodivergent expression are not only accepted but *encouraged*. Neuroqueering research (and other elements of knowledge creation and dissemination) can uplift the voices of gender-diverse Autistic people: our experiences are so vast; so too should be the research about us.

How can we continue to shift research paradigms?

There are many ways in which we can continue to shift research paradigms in gender-diverse Autistic research. This section explores some of these methods. First and foremost is the centering of gender-diverse Autistic experiences and expertise; this allows for more accurate information that improves general understanding of our experiences and can help improve support services. Additionally, research outputs need to align with the needs and interests of gender-diverse Autistic people. Research would also benefit from better inclusion and representation, including ethnic and racial diversity and representation of those who live outside of the gender binary. Another important aspect of all research is facilitating the individual sharing of stories in as safe a way as possible. Participants within Munday (2022) were specifically asked their recommendations for future research on our lived experiences; their recommendations are weaved throughout this section.

Centering gender-diverse Autistic experiences and expertise

Autistic individuals are often framed as lacking epistemic authority (the ability to contribute to knowledge on autism) because we are *too close* to the "issue" of autism. We are judged as producing unreliable knowledge on Autistic embodiment, suggesting that non-Autistic people should have authority over our stories as "bias-free" observers (Hacking, 2009; Hens et al., 2019). Although it is important to talk to those around us to understand how they can scaffold our support and care, consistently circumventing gender-diverse Autistic people means we lose autonomy over our knowledge, stories, and culture (Botha, 2021). Research, and those of us affected by it, would benefit from championing the voices of Autistic individuals as the experts of our own experiences, instead of relying on non-Autistic others to act as an authority over us (Sparrow, 2020; Yergeau, 2018). Many of the recommendations within Munday (2022) focused on the importance of talking to gender-diverse Autistic children and adults directly:

> *You want to know what it's like [to be trans and Autistic]? Ask us! You know, we are here. I know a lot of us would be comfortable answering questions and would quite happily answer questions to help people. [Give us] that option to help educate people.*
>
> *(Derek, 20, trans man, UK)*

> *Just talk to more of us, I guess and have it coming from us, and not make things up about us when you've not talked to us. . . . Yeah, just get more stories out there. It's fantastic for young people coming out, I think it's really important. If they could see themselves represented.*
>
> *(Kim, 50, nonbinary, UK)*

By making the information easier to find and access, as well as having people actually part of the communities providing the information.

(David, 21, trans man, US)

I think the first thing, the most important thing [in research] is to find transgender Autistic people who are willing to share their stories, and then just listen to them, just except that that is their experience. That that is what they have gone through and be accepting of it and not dismissive of it. That's basically all you can do, anything outside of that would be exclusionary of them within their experience, which just doesn't help.

(Scott, 31, man, South Africa)

Participants recommended that gender-diverse Autistic individuals are included in work around our experiences, following the disability rights movement ideal of "nothing about us without us" (Charlton, 2000). Derek suggested that trans Autistic people should be given more options to engage in research, giving us the option to help educate others from our lived experiences. Similarly, Kim highlighted the importance of representation especially for young people who are still "figuring themselves out". Scott explained that lived experience voices need to be centered, listened to, and appreciated.

When engaging with gender-diverse Autistic people, researchers must adopt a curious mind rather than a combative attitude. Critically, no matter how knowledgeable or well meaning a researcher is, if they are not part of the group they are researching, they cannot know these experiences and identities with the same depth and intimacy (Weiting, 2023). This also relates to non-Autistic cisgender parents, carers, and professionals, as this can undermine the gender-diverse Autistic person's autonomy. As Sam, a 27-year-old agender person from the UK, reflected,

I think, in general, it would just be "stop asking people's parents" for one [laughs]. Because I think just generally autism research is so bad because we only study children and speak to Autistic people's parents.

Centering the voice of anyone outside of our community means that many of us feel like we are being experimented *on*, not with. As Scott, a 31-year-old man from South Africa, reflected,

It's very much like . . . I am one of those science boxes, so like the kids get to make slime, and everyone just gets to poke the slime, but I'm not a science experiment; I'm a human being! I don't want to be treated like I am a test tube filled with who knows what; I just want to be treated as a person that's it, but it doesn't happen often, unfortunately, in a lot of research and even in a lot of the support groups, sometimes because they're run by cisgender neurotypical abled people, then they're just always poking and it's – I'm, not an experiment, I am a living, breathing, feeling, human being.

Scott shared his constant frustration with being treated like an experiment rather than a human being. He reflected that people "poke the slime" within research due to the normative identities of those who lead research projects. Autistic people are not here to be educational "self-narrating zoo exhibits" (Shore, 2003, p. 184). We should share our stories as and when we feel comfortable and should not have them shared on our behalf. Robin, a 26-year-old nonbinary trans masculine person from the United States, recommended,

> *Research needs to be including the voices of Autistic and trans/nonbinary individuals at minimum, as like a leadership voice, if they're not running the project, they need to at least be strongly listened to and their ideas incorporated and leading the research. Ideally, Autistic and trans people are leading the research themselves, and therefore their voices by default are part of the planning and implementation of said research. I think once that happens, like you don't have to worry about a lot of other stuff, like it just falls into place.*

Robin explained that issues in current research could be circumvented by including trans Autistic people, especially within research leadership roles. He suggested that such work would focus on participant voices viewed through a trans- and Autistic-affirming lens. Centering the experiences of gender-diverse Autistic people within research teams and participant pools challenges the pathology paradigm and trans normativity, and the inappropriate language that comes with them.

Aligning outputs with the needs and interests of gender-diverse Autistic people

Research must distance itself from the rates of co-occurrence or begin to use these figures to create change in services that support gender-diverse Autistic people. Understanding that there are increased rates of Autistic people engaging in gender-identity healthcare needs to underpin the practice within such services (Bruce et al., 2023; Strang et al., 2016; 2018). Turning aside work that reduces Autistic and transgender experiences to *issues* and *deficits* will facilitate research that accurately reflects our lived lives. As Greg, a 25-year-old trans man from the United States, reflects,

> *While I think a lot of this research could be misguided, looking more at why are Autistic people trans or something, rather than how to help trans Autistic people access better and more affirming healthcare or access mental health services. . . . The study and the researchers need to be*

affirming and informed on autism, trauma, and transgender experiences, I think, for accuracy in the resulting publications. Research in this area needs to be about helping, not just to satisfy curiosity.

Greg suggested that it was unacceptable to merely study the overlap of our identities without exploring how to make our lives better through systemic change. He also shared that researchers need to be better informed to create work that is accurate and change making. Similar recommendations were found in Brooks (2022) where nonbinary Autistic participants outlined that research should be led by the community. Research by some transgender Autistic professionals highlight not only the needs of our community but how these can be appropriately supported by professionals across health and social care settings (Gratton, 2020; Kourti, 2021).

Improving inclusion and representation

It is important to enable more diverse people to be uplifted in gender-diverse Autistic research. Research that centers white European participants and ideals upholds the colonial concept of the gender binary, which is used to control dynamics and production within capitalism (Lugones, 2007). The very gender categories and ideas we use in gender-diverse research may be inadvertently adding to the marginalisation of oppressed peoples. "Neuroaffirming" words can cause similar issues and barriers, the use of "neurodivergent" and "neurotypical" centers white normativity and does not accurately describe Black bodyminds, which have never been considered "neurotypical" (Schalk, 2018). The power dynamics within all aspects of our societies need to be understood to make work that encompasses more experiences, cultures, and languages. The importance of sharing intersectional stories was contemplated by Anthony, a 33-year-old trans male from Australia:

> *It's just the usual issues of whether you're reaching a wide enough participant group. For example, I'm white, English-speaking, well-educated, and come from a wealthy family, so am pretty stock standard in terms of the type of people you would find hanging around trans and Autistic Facebook groups, which tend to be fairly white, English-speaking, and middle class (at least from what I've observed). I'm not sure how to solve this issue, though, as I've never been involved in recruitment.*

Anthony brought up an ongoing issue within Euro-colonial academic research: that many participants are white, English speaking, well educated, and relatively wealthy. Those with higher formal qualifications are also more likely to be participants in research, which erases the voices of those who experience poverty and have less access to education (Henrich et al., 2010). There is a growing area of academic work on the intersection of race, gender diversity, and autism, which appreciates that these identities do not exist within a vacuum (Brown, 2016 Kielsgard & Brown, 2021).

Additionally, research often overlooks nonbinary individuals, as one participant in Munday (2022) shared: "I have not seen [research] that included nonbinary people. It doesn't mean it doesn't exist, but I haven't seen it" (Jay, 31, agender, US). This has been echoed by participants in other gender-diverse Autistic work, such as Kay, a trans masc nonbinary participant in Brooks (2022):

> *Everything [in research] is just cis white boys, so that's crap, nonbinary Autistic work – that doesn't exist. . . . Where are the agender folk? Where are the nonbinary folk? Where are the genderfuck folk? Where are the gendervagues?*

Kay suggested that research focused on cisgender white boys and men erases the experiences of other cultures, backgrounds, and genders. Despite the understanding that Autistic people are more likely to be transgender than our non-Autistic counterparts (Brown, 2016; Walsh et al., 2018), these terms are still focused on the gender binary of trans men and trans women. This focus overlooks participants who identify along, outside of, or between genders, such as those with gendervague identities – in which an individual cannot separate their gender from their neurodivergence (Brown, 2016). For some Autistic people, the words "gendervague" and "autigender" (Adams, 2022) make more sense than gender-diverse terms created by neuronormative people. To better appreciate how Autistic people understand or neuroqueer gender, we must give participants the space to explain their gender without judgment or restriction. One participant in Munday (2022) suggested that they would have ticked a "nonbinary" box had they not been given the opportunity to explain their gender more specifically: "I sort of say 'nonbinary' for everybody else, but I mean, the more specific, accurate label would be 'agender'" (Scott, 27, agender, UK). Researchers could be missing vital elements of people's identities and narratives by using predetermined tick-box answers, saying nothing of inclusion and validation of participants.

There are many who live at the intersection of ethnic, gender, and neuro marginalisation minority, and their support and care must be tailored to their cultural contexts. Gender-diverse Autistic work that continues to center white European, middle-class individuals is no longer "breaking new ground", rather continuing the ostracization of the global majority. Future studies of Autistic gender-diverse experiences should include greater ethnic variability of participants, with global majority researchers at the center of work around their experiences. Improving gender and racial diversity can decenter white European perspectives in research and policy, making more appropriate and representative research for *all* trans Autistic people.

Use your privilege to uplift gender-diverse Autistic stories

An important part of shifting research paradigms is creating a safer, validating, and uplifting space for people to share their stories. Many of the participants in Munday (2022) understood the importance of being able to share their stories:

> I do not think that trans Autistic stories are common enough. It's easy-ish to find them within the online Autistic community, but I think that outside of that the general public never hears of them. There is also a lot of potential for research in this area that I feel is being overlooked because these stories are not as public. . . . I think just having more trans Autistic stories out there would be helpful and make it more accessible. More people should consider writing blogs or books or articles to share their stories. The more they're shared and discussed, the more I think people will be able to understand them. I feel like these stories are both complicated and very uncomplicated; like they are personally complex, it's hard to figure out your identity, but seeing the connections between autism and transgender experiences just seems simple to me.
>
> (Greg, 25, trans man, US)

> My hope is that through storytelling we can humanise trans Autistic people more for a wider audience. It's why I think it's so important to improve representation. People really connect with stories – whether film or books or videogames – so my hope is that by having more trans and Autistic characters . . . we can dislodge some of those old stereotypes and biases people have.
>
> (Anthony, 33, trans male, Australia)

> I want changes to happen, and things only happen when people can actually share their stories and thoughts, and I have many thoughts, and I have many stories.
>
> (Sam, 27, agender, UK)

Greg suggested that our stories are not "common enough"; he recommended more people share their experiences online and in print to improve representation. Similarly, Anthony suggested that representation should be improved in media, with trans Autistic people becoming typical characters across film, TV, and books. Greg, Anthony, and Sam all reflected that change can only occur when people's narratives are heard and shared, appreciating that gender-diverse Autistic people should be at the center of the storytelling and knowledge-sharing experience. The ability to safely share our stories is a privilege that is not afforded to everyone, therefore researchers who facilitate the sharing of these stories must critically reflect on their position of power and what they hope to achieve with the knowledge generated from their research and for whom

(Weiting, 2023). When working with gender-diverse Autistic participants in research, allies should do the following:

- Think about why you are doing the work you plan to. Be clear on your positionality, both with yourself and the participants – why are you doing this work?
- Ask yourself, what will gender-diverse Autistic people benefit from this work? How can the knowledge gained be useful in the real world?
- Appreciate that many of your participants will be multiply marginalised and remain sensitive to this throughout your work with them.
- Offer your pronouns and name to participants before you ask them theirs. Pronouns and names need to be respected and used throughout your work. You can also share your pronouns in your email signature, as this normalises the sharing and understanding of such information.
- Make information and expectations clear. Plain-language versions of participant information sheets and so forth should be offered at the same time as more detailed ones. Surveys need to use clear language with any nomenclature explained.
- Appreciate that your participants are likely to be multiply-neurodivergent, which means their needs may lie outside the "typical" – for example, large-print versions of paperwork for those who are Blind or Visually Impaired.
- Encourage participants to share information on how to best accommodate their needs.
- Give choices in how to engage – some participants may like to talk using spoken word, some may need to type or use augmented and alternative communication (e.g., signing or spelling). Some may be comfortable having conversational interviews and some may need more defined structure.
- Compensation (or lack thereof) should be stated clearly at the beginning of work as this can complicate finances for those on capped income who are receiving financial aid.
- Recruit people in a meaningful way to improve diversity within your participant pool.
- Encourage individuals to share their stories by creating spaces that are safer, validating, and uplifting.
- Experiment with neuroqueering your practice and your understanding of both neurology and gender.
- Believe and support Autistic gender-diverse team members and participants when we advocate for something, even if what we ask for seems "trivial".
- Immerse yourself in the rich work that already exists. Keep up to date with new writers, bloggers, and social media admins, as well as academic work (and cite these creators when you can). Academic work is usually behind in terms of what is happening in the Autistic and gender-diverse community: the creation and re-creation of information and culture happens within communities, not just academia.

- Center gender-diverse Autistic experiences and presume competence – we are the experts on our lived experiences.

Looking to the future

Autistic gender-diverse people are playing a growing role in the development of research, creation of knowledge, and the implementation of best practice across sectors (Adams & Liang 2020; Bruce et al., 2023; Brooks 2022; Brown, 2016; Dale, 2019; Gratton, 2020; Kourti, 2021; Kourti & MacLeod, 2019; Purkis & Lawson, 2021; Sparrow, 2020). Some of us are privileged enough to share our stories globally, including Laura Kate Dale's (2019) autobiography of her life as a gay Autistic trans woman; Maxfield Sparrow's (2020) and Adams and Liang's (2020) edited collections of stories from Autistic transgender people; and Lawson and Lawson's (2017) autobiography on their gender journey as a couple.

We are slowly and steadily shifting knowledge and professional practice toward greater transgender and Autistic cultural awareness and responsiveness, but it is not something we can – or should – do alone. We need researchers and practitioners from outside of our community to become *active* allies, who get used to feeling uncomfortable and use these feelings to explore their own prejudices and gaps in knowledge (Huggett, 2023). The responsibility to shift paradigms in gender-diverse Autistic research belongs to all of us.

Note

1 Trans-normativity relies on conformity to a medical model of transition which emphasises a "born in the wrong body" discourse. Trans-normativity creates a hierarchy of legitimacy which demands medical transition to *prove* one is trans (Johnson, 2016).

References

Adams, N. (2022). Autistics never arrive: A mixed methods content analysis of transgender and Autistic autobiography. *Bulletin of Applied Transgender Studies*, 1(1–2),145–161. https://doi.org/10.57814/de1e-gj97.

Adams, N., & Liang, B. (2020). *Trans and Autistic*. Jessica Kingsley.

Bailar, S. (2023). *He/she/they: How we talk about gender and why it matters*. Penguin.

Botha, M. (2021). Academic, activist, or advocate? Angry, entangled, and emerging: A critical reflection on autism knowledge production. *Frontiers in Psychology*, 12. https://doi.org/10.3389/fpsyg.2021.727542.

Brooks, C. (2022). *Exploring views on future directions of research involving nonbinary Autistic people through lived experience* [Master's dissertation, University of Birmingham]. https://doi.org/10.13140/RG.2.2.22251.82725.

Brown, L. X. Z. (2016, June 22). Gendervague: At the intersection of Autistic and trans experiences. *Autistic Hoya*. https://www.Autistichoya.com/2020/05/gendervague-at-intersection-of-Autistic.html.

Bruce, H., Munday, K., & Kapp, S. K. (2023). Exploring the experiences of Autistic transgender and non-binary adults in seeking gender identity healthcare. *Autism and Adulthood*, 5(2), 191–203. http://doi.org/10.1089/aut.2023.0003.

Brugha, T. S., Spiers, N., Bankart, J., Cooper, S.-A., McManus, S., Scott, F. J., Smith, J., & Tyrer, F. (2018). Epidemiology of autism in adults across age groups and ability levels. *British Journal of Psychiatry*, 209(6), 498–503. https://doi.org/10.1192/bjp.bp.115.174649.

Budge, S. L., & Pankey, T. L. (2016). Ethnic differences in gender dysphoria. *Current Psychiatry Reviews*, 12(2) 175–180.

Bush, H. H. (2016). *Self-reported sexuality among women with and without autism spectrum disorder (ASD)* [Doctoral dissertation, University of Massachusetts].

Charlton, J. I. (2000). *Nothing about us without us: Disability oppression and empowerment*. University of California Press.

Conell, C. (2010). Doing, undoing or redoing gender? Learning from the workplace experiences of transpeople. *Gender and Society*, 24(1), 31–55.

Dale, L. K. (2019). *Uncomfortable labels: My life as a gay Autistic trans woman*. Jessica Kingsley.

Davidson, J., & Tamas, S. (2016). Autism and the ghost of gender. *Emotion, Space and Society*, 19, 59–65. https://doi.org/10.1016/j.emospa.2015.09.009.

Edelman, L. (1994). *Homographesis: Essays in gay literary and cultural theory*. Routledge.

George, R., & Stokes, M. A. (2016). Gender is not on my agenda: Gender dysphoria and autism spectrum disorder. In L. Mazzoni & B. Vitiello (Eds.), *Psychiatric symptoms and comorbidities in autism spectrum disorder* (pp. 121–134). Springer.

Grant, J. M., Mottet, L. A., Tanis, J., Harrison, J., Herman, J. L., & Keisling, M. (2011). *Injustice at every turn: A report of the national transgender discrimination survey*. National Center for Transgender Equality and the National Gay and Lesbian Task Force.

Gratton, F. V. (2020). *Supporting transgender autistic youth and adults: A guide for professionals and families*. Jessica Kingsley.

Hacking, I. (2009). Autistic autobiography. *Philosophical Transactions of the Royal Society Biological Sciences*, 364(1522), 1467–1473. https://doi.org/10.1098/rstb.2008.0329.

Henrich, J., Heine, S. J., & Norenzayan, A. (2010). The weirdest people in the world? *Behavioral and Brain Sciences*, 33(2–3),61–83. https://doi.org/10.1017/S0140525X0999152X.

Hens, K., Robeyns, I., & Schaubroeck, K. (2019). The ethics of autism. *Philosophy Compass*, 14(1). https://doi.org/10.1111/phc3.12559.

Herman, J. L., Flores, A. R., Brown, T. N. T., Wilson, B. D. M., & Conran, K. J. (2017). *Age of individuals who identify as transgender in the United States*. The Williams Institute.

Huggett, B. (2023). Autism research at the crossroads. *Spectrum*. doi:10.53053/TCFY1384.

Johnson, A. H. (2016). Transnormativity: A new concept and its validation through documentary film about transgender men. *Sociological Inquiry*, 86(4), 465–491.

Kielsgard, T. R., & Brown, L. X. Z. (2021). Living at the intersection of autism, race and gender diversity. In M. Kourti (Ed.), *Working with Autistic transgender and non-binary people: Research, practice and experience* (pp. 71–86). Jessica Kingsley.

Kourti, M. (2021). *Working with autistic transgender and non-binary people: Research, practice and experience*. Jessica Kingsley.

Kourti, M., & MacLeod, A. (2019). "I don't feel like a gender, I feel like myself": Autistic individuals raised as girls exploring gender identity. *Autism in Adulthood*, 1(1), 52–59.

Lawson, W. B., & Lawson, B. M. (2017). *Transitioning together: One couple's journey of gender and identity discovery*. Jessica Kingsley.

Lehmann, L., Rosato, R., McKenna H., & Leavey, L. (2020). Autism trait prevalence in treatment seeking adolescents and adults attending specialist gender services. *European Psychiatry*, 63(1). doi:10.1192/j.eurpsy.2020.23.

Lugones, M. (2007). Heterosexualism and the colonial/modern gender system. *Hypatia*, 22(1), 186–209. http://www.jstor.org/stable/4640051.

McBee, T. P. (2012). Trans but not like you think. *Salon*. https://www.salon.com/2012/08/07/trans_but_not_like_you_think/.

Miller, R. A. (2019). "I feel like they are all interconnected": Understanding the identity management narratives of Autistic LGBTQ college students. *College Student Affairs Journal, University of North Carolina.*

Munday, K. (2022). *Stories from under the "double rainbow": Trans and non-binary Autistic narratives* [Postgraduate thesis]. doi:10.13140/RG.2.2.34886.75843.

NHS. (2022). *Gender dysphoria.* https://www.nhs.uk/conditions/gender-dysphoria/.

Purkis, Y., & Lawson, W. (2021). *The Autistic trans guide to life.* Jessica Kinglsey.

Rider, N., McMorris, B., Gower, A., Coleman, E., & Eisenberg, M. (2018). Health care utilisation of transgender and gender non-conforming youth: A population-based study. *Paediatrics*, 141(3), 23–38.

Schalk, S. (2018). *Bodyminds reimagined: (Dis)ability, race, and gender in Black women's speculative fiction.* Duke University Press.

Serano, J. (2007). *Whipping girl: A transsexual woman on sexism and scapegoating of femininity.* Seal Press.

Shore, S. (2003). *Beyond the wall: Personal experiences with Autism and Asperger syndrome.* Autism Asperger Publishing.

Son, E., Magana, S., Pedraza, F. D. M., & Parish, S. L. (2020). Providers' guidance to parents and service use for Latino children with developmental disabilities. *American Journal of Intellectual and Developmental Disabilities*, 25(1), 64–75.

Sparrow, M. (2020). *Spectrums: Autistic transgender people in their own words.* Jessica Kingsley.

Strang, J. F., Kenworthy, L., Daniolos, P., & Case, L. (2016). Depression and anxiety symptoms in children and adolescents with autism spectrum disorders with intellectual disability. *Research in Autism and Spectrum Disorders*, 6(1), 406–412.

Strang, J. F., Powers, M. D., Knauss, M., Sibarium, E., Leibowitz, S. F., Kenworthy, L., Sadikova, E., Wyss, S., Willing, L., Caplan, R., Pervez, N., Nowak, J., Gohari, D., Gomez-Lobo, V., Call, D., & Anthony, L. G. (2018). "They thought it was an obsession": Trajectories and perspectives of Autistic transgender and gender-diverse adolescents. *Journal of Autism and Developmental Disorders*, 48(12), 4039–4055.

Walker, N. (2021). *Neuroqueer heresies: Notes on the neurodiversity paradigm, Autistic empowerment, and post-normal possibilities.* Autonomous Press.

Walker, N., & Raymaker, D. M. (2021). Toward a neuroqueer future: An interview with Nick Walker. *Autism in Adulthood*, 3(1). doi:10.1089/aut.2020.29014.njw.

Wallisch, A., Boyd, B. A., Hall, J. P., Kurth, N. K., Streed, C. G., Mulcahy, A., McMaughan, D. J., & Batza, K. (2023). Health care disparities among autistic LGBTQ+ people. *Autism in Adulthood*, 5(2). doi:10.1089/aut.2022.0006.

Walsh, R. J., Krabbendam, P., De Winter, J., & Begeer, S. (2018). Brief report: Gender identity in Autistic adults: Associations with perceptual and socio-cognitive profiles. *Journal of Autism and Developmental Disorders*, 48(12), 4070–4078.

Weiting, D. (2023). Early-career autism researchers are shifting their research directions: Tragedy or opportunity? *Autism in Adulthood*, 5(3). doi:10.1089/aut.2023.0021.

Yergeau, M. (2018). *Authoring autism.* Duke University Press.

5

THE POWER OF COMMUNITY-GENERATED DATA FOR AN EPISTEMIC SHIFT IN AUTISTIC SEXUALITY

From Stigmatised to Neuroaffirming Sex

Sara Rocha and Mayne Benedetto

Introduction

Sexuality, as emphasized by Foucault (1977), is a construct influenced by discourse, underscoring the importance of examining predominant voices. Historically, the voices defining sexuality have primarily been allistic, resulting in the pathologization and labeling of autistic sexual behaviors as abnormal or deviant. This has led to the medicalisation of the sexual experiences, preferences, and behaviors of autistic individuals (Schöttle et al., 2017; Kolta & Rossi, 2018).

For that reason, we advocate a novel approach to reframe research on autistic sexuality through the utilization of a community-driven methodology. Our aim is to delve into the lived experiences and narratives of autistic women and nonbinary individuals, with the goal of contributing to conversations aimed at establishing a community-led framework for fostering neuroaffirming perspectives on the sexual experiences, preferences, and behaviors of autistic individuals. The intersections involving womanhood, being assigned female at birth (AFAB), or being perceived as a woman frequently coincide with experiences of victimization and negative encounters within the realm of sexuality. We emphasize that the responsibility for any victimization or sexual assault and violence rests solely with the perpetrator.

Although it is recognized that autistic men also face elevated levels of violence, research indicates a higher incidence of physical violence among women and girls (Cazalis et al., 2022) along with increased exposure to negative sexual experiences (Gibbs et al., 2023). Despite this, there is a notable scarcity of studies examining the experiences of autistic women, and virtually none focusing on autistic nonbinary individuals. Consequently, this survey aimed to specifically explore this intersection, encompassing cisgender or transgender women, nonbinary individuals, and any other gender minorities.

DOI: 10.4324/9781003440154-7

The research carried out by Associação Portuguesa Voz do Autista (Rocha et al., 2023), a Portuguese organization led by autistic individuals, offers valuable insights into the sensory and communicational dynamics experienced by women and nonbinary autistic individuals during sexual encounters. This study introduces an innovative methodology, particularly relevant for regions with limited participatory research infrastructure. Primarily, this chapter aims to showcase the potential of community-led studies and methodologies that destigmatize autistic sexuality and empower the autistic community. This approach is applicable across diverse cultural contexts and knowledge bases, contributing to the advancement of the neurodiversity movement and enhancing the current understanding of neurodivergence.

Methodology: Epistemic shift and community-generated data

Although established concepts in autism research within a neurodiversity paradigm (Walker, 2021) are important, many English and academic frameworks may not fully resonate with other social, cultural, and community perspectives. In Portugal, the lack of established and funded projects led by, or involving, autistic researchers in academia has resulted in a dependence on community-driven initiatives by autistic-led organizations and groups. These initiatives aim to advocate for and address community barriers and needs, diverging from research frameworks that predominantly center on academic-led initiatives.

In certain regions where space for neuroaffirming research within academia is limited, the community is taking on the responsibility of driving knowledge forward. Emerging alternative methodologies are shifting the focus from viewing the community as merely the subject of research to positioning it as a leader in the process. One such approach is citizen-generated data, where individuals or organizations representing minority groups, such as the autistic community, actively produce and collect data. These data serve to deepen understanding of their experiences, track progress on their rights, and directly address issues affecting them. Citizen-generated data complement academic or institutional data and empower communities to gather information where data and research are lacking (Datashift, 2017; Meijer & Potjer, 2018).

This method empowers advocates and grassroots organizations to take control of data collection, thereby strengthening their capacity to advocate for their needs and rights and ultimately enhancing their quality of life. This framework holds particular significance in countries where existing research exhibits significant gaps in understanding the situations and daily experiences of individuals from minority communities, which are often unaddressed by academic or institutional research. It has the potential to contribute to research by acknowledging diverse cultural, linguistic, and legal realities. By enabling the community to define priorities and research questions and utilizing study results to inform policy and advocacy, this approach further amplifies its impact.

Various forms and levels of community engagement in research exist, ranging from contributory and collaborative to cocreated data (Shirk et al., 2012). Participatory research in autism is becoming increasingly prevalent, involving autistic individuals and their families in decision-making processes (Keating, 2021). However, the degree of community inclusion and influence over changes varies significantly across different projects. Autistic individuals may find themselves expected to contribute without meaningful opportunities to influence aspects they disagree with.

Community-generated data can be viewed as a form of participatory research, but they transcend mere participation by placing the community in a leadership role throughout the research process. This involves data and projects generated by autistic individuals for autistic individuals. Given that historically, research has often neglected topics important to many autistic individuals, such as autistic sexuality and maternity, and considering the substantial delay, an average of 17 years (Morris et al., 2011) for research evidence to impact clinical practice, community-generated data represent a shift toward research led by autistic organizations and advocates. This shift enables the community to address questions they consider vital for improving policy and asserting their rights.

The study presented here was crafted within the framework of community-driven data and spearheaded by an autistic self-advocacy organization. An online survey, developed collaboratively by autistic advocates and researchers, was extended to autistic women and nonbinary individuals. This survey encompassed both quantitative and qualitative inquiries, exploring their encounters with sexuality, sex education, sensory challenges, and experiences of sexual violence. Furthermore, ample space was provided for participants to raise questions or address issues they deemed important but were not explicitly addressed.

The formulation of questions and the design of the survey were guided by the human rights model of disability. This ensures that the outcomes can be analyzed and channeled into policy recommendations and the development of initiatives that directly address the issues highlighted in the survey. Approximately 160 autistic individuals responded to the survey, with 88% identifying as women and 12% as nonbinary or belonging to other minority genders. Most respondents hailed from Portuguese-speaking countries, notably Brazil and Portugal.

The qualitative findings regarding sensory experiences underwent thematic analysis (Braun & Clarke, 2006), yielding several emergent topics that will be explored in this chapter. Building on these central themes derived from our empirical data, the chapter will emphasize the challenges and opportunities associated with sensory experiences. Specifically, it will delve into topics such as sensory seeking or avoidance, the complexities of hypersensitivity and hyposensitivity, and the delicate balance between enjoyable sensory experiences and overwhelming sensory overload. In the subsequent section, we will contextualize these themes within the broader landscape of research on autistic sexuality.

From stigmatised to neuroaffirming sex

Recent studies have indicated that a significant proportion of autistic individuals perceive their knowledge of sexuality to be limited, primarily sourced from social avenues, with various barriers hindering access to comprehensive sex education (Brown et al., 2014; Barnett & Maticka-Tyndale, 2015; Joyal et al., 2021; Pedgrift & Sparapani, 2022). Our study revealed that most participants acquired sex education through informal means, such as friends (52%) and online platforms or media sources (35%). Although approximately 32% reported receiving sex education through formal classes, respondents uniformly expressed dissatisfaction with the adequacy of the information received.

Fifty-seven percent of the respondents reported not receiving education on consent, while a staggering 91% expressed dissatisfaction with the level of sex education they had received. When queried about their preferences for additional learning, participants stated:

> It wasn't an educational experience that enabled me to grasp the intricacies of consent. There were nuances within the realm of consent that eluded my initial understanding.

> I am still navigating the concept of what constitutes abuse within a relationship. I am also seeking clarity on what types of sexual experiences are considered normal and what defines a healthy sexual relationship.

The lack of information regarding what is considered "normal" was a prevalent sentiment among experiences shared. Furthermore, the absence of resources to articulate and validate autistic bodily and sensory experiences may contribute to a disconnection from our own experiences. With the prevailing standard of bodily experiences being allistic, coupled with the lack of validation for autistic bodily experiences, autistic individuals may inadvertently adopt a phenomenon known as masking (Miller et al., 2021; Pearson & Rose, 2021) that involves autistic individuals camouflaging their innate characteristics, prioritizing the comfort of allistic individuals over their own well-being.

This masking process often results in the neglect of autistic individuals' own needs and boundaries, as they conform to the expectations and comfort of their social environment (Hull et al., 2017). Autistic individuals frequently encounter situations where their boundaries and needs are invalidated, leading to heightened difficulties in both recognizing and asserting them when necessary and even feeling reluctant to do so. Reflecting on these challenges, participants in our study conveyed,

> I became so accustomed to feeling uncomfortable with everything – smells, sounds, tastes, textures – that distinguishing between someone being abusive toward me and my inability to fulfill my social role becomes challenging.

Women are taught to obey and agree. For an autistic woman, conforming to these norms is not merely social guidance; it's a rigid rule dictating what is expected of her.

In intimate relationships, acknowledging the sensory and emotional experiences of autistic individuals is paramount for obtaining informed consent. However, differences between autistic individuals and their allistic counterparts are frequently overlooked or misunderstood by those who are allistic. This lack of recognition can create ambiguity, particularly as verbal communication is commonly accepted as consent within allistic communities.

Autistic individuals may rely on feelings of uncertainty, discomfort, or distress to convey or retract consent, which can pose challenges in verbal articulation, especially during moments of overwhelm (Lewis & Stevens, 2023). Moreover, even when an autistic individual does not explicitly express consent or directly denies it, their actions may not be perceived as such, aligning with societal expectations regarding allistic sexual behavior. Without clear consent, any sexual activity constitutes assault. Even if the autistic person's nonverbal communication of nonconsent may not align with typical sexual expectations, this does not absolve the perpetrator of responsibility for sexual assault; without unequivocal consent, any sexual activity should not proceed. This underscores the importance of exploring the concept of autistic embodiment (De Jaegher, 2013; Mackinlay, 2019) and considering how societal perceptions shape autistic individuals' understanding of themselves in relation to stimming, emotional regulation, and co-regulation.

Discrepancies in emotional regulation among autistic individuals underscore the pervasive neglect of their needs within their social circles. Two fundamental concepts – emotional awareness and interoceptive awareness – shed light on this matter. Recent studies challenge the notion of "disordered emotional processing" in autism, instead attributing it to a distinct display of emotional responses often labeled as alexithymia (Bird & Cook, 2013; Kinnaird et al., 2019; Gormley et al., 2022).

Autistic individuals possess a unique comprehension of bodily sensations, not due to inherent impairment but rather due to limited agency over their experiences and a lack of vocabulary to articulate them. Despite the absence of structural differences, research indicates higher levels of emotional deregulation among autistic children compared to their allistic peers (Barbier et al., 2022). Historically, autistic children have relied on external co-regulation to navigate social situations and learn self-regulation, while their self-soothing strategies, such as stimming, have often been suppressed (Rincover, 1978).

Failure to acknowledge these differences in emotional and interoceptive awareness as part of the autistic experience can lead to autistic bodies and emotions being pathologized as indicative of emotional dysregulation. Consequently, one of the most effective methods of self-regulation for autistic individuals is deemed "unwanted" and suppressed, with attempts made to substitute it with allistic forms of regulation that are considered more socially acceptable. When these methods fail to regulate autistic individuals in the same manner as allistic individuals, they are erroneously branded as disordered.

Stimming, characterized by repetitive self-stimulatory behaviors, serves as a crucial mechanism for autistic individuals to regulate their sensory, emotional, and cognitive experiences, as well as to express various emotional states, including distress (Kapp et al., 2019). This repetitive behavior functions as both a means of self-regulation and a form of communication, enabling individuals to release and manage emotions such as distress, happiness, pleasure, and excitement (Charlton et al., 2021). Stimming typically involves repetitive movements, sounds, or actions and is commonly observed among autistic individuals. Unfortunately, stimming is sometimes perceived as involuntary or disruptive, leading to societal pressures for autistic individuals to suppress these behaviors to avoid embarrassment. When stimming is pathologized and suppressed, autistic individuals may struggle to recognize it as a legitimate means of expressing happiness or distress in specific situations, hindering their ability to effectively manage their emotions or soothe themselves.

In this study, several autistic individuals reported that they only began to understand their feelings once they discovered they were autistic, as there is a supportive community dedicated to "translating" these experiences and interpreting them using allistic behavior. However, being born with a unique "sensorium" and possessing distinct subjective sensory experiences and processing abilities (Murray et al., 2023) means that certain types of touch during sexual encounters, for instance, may be physically painful for autistic individuals. This perspective also disregards variations in the origins, types, and intensities of distress, failing to acknowledge sensory, cognitive, and emotional overload that allistic individuals may not encounter at all (Milton, 2012; Miyawaki et al., 2016; Lewis & Stevens, 2023). For instance, an autistic individual may lack adequate co-regulation support or may face the invalidation of their distress, hindering the development of self-regulation skills.

Co-regulation relies on both nonverbal and vocal cues to navigate emotions, sensory experiences, and physical connections within relationship dynamics (Hilpert et al., 2022). Addressing this aspect has the potential to foster positive co-regulation and instill a sense of physical and emotional security within relationships involving individuals with diverse neurotypes. Considering the variations in communication styles and preferences, including differences in love languages such as words of affirmation, acts of service, physical touch, quality time, and receiving gifts among allistic individuals (Chapman, 1992; McDermott, 2022), it is common for allistic individuals to hold expectations regarding how emotions are communicated and regulated, often anticipating specific nonverbal or verbal behaviors from their autistic partners.

When couples encounter difficulties in effectively co-regulating each other's emotions, unmet needs from both parties can perpetuate a negative cycle, compromising their regulatory abilities (Hilpert et al., 2022). In the subsequent section, we will delve deeper into the experiences and narratives surrounding the navigation of sensory experiences among the participants in our study.

Sensory experiences: Seeking or avoiding?

The unique sensory experiences of autistic individuals significantly influence their perceptions and engagement in sexual encounters, shaping their connection with both their own bodies and their partner's. Although previous research has explored the impact of sensory experiences on the sexuality of autistic adults, there remains a dearth of studies addressing the comprehensive integration of physical, emotional, relational, and social aspects of sexuality with sensory experiences, recognizing their interconnectedness (Barnett et al., 2015; Gray et al., 2021; Sibeoni et al., 2022).

In our study, 85% of autistic women and nonbinary individuals reported encountering sensory issues during sexual activity. Whereas some individuals viewed these sensory challenges positively, enhancing pleasurable sensations, the majority described negative impacts, expressing uncertainty about how to alleviate these challenges. Approximately 5% expressed uncertainty regarding whether sensory issues affected them during sexual encounters.

To address these findings, we categorized the sensory experiences of autistic individuals into three distinct categories based on their experiences of hypo- or hypersensitivity during sexual encounters. These categories, informed by narratives from the qualitative analysis, serve to illustrate the thematic analysis: feeling more, seeking less as hypersensitivity, feeling less, seeking more, hyposensitivity, and balancing the fun sensory experience with sensory overload. Following this, we introduce strategies for sensory regulation, drawing from community-led insights on managing sensory overwhelm or sensory seeking behavior.

Feeling more, seeking less: Hypersensitivity

Among autistic individuals who reported heightened sensitivity to specific sensory experiences, particularly touch, many expressed difficulties in responding positively to light touches, often describing them as painful. In contrast, they indicated a preference for and enjoyment of more pressure and firmer touch. One participant articulated, "I dislike being lightly caressed; I prefer touches with greater pressure, and I generally prefer sexual encounters with less foreplay as it makes me feel deeply uncomfortable". Additionally, some participants noted that their hypersensitivity made it easier for them to become sexually aroused, sometimes leading to perceptions of being more sexually willing. As one participant commented,

> Hypersensitivity makes me get aroused more easily, and this may lead to judgments of me being "easy".

In these conversations, a crucial distinction emerged between touch and pressure. Proprioception, a complex sensory system encompassing body awareness, muscle force, and pressure (Taylor, 2009), was discussed as a potentially regulatory sense. This became evident when participants expressed their preference for stronger, more pressurized sexual experiences. One participant stated,

> I enjoy more intense, pressure-based sexual encounters; otherwise, it doesn't work for me.

Several participants indicated that light touch could sometimes lead to overstimulation and engaged with a sense that offers more regulatory input, such as pressure, to manage their sensitivity to touch.

Feeling less, seeking more: Hyposensitivity

On the opposite side, some autistic individuals described feeling less sensitivity to certain sensory experiences, as touch, potentially leading to situations where they unintentionally harmed themselves. One individual shared, "There are times I've hurt myself without even realizing it. I carry on, only to discover afterward that I've crossed a line when I see bruises and blood". This reduced sensitivity could also impact sexual climax, as reported by participants who mentioned difficulty achieving orgasms. One participant stated, "I require a longer time to achieve orgasms with clitoral stimulation", while another expressed "difficulty in experiencing pleasure". Being less sensitive can lead to dangerous situations or make it more difficult to identify situations of sexual assault, as it was the case that one individual recounted:

> I've been stealthed[1] because I didn't realize the guy had taken off his condom. To this day, I don't feel the difference; when it happens, I have to look or check with my hand because I think it's going to happen again.

A few participants expressed the need for increased touch due to their higher sensory threshold, with some revealing that they used sexual activities as a self-regulatory or stimming strategy. One individual explained,

> I find great comfort in engaging in sexual activities and masturbation, using them as a form of stimming to meet my body's need for pressure and touch. However, this can sometimes lead me into risky situations, as I might engage in sexual activities out of the need for stimming rather than a genuine desire for sexual contact.

This shows the importance of identifying and understanding our sensory profile needs and how to meet them in safe ways, as well as to receive more information on less talked about forms of assault. Sexual assault is always the fault of the perpetrator, but providing knowledge on recognising their own body could provide tools to support them in identifying assault if it happens.

Bondage/discipline, dominance/submission, and sadomasochism (BDSM), for instance, emerged as a method to exert more control over, or play and explore, sensations and pressure, as one of the participants shared:

> Engaging in BDSM . . . I leverage my skin's specific sensitivity for alternative stimuli.

Some autistic people who engaged in BDSM have reported that their distinct sensory requirements during sexual activity are more effectively addressed through alternative stimuli and sexual play. Additionally, having a predefined script or agreed-upon framework allows them to provide prior consent for all anticipated actions, thereby reducing the need for real-time information processing during sexual encounters. However, another participant mentioned that a partner had mistakenly associated their hyposensitivity with sadism, resulting in physical harm, underlining the danger if partners attempt to engage in BDSM without knowledge and previous communication and consent.

The fun sensory experience versus the overload

Some participants also highlighted the positive aspects of having a different sensory threshold. Participants mentioned:

> I always have intense experiences, and so far, that's been really cool.

> At the onset of my sexual exploration, I encountered difficulty in achieving comfort and embracing sensations of pleasure. However, my initial partner demonstrated respect for my boundaries, facilitating the gradual overcoming of these challenges.

In the pursuit of fulfilling sexuality, autistic individuals often rely on their partners' comprehension and accommodation of their sensory requirements and personal boundaries. However, the absence of articulate descriptions, particularly in cases where the partner is allistic, can engender misunderstandings. In instances where such understanding is deficient and the volume of information to be assimilated becomes overwhelming, individuals may experience heightened distress, potentially culminating in "shutdowns" or "meltdowns".

A number of participants highlighted that experiencing a shutdown could impede the ability to provide or sustain consent, as it manifests through dissociation and "zoning out" rather than a clear external response. Some individuals noted challenges in verbal communication, responsiveness, interaction, or cognitive processing during these episodes. Moreover, one participant elucidated how even in ostensibly positive encounters, overwhelming sensory stimuli could precipitate a shutdown.

> People engaged in sexual activity with me without regard for my consent, persisting even when I was experiencing an autistic shutdown or feeling frozen.

> When I experience an unexpected touch, I feel invaded and uncomfortable, even though I initially consented to trying. After a certain point, everything bothers me, and I feel like running away, but I can't react.

These accounts underscore the significant influence of overwhelm and shutdowns on an individual's capacity to provide consent. Moreover, they highlight the potential for perpetrators to exploit initial consent and perpetrate sexual assault against autistic individuals, particularly when they lack the language to comprehend their experiences as nonconsensual. Alarmingly, some autistic individuals disclosed engaging in sexual activity to appease their partners despite their lack of desire to do so. One individual articulated,

> I find tongue kissing uncomfortable due to its texture and the presence of bodily fluids, which elicits a sense of repulsion in me. Unfortunately, my boyfriend frequently expresses his desire for it, leading to frustration and arguments between us. In many instances, I reluctantly comply just to appease him, only to face the consequences of a meltdown in the days that follow.

It is important to highlight that if a partner pressures you into engaging in any type of sexual activity, especially if they know it will cause you to become overwhelmed, they prioritise their own sexual satisfaction over your physical and emotional well-being, which is a clear sign of an abusive relationship and consent violation. Sensory overload during sexual encounters has the potential to turn a positive experience negative, even when the individual was initially willing and consenting.

Recognising and expressing these needs as boundaries can be difficult, especially if they are not aware they are autistic, do not know how to name those feelings, or are invalidated because they are different than the allistic ones, but it is essential to allow them to better understand their desires, needs, boundaries, and triggers, as well as their own bodies and those of their partners. As participants shared,

> What helped me was discovering that I'm autistic. I set limits myself and I know what's causing discomfort now. Before, I thought it was my problem, in the bad sense of the word.

> I am in a process of self-knowledge, and perhaps if I had been diagnosed earlier, I would have a better understanding.

This underscores the significance of diagnosis or self-awareness in fostering personal and individual knowledge. The minimisation of autistic needs as impairment rather than differences from allistic people cannot support autistic individuals in embracing and exploring their sexuality. This approach brands our sexuality as a "deficit" and implies an inherent need for normalization, rather than accepting and validating our experiences to enhance understanding of our needs and boundaries in sexuality and relationships as autistic individuals.

Strategies for sensory regulation

To delve further into the experiences of the participants, we asked about the strategies they use to manage sensory stimuli effectively. The sensory regulatory mechanisms identified were as follows:

1. *Communication and intimacy*: "To navigate this, I engage in open communication with my partner, and conduct 'check-ins' during our interactions to ensure both of us are comfortable or if we need to pause."
2. *Desensitization and time to process*: "I've discovered that I can manage this by preparing my mind. Consequently, sexual experiences may take longer. If discomfort arises, I request a pause, step back, and change the course. At times, I skip certain caresses to allow time for desensitization. When I feel ready, I invite touch again."
3. *Autistic diagnosis and self-knowledge*: "Investing in self-exploration and self-awareness has significantly alleviated these challenges."
4. *Boundaries*: "I proactively establish boundaries for myself, recognizing what currently causes discomfort."
5. *Alternative sex and BDSM*: "Today I practice BDSM, which is an activity that can include sexual activity, but everything is consensual and agreed beforehand, there's a script to follow, a predictability that helps me."
6. *Alcohol*: "I find it challenging to tolerate touch unless I have consumed alcohol."

However, numerous participants expressed uncertainty regarding the management of their sensory issues, leading to avoidance of sexual experiences. Learning sensory strategies tailored to autistic needs can enhance their sex lives by providing guidance on adapting encounters. Nonetheless, caution is necessary with strategies that affect a person's health, such as alcohol or drugs, as they may lead to addiction or other health issues and impair their ability to consent.

Some individuals mentioned resorting to alcohol or drugs to alleviate sensations and anxiety in order to engage in sexual activity. One participant, who experienced sexual assault after using a substance, suggested that this may have heightened their vulnerability to the incident. We emphasise that it is the partner's responsibility to ensure there is clear consent when the other person is under the influence of drugs or alcohol and to determine whether that person is capable of consenting. Autistic individuals may employ tools to cope with ableist societal frameworks (Pearson & Rose, 2021), often bearing the increased burden of choices that can make them more susceptible to violence. Research in this area is limited and urgently needed. That said, gaining insights into helpful and supportive strategies from other autistic individuals can aid them in recognising toxic relationships, such as those where they feel pressured into sex to the extent of needing to numb themselves and in identifying healthy, supportive relationships where they can communicate their boundaries and needs to their partner without pressure.

Considering the previous results, it is not surprising that an overwhelming 90% of participants highlighted a lack of adequate sexual education, specifically regarding consent, dating, and social norms related to sexuality. They underscored the importance of comprehensive sexual education encompassing a healthy sexual life, relationship dynamics, boundaries, consent, recognising signs of abuse, understanding sexual orientation and gender identity, and gaining knowledge about body autonomy.

Recognising the diversity in communication and sensory profiles among autistic individuals is crucial for understanding discomfort, desires, and bodily needs. The absence of this awareness heightens the vulnerability of autistic individuals to experiences of sexual violence, by denying them words to describe their experiences and to recognise and identify their needs and boundaries and when these are crossed and violated. This provides abusers and perpetrators the possibility to hide behind the myth of "normal" forms of consent and relationships to attempt to hide their abuse; however, as previously stated, clear consent should be continuously negotiated between the individuals involved rather than relying on normative assumptions about how consent is expressed. What matters is how each person gives continuous consent.

Our findings revealed that 81% of participants had been in an abusive relationship at some point, with 86.6% of women and 77.8% of nonbinary individuals reporting experiences of sexual violence. About 95.8% of autistic women and all nonbinary individuals had encountered negative sexual experiences in their lives. This highlights the urgent need for comprehensive and inclusive sexual education that addresses consent, boundaries, abuse, and the nuances of social and sexual relationships.

Table 5.1 illustrates why autistic individuals felt their sexual experiences were negative: some reported feeling unable to say no, not wanting to or feeling pressured to engage in those experiences, difficulty identifying discomfort, later regretting those experiences, or being afraid of losing a relationship.

The societal pressure on autistic individuals to adhere to conventional norms and communication standards, which are primarily based on allistic perspectives of consent and interaction rather than acknowledging, valuing, and educating about autistic modes of expression, could potentially contribute to instances of sexual violence within the autistic community. Further research is necessary to explore this issue in depth.

Closing reflections

The recognition of autistic sexuality and its distinct manifestations initiated a reassessment of the essence of autism and its various presentations. We offer

TABLE 5.1 Responses of why autistic individuals felt their sexual experiences were negative, by gender

Why were the sexual experiences negative?	Women N (%)	Nonbinary N (%)	Total N (%)
felt I couldn't say no	102 (71.83)	15 (83.33)	117 (73.13)
unwanted sexual experiences	100 (70.42)	14 (77.78)	114 (71.25)
felt discomfort but didn't know it was discomfort	90 (63.38)	14 (77.78)	104 (65)
was pressured into it	91 (64.08)	10 (55.56)	101 (63.13)
sexual experiences that were later regretted	88 (61.97)	10 (55.56)	98 (61.25)
felt I would lose a friendship if I said no	39 (27.46)	9 (50)	48 (30)
the person was in a position of power (work, professor, etc.)	33 (23.24)	3 (16.67)	36 (22.5)
didn't answer	3 (2.10)	0	3 (1.88)

insights derived from the firsthand experiences and narratives of autistic individuals, aiming to foster novel perspectives and methodologies in comprehending autistic sexuality. This study employed a methodology conducive to data collection by autistic-led organizations for advocacy purposes. The findings of this study have been leveraged to advocate for enhanced inclusive sex education programs, further research on the sexuality of autistic individuals, and the development of neuraffirmative support services.

The transition toward community-led research has empowered autistic participants to express what they deem important, thus unveiling previously unexplored themes. These themes include, for example, the impact of overwhelm and shutdowns on consent, challenges in recognizing and articulating discomfort, and struggles in establishing and maintaining boundaries. By empowering autistic individuals to understand and communicate their sensory and emotional needs, we can enhance their capacity to express their desires and requirements effectively. Derived from this study on the sexuality of autistic individuals and their sexual encounters, we are able to discuss several pivotal insights.

Access to sex education among autistic individuals

Autistic individuals frequently encounter barriers to accessing comprehensive sex education, often resorting to informal sources such as peer networks and online platforms. Existing sexual education initiatives appear insufficient in addressing critical topics, particularly pertaining to consent and the nuanced distinctions between autistic and allistic communication patterns.

Addressing these disparities necessitates a reconceptualization of sexual education frameworks to incorporate considerations for autistic communication styles, highlighting the importance of accommodating diverse forms of expression beyond verbal communication. This approach aligns with the principles of the double empathy theory (Milton, 2012), emphasizing mutual understanding and recognition of differences in communication modalities between autistic and non-autistic individuals.

Understanding and expressing consent

Effective sexual education interventions should encompass strategies for navigating consent that transcend traditional spoken communication methods, thereby ensuring inclusivity and accessibility for autistic individuals within sexual education discourse. Deficient sexual education has multifaceted repercussions on the experiences of autistic individuals. It is evident from participants' accounts that they encounter challenges in comprehending and communicating consent, ranging from describing sensations of discomfort to expressing uncertainty when navigating sexual interactions.

This lack of clarity significantly heightens the risk of sexual assault or coercion, particularly among autistic women and nonbinary individuals. It is imperative that further research endeavors to delve into the nuances of consent within the autistic community, aiming to offer a comprehensive understanding of this issue and devising mitigation strategies to reduce instances of violence stemming from difficulties in expressing and understanding consent.

Masking and boundaries

Autistic individuals may adopt masking behaviors to adhere to social norms, often resulting in the neglect of their own needs and boundaries. Consequently, this can exacerbate challenges in identifying and asserting boundaries within intimate relationships. It is crucial to advocate for neuro-friendly environments and combat systemic ableism, including addressing diagnostic discrepancies. By doing so, autistic individuals can authentically express themselves rather than resorting to coping mechanisms like masking, which only exacerbates issues related to boundary setting and interpersonal dynamics.

Emotional regulation and sensory experiences

Recognising and accommodating the distinctive sensory requirements of autistic individuals is paramount for cultivating enriching sexual encounters and facilitating informed consent. As outlined previously, strategies for sensory regulation, including effective communication, consent, and boundary setting, are pivotal in achieving this goal. Disparities in emotional and interoceptive awareness can contribute to misunderstandings and misinterpretations of needs by allistic individuals. The sensory experiences of autistic individuals significantly influence their perceptions and participation in sexual encounters.

Recommendations

In summary, this study highlights the importance of recognising and addressing the diverse needs and experiences of autistic individuals in sexual education and intimate relationships, with the aim of ensuring their safety, well-being, and autonomy. In response to these findings, we provide the following range of recommendations:

1. Conduct studies focusing on the needs, barriers, experiences, and priorities of autistic individuals in sexuality and relationships, ensuring active participation from the autistic community.
2. Develop and implement inclusive and empowering sex education programs covering topics such as relationships, consent, personal boundaries, sexual orientation, and gender identity, contextualized within the broader social aspects of autistic sexuality. Ensure these programs are accessible to children, adolescents, and adults alike.
3. Create accessible information, education, and communication materials specifically tailored for autistic children, young people, and adults to enhance their understanding of sexual health and violence, as well as available support services.
4. Provide trauma-informed mental health and neurodiversity services tailored to the needs of autistic individuals who have experienced violence.
5. Establish peer support groups for autistic survivors of violence, led by autistic individuals and supported by mental health professionals.
6. Advocate for the criminalization of harmful practices that violate the sexual and reproductive rights of people with disabilities, including sterilization and forced abortion.
7. Integrate specific training on autism and neurodiversity into the education of healthcare professionals to promote rights-based practices and improve access to healthcare services.
8. Expand the availability and accessibility of mobile clinics specifically adapted for autistic individuals by sexual health and violence service providers.

Note

1 Stealthing: when someone removes a condom during sex without the other person's consent or lies about having put one on in the first place. It is considered an offense under the Sexual Offences Act 2003 in the United Kingdom.

References

Barbier, A., Chen, J. H., & Huizinga, J. D. (2022). Autism spectrum disorder in children is not associated with abnormal autonomic nervous system function: Hypothesis and theory. *Frontiers in Psychiatry*, 13, 830234.

Barnett, J. P., & Maticka-Tyndale, E. (2015). Qualitative exploration of sexual experiences among adults on the autism spectrum: Implications for sex education. *Perspectives on Sexual and Reproductive Health*, 47(4), 171–179. https://doi.org/10.1363/47e5715.

Bird, G., & Cook, R. (2013). Mixed emotions: The contribution of alexithymia to the emotional symptoms of autism. *Translational Psychiatry*, 3, e285.

Braun, V., & Clarke, V. (2006). Using thematic analysis in psychology. *Qualitative Research in Psychology*, 3(2), 77–101.

Brown-Lavoie, S. M., Viecili, M. A., & Weiss, J. A. (2014). Sexual knowledge and victimization in adults with autism spectrum disorders. *Journal of Autism and Developmental Disorders*, 44(9), 2185–2196. https://doi.org/10.1007/s10803-014-2093-y.

Cazalis, F., Reyes, E., Leduc, S., & Gourion, D. (2022). Evidence that nine autistic women out of ten have been victims of sexual violence. *Frontiers in Behavioral Neuroscience*, 16, article 852203.

Chapman, G. (1992). *The five love languages: How to express heartfelt commitment to your mate*. Northfield Publishing.

Charlton, R. A., Entecott, T., Belova, E., & Nwaordu, G. (2021). It feels like holding back something you need to say: autistic and non-autistic adults' accounts of sensory experiences and stimming. *Research in Autism Spectrum Disorders*, 89, 101864.

Datashift. (2017). *Using citizen-generated data to monitor the SDGs: A tool for the GPSDD data revolution roadmaps toolkit*. Global Partnership for Sustainable Development Data. http://www.data4sdgs.org/resources/making-use-citizen-generated-data.

De Jaegher, H. (2013). Embodiment and sense-making in autism . *Frontiers in Integrative Neuroscience*, 7, article 15. https://doi.org/10.3389/fnint.2013.00015.

Foucault, M. (1977). *The history of sexuality*. Pantheon Books.

Gibbs, V., Hudson, J., & Pellicano, E. (2023). The extent and nature of autistic people's violence experiences during adulthood: A cross-sectional study of victimisation. *Journal of Autism and Developmental Disorders*, 53, 3509–3524. https://doi.org/10.1007/s10803-022-05647-3.

Gormley, E., Ryan, C., & McCusker, C. (2022). Alexithymia is associated with emotion dysregulation in young people with autism spectrum disorder. *Journal of Developmental and Physical Disabilities*, 34, 171–186.

Gray, S., Kirby, A. V., & Graham Holmes, L. (2021). Autistic narratives of sensory features, sexuality, and relationships. *Autism in Adulthood: Challenges and Management*, 3(3), 238–246. https://doi.org/10.1089/aut.2020.0049.

Hilpert, P., Butner, J. E., Atkins, D. C., Baucom, B., Dellwo, V., Bodenmann, G., & Bradbury, T. N. (2022). Stress crossover in intimate relationships: A new framework for studying dynamic co-regulation patterns in dyadic interactions. *PsyArXiv Preprints 5sjgk*, University of Zurich.

Hull, L., Petrides, K. V., Allison C., Smith, P., Baron-Cohen, S., Lai, M. C., & Mandy, W. (2017). "Putting on my best normal": Social camouflaging in adults with autism spectrum conditions. *Journal of Autism and Developmental Disorders*, 47(8), 2519–2534.

Joyal, C. C., Carpentier, J., McKinnon, S., Normand, C. L., & Poulin, M. H. (2021). Sexual knowledge, desires, and experience of adolescents and young adults with an autism spectrum disorder: An exploratory study. *Frontiers in Psychiatry*, 12, 685256. https://doi.org/10.3389/fpsyt.2021.685256.

Kapp, S. K., Steward, R., Crane, L., Elliott, D., Elphick, C., Pellicano, E., & Russell, G. (2019). "People should be allowed to do what they like": Autistic adults' views and experiences of stimming. *Autism*, 23(7), 1782–1792. https://doi.org/10.1177/1362361319829628.

Keating, C. T. (2021). Participatory autism research: How consultation benefits everyone. *Frontiers in Psychology*, 12, 713982. https://doi.org/10.3389/fpsyg.2021.713982.

Kinnaird, E., Stewart, C., & Tchanturia, K. (2019). Investigating alexithymia in autism: A systematic review and meta-analysis. *European Psychiatry*, 55, 80–89.

Kolta, B., & Rossi, G. (2018). Paraphilic disorder in a male patient with autism spectrum disorder: Incidence or coincidence? *Cureus*, 10(5), e2639.

Lewis, L. F., & Stevens, K. (2023). The lived experience of meltdowns for autistic adults. *Autism*. Advance online publication.

Mackinlay, E. (2019). *Critical writing for embodied approaches: Autoethnography, feminism and decoloniality*. Palgrave Macmillan.

McDermott, C. (2022). Theorising the neurotypical gaze: Autistic love and relationships in The Bridge (Bron/Broen 2011–2018). *Medical Humanities*, 48(1), 51–62. https://doi.org/10.1136/medhum-2020-011906.

Meijer, A., & Potjer, S. (2018). Citizen-generated open data: An explorative analysis of 25 cases. *Government Information Quarterly*, 35. https://doi.org/10.1016/j.giq.2018.10.004.

Miller, D., Rees, J., & Pearson, A. (2021). "Masking is life": Experiences of masking in autistic and nonautistic adults. *Autism in Adulthood*, 3(4), 330–338. https://doi.org/10.1089/aut.2020.0083.

Milton, D. E. M. (2012). On the ontological status of autism: The "double empathy problem." *Disability & Society*, 27(6), 883–887.

Milton, D., & Bracher, M. (2013). Autistics speak but are they heard? *Medical Sociology Online*, 7(2), 61–69.

Miyawaki, D., Iwakura, Y., Seto, T., Kusaka, H., Goto, A., Okada, Y., Asada, N., Yanagihara, E., & Inoue, K. (2016). Psychogenic nonepileptic seizures as a manifestation of psychological distress associated with undiagnosed autism spectrum disorder. *Neuropsychiatric Disease and Treatment*, 12, 185–189.

Morris, Z. S., Wooding, S., & Grant, J. (2011). The answer is 17 years, what is the question? Understanding time lags in translational research. *Journal of the Royal Society of Medicine*, 104(12), 510–520. https://doi.org/10.1258/jrsm.2011.110180.

Murray, D., Milton, D., Green, J., & Bervoets, J. (2023). The human spectrum: A phenomenological enquiry within neurodiversity. *Psychopathology*, 56(3), 220–230. https://doi.org/10.1159/000526213.

Pearson, A., & Rose, K. (2021). A conceptual analysis of autistic masking: Understanding the narrative of stigma and the illusion of choice. *Autism in Adulthood*, 3(1), 52–60. https://doi.org/10.1089/aut.2020.0043.

Pedgrift, K., & Sparapani, N. (2022). The development of a social-sexual education program for adults with neurodevelopmental disabilities: Starting the discussion. *Sexuality and Disability*. Advance online publication. https://doi.org/10.1007/s11195-022-09743-1.

Rincover, A. (1978). Sensory extinction: A procedure for eliminating self-stimulatory behavior in developmentally disabled children. *Journal of Abnormal Child Psychology*, 6(3), 299–310. https://doi.org/10.1007/BF00924733.

Rocha, S., Benedetto, M., Serra, R., Simões, J., & Rocha, M. (2023). *Experiences of sexuality and relationships in autistic women and nonbinary people*. Associação Portuguesa Voz do Autista. https://vozdoautista.pt/sexuality.

Shirk, J. L., Ballard, H. L., Wilderman, C. C., Phillips, T., Wiggins, A., Jordan, R., McCallie, E., Minarchek, M., Lewenstein, B. V., Krasny, M. E., & Bonney, R. (2012).

Public participation in scientific research: A framework for deliberate design. *Ecology and Society*, 17(2). http://www.jstor.org/stable/26269051.

Sibeoni, J., Massoutier, L., Valette, M., Manolios, E., Verneuil, L., Speranza, M., & Revah-Levy, A. (2022). The sensory experiences of autistic people: A metasynthesis. *Autism*, 26(5), 1032–1045. https://doi.org/10.1177/13623613221081188.

Schöttle, D., Briken, P., Tüscher, O., & Turner, D. (2017). Sexuality in autism: Hypersexual and paraphilic behavior in women and men with high-functioning autism spectrum disorder. *Dialogues in Clinical Neuroscience*, 19(4), 381–393. https://doi.org/10.31887/DCNS.2017.19.4/dschoettle.

Taylor, J. L. (2009) Proprioception. In *Encyclopedia of Neuroscience* (pp. 1143–1149). Academic Press.

Walker, N. (2021). *Neuroqueer heresies: Notes on the neurodiversity paradigm, autistic empowerment, and postnormal possibilities*. Autonomous Press.

PART II

Evolving Understandings: Naming the Nameless So It Can Be Thought

6

AUTIQUEER EXPERIENCES OF BDSM

Desire, Communication, and Terminology for BDSM Practices

Mika Hagerlid

Introducing my standpoint and central concepts

What does it mean to be autiqueer?

I write this chapter from an *autiqueer* standpoint. Broadly speaking, autiqueer is defined as "a queer orientation which can only be understood in the context of being autistic, when one's autism greatly affects one's queerness" (LGBTQIA + wiki, 2023). In my personal experience, being autiqueer profoundly impacts how I exist and come into being in my everyday life. Drawing from intersectional and feminist theory (Haraway, 1988,1997; McCall, 2005), I explore the situated knowledge of my autiqueer experiences and perspectives on BDSM. This exploration also includes examining alternative terminology for many common BDSM practices; the purpose is to develop a terminology that better mirrors my autiqueer experience. By doing so, I hope to offer more authentic terminologies for others who also feel the gap between markers commonly used to refer to BDSM practices and their own embodied experiences of BDSM. I also hope that others feel inspired to develop their own terminologies.

Describing the norms: Neuroconventionality, heteronormativity, and vanilla sex

Aside from the term *autiqueer*, I also use the terms *neuroconventional, heteronormative sexuality*, and *vanilla sex*. In this chapter, the term *neuroconventional* describes norms that pathologize neurodivergent ways of doing sex and relationships (McDermott, 2022). This chapter can be seen as a critical counternarrative that describes autiqueer BDSM practices from a perspective of enrichment and legitimacy.

DOI: 10.4324/9781003440154-9

Heteronormative sexuality is an object-oriented sexuality where the biological sex and the gender expression in a person are the central objects of sexual desire. For example, this includes attraction toward secondary gender characteristics such as breasts or facial hair, primary gender characteristics such as genitalia, and a cisnormative gender appearance. My own autiqueer sexuality does not work in this way. Rather than being object oriented, my sexuality is primarily action oriented, which means directed toward performing specific acts (Bertilsdotter Rosqvist & Jackson-Perry, 2020).

Finally, I use the term *vanilla sex* as a marker for a set of sexual practices believed to be so generic that they do not need to be discussed or agreed on before engaging in them. This does not mean that engaging in vanilla sex does not require or involve consent practices, but the focus is generally on consenting to the *initiation* of sex rather than the actual *content* of sex. These practices take place in a dyad of two persons of any gender or sex constellation who have a romantic interest in each other. Moreover, the acts that constitute vanilla sex are usually marked as an expression of mutual love. In contrast, BDSM practices require by their very nature explicit communication, risk awareness, and informed consent. Additionally, BDSM does not necessarily involve the types of genital stimuli, such as penetration, that is usually defined as sex. A BDSM scene might, for example, include impact play and discipline but no genital sex.

Setting the scene

Estrangement

On the occasions when I have been expected to engage in neuroconventional and heteronormative vanilla sex, I have felt crammed into an excruciatingly narrow set of arbitrary conventions. This is true even in cases when there is room to "experiment". I become isolated and separated, not only from my sexual partner but also from myself and the nature of my desires. This is because my autiqueer and BDSM-oriented sexual foundation is qualitatively different from one that originates in neuroconventional and heteronormative vanilla sex. I could in theory perform normality but only at the cost of repressing essential parts of my core self. Consequently, there are clear parallels between my encounters with neuroconventional and heteronormative vanilla sex and Goffman's (1963) concept of stigma. In this work, Goffman (1963) describes the harm done to, for example, sexual minorities, when forced to stage heteronormativity out of fear of social repercussions. However, inclusion only applies insofar that the individual pretends to be something that they are not.

There is a gap between my own autiqueer sexuality and a set of norms that marks it as inconceivable. This personal experience of mine echoes the content of publications on sexuality and autism that have been conducted within the neurodiversity paradigm. They highlight the gap between neuronormative couple-oriented sexuality with established sociosexual scripts and autistic sexualities (Bertilsdotter Rosqvist & Jackson-Perry, 2020; Pliskin, 2022).

Norms as a secondhand experience

Some encounters with sexual partners have led me to start thinking of neuroconventional heteronormative vanilla norms as a personified narrator who demands the right to mark acts, lusts, and desires with normative meaning. A useful distinction here is that between the self and what Mead (1934) referred to as the *generalized other*. The generalized other can be summarized as external social expectations, while the self includes ideas about the expectations of the generalized other (the *me*), as well as the individual identity that arises from responding to those expectations (the *I*). The narrator that I describe is one face of the generalized other in that it represents an abstract and collective expectation that places value on sexual behavior. The strange thing for me as an autistic person is that I have never personally interacted with this narrator or generalized other.

I only encounter the narrator indirectly through other people. These indirect encounters with the narrator manifest in the reactions that I arouse in partners, which span from perplexed to ecstatic when I (often unknowingly) cross the boundaries of established sexual norms. The narrator I encounter is the internal audial experience of what McDermott (2022) refers to as the *neurotypical gaze*, which she defines as "a vision of neurotypical mourning for the perceived loss of normalcy" (McDermott, 2022, p. 54). I think of the neurotypical gaze as yet another face of Mead's (1934) generalized other. McDermott (2022) further describes that when autistic sexuality is viewed through the neurotypical gaze, it needs to be addressed and "fixed" so that normalcy can be upheld. Although she focuses on vanilla sex, this notion could also be extended to the qualitative difference that can arise between neuroconventional sexuality and alternative autistic sexualities, such as asexuality, nonmonogamy, queerness, or BDSM. When autistic ways of loving and desiring are observed from this point of view, they do not reach the normatively set criteria for what such acts should look like and are therefore dismissed and pathologized (McDermott, 2022).

Finding a space, community, and vocabulary for autiqueer sexuality

I find neuroconventional and heteronormative vanilla sex boring at best and at worst deeply disagreeable and directly harmful. Because of this, there is a startling dissonance when the normative narrator marks certain acts as "loving", "warm", and "desirable", and I instead find myself experiencing boredom, disgust, or discomfort. Similarly, sexual acts that I thoroughly enjoy and that are common within BDSM carry markers such as "ugly", "violent", or "destructive". I am left with the impression that the narrator is a rather unpleasant person and, to be frank, a bully. In contrast to that bully, the BDSM scene has provided me with a space and community where my autiqueer sexuality is not stigmatized.

Like many other BDSM practitioners, I use a different set of markers than the narrator does when describing my sexual practice. For me, BDSM is about being deeply interested and invested in interpersonal encounters beyond norms and conventions. A substantial part of my autiqueer sexuality consists of a longing for mental states and activities that do not fit well into my neatly arranged everyday routines; I am nevertheless attracted to them. Examples I will explore further in this chapter are *autistic fusing* where a self merges with that of others (Bertilsdotter Rosqvist et al., 2023), and the euphoric flow of Dom/me- or subspace (Carlström, 2019). Unlike vanilla sex, BDSM offers a space in which I can interact with others beyond many of the norms that confuse me and that I cannot relate to.

Having provided a brief summary how neuroconventional and heteronormative vanilla norms do not fit well with my own autiqueer sexuality, I proceed to a textual exploration of an autiqueer love for BDSM. This also involves exploring an alternative vocabulary that mirrors my own embodied and autiqueer experiences of BDSM. The topics covered below are (1) desire for authentic wholeness, (2) communication as the invocation of lust, and (3) developing a terminology for BDSM practices that align with autiqueer experiences.

Desire for authentic wholeness

Ergi as metaphor for desire

My desire alters my state of mind and opens a door for an exploration of experiences that are sometimes so otherworldly that they can be hard to describe in hindsight, including the experience of ego death. While my self dissolves, it also expands, merging with my actions and with the intentions, feelings, and physical sensations of my partner. In these altered states of mind, I do not necessarily perceive time as linear and often have an altered perception of space.

This process of merging with others is sometimes referred to as *autistic fusing* (Bertilsdotter Rosqvist et al., 2023). In a sexual context, autistic fusing combined with a state of *ergi* can capture the intense transcendental intimacy, trust, connection, and love that I explore and experience in my BDSM scenes. These experiences are in sharp contrast to the cultural representations of autistic people as unable to experience profound connection and love, as described in McDermott's (2022) work.

In old Norse, ergi is a complex term that broadly refers to sexual lust in a receptive capacity. Conceptually, ergi closely captures the way in which I experience desire. Price (2019) translates *ergi* as "extreme lust" but also emphasizes that because ergi as a concept was intimately linked with the practice of *seiðr* (magic), it moves far beyond the modern concept of lust. In the context of seiðr, ergi refers to a state of mind that resides at the intersection of intense arousal and ritual practice; ergi allows its practitioner to enter realms beyond our own. This state of mind comes with strong connotations of the practitioner's sexual receptiveness.[1] Some have argued that this receptiveness refers to the body as well as the mind, the latter playing an essential role in spirit invocation, channeling, and ritual possession work (Price, 2019). The state of ergi is physical receptivity in a sexual sense when combined with the spiritual openness that allows the practitioner to journey beyond the fabric of what we normally refer to as reality.

Rooted in ergi, I want my BDSM scenes to be ecstatic, inter-, intra-, and beyond physical at the same time. Practicing BDSM through the state of ergi provides me with a context that allows me to expand both within and beyond myself. For me, the concept of ergi also emphasizes the spiritual dimension of BDSM, a connection that has been theorized and observed in recent research (cf Greenberg, 2019; Klement et al., 2017; Mueller, 2018).

Altered states of mind and autism

Both qualitative and quantitative research find support for altered states during BDSM play (Ambler et al., 2017; Turley, 2016). My experience of desire as ergi falls into what is sometimes referred to as *monotropic flow* (McDonnell & Milton, 2014; Murray, et al., 2005). McDonnell and Milton (2014) describe monotropic autistic flow as the complete immersion in a task, intense enjoyment in a task, and altered perception (e.g., of bodily input and the passing of time). Moreover, my experiences of ego death show a resemblance to *collective monotropic flow* (Jackson-Perry et al., 2020) in the sense of an experience of collectively engaging in an activity while being in autistic hyperfocus.

For autistic people, monotropic flow states are intrinsically linked to stimming (McDonnell & Milton, 2014; Pliskin, 2022), an activity that produces sensory input that allows autistic people to regulate otherwise overwhelming input and experiences (Kapp et al., 2019; Pliskin, 2022). BDSM is part of how I stim and self-regulate, and my need to engage in BDSM tends to be higher under periods of high stress (cf Boucher, 2018; Grey et al., 2021; Jones, 2020). This is in direct opposition to how many neurotypical people instead experience lower sexual desire during periods of stress (for a recent review, see Jansen & Bancroft, 2023). Moreover, self-regulation is a very different sexual driving force than that of heteronormative reproduction.

Authentic wholeness

The altered mental states that I want to achieve by practicing BDSM through ergi feel much more "true", "whole", and "natural" compared to my everyday mode in social interactions, which is primarily characterized by masking and friction. I have an intense yearning for interpersonal encounters where my desire does not cause confusion or call for immediate intervention to remove what the narrator has marked "bad" from the context. My BDSM desires are also strongly linked to a very specific desire to not only being allowed but being *actively encouraged* to explore and express so called conflicting emotions and mental states without the friction of neuroconventional and hetero-normative vanilla norms. This can include exploring the dynamic between fear/safety, attraction/rejection, pain/pleasure, sadism/love, and so on. The BDSM community has given me a space where my autiqueer sexuality creates intense emotional connection instead of estrangement; it allows my sexuality to exist in its entire nuance and complexity. I want a space where I am allowed to explore both what the narrator has marked "good" (e.g., pleasure and love) and "bad" (e.g., pain and sadism) since the marking of these concepts rarely reflect autistic sensory profiles or intimacy needs (Boucher, 2018; Grey et al., 2021; Pearson & Hodgetts, 2023). I desire experiences of authentic and genuine connection with someone else with whom I can share and explore. In short, I desire an open-minded and open-bodied exploration beyond the flat dichotomies proclaimed by the narrator. Similarly, the autistic BDSM practitioners in Pearson and Hod-getts's (2023) also pointed out how BDSM provided them with a space where they could be genuinely authentic and accepted for who they were at their most vulnerable.

Rooted in my physical, emotional, and mental experiences is a knowledge that many of the experiences marked as opposites rarely are neither contra-dictory nor antithetical. Instead, as a practice that endorses the exploration of complex emotions and physical experiences in intense focus and flow, BDSM is one of the few practices that allows for all of me to exist at the same time. As such, my desire and driving force to practice BDSM is largely a desire for wholeness and intense interpersonal connection.

Communication as the invocation of lust

Mute sexualities

When I grew up, the narrator had dictated that the sexual ideal was a mute one except for an occasional gasp or moan. The agreement that a sexual encounter was going to take place and what that sexual encounter would entail was supposed to happen in a kind of idealized silent and telepathic consensus. Although Swedish culture has been comparatively sexually liberal since the 1950s, sex-positive values were only applied if the sex in question could be considered "good sex" and socially condoned (Kulick, 2005). This meant that it should happen in an already established relationship between two consenting heterosexual adults who are "more or less sociological equals" and should not include any power dynamic, even in the form of role play (Kulick, 2005, p. 208). These notions of "good sex" persist to some degree in a more recent large ethnographic study among Swedish BDSM practitioners (Carlström, 2018). My personal experiences are not much different. In my teenage years, for example, my classmates said that talking during or prior to sex would "ruin the moment" and "break the spell". It was as if sexual lust was the most fragile of spells, doomed to wither into nothingness in the mere presence of words.

Autism-friendly communication and consent practice

For obvious reasons, this approach was not one that suited my autiqueer BDSM desires. Instead, I want and need explicit communication from my partners (cf Boucher, 2018; Pearson & Hodgetts, 2023; Pliskin, 2022). Additionally, the practices that I am primarily interested in require informed consent. In contrast to neuroconventional and heteronormative vanilla norms, the broader BDSM culture provided me with an empowering context in which my needs for explicit communication were not only normalized but marked as cherished and treasured parts of sexual encounters. An example of this is the widespread acknowledgment of the acronym RACK: risk-aware consensual kink. RACK represents the philosophy that engaging in BDSM sometimes involves risks and highlights the importance of making informed decisions about those risks. Consequently, conversations about kinks, sexual driving forces, and previous experiences are all normal parts of getting to know a new partner, be it for a single scene, regular meetings, or a long-term relationship. The practice of making desires explicit in BDSM is a prerequisite for getting those needs met and explored. Words are not labeled a banishing spell but an invocation carried by both lust and joy.

Some have argued that the BDSM scene might be uniquely accommodating for autistic sexual needs because of the large proportion of neurodivergent practitioners (cf Pliskin, 2022; Price, 2022). In other words, neurodivergent people have not entered into an already existing culture of explicit sexual communication but actively participated in the development of that culture (Price, 2022).

In general, a healthy consent culture focuses not only on what a person likes but also explicitly highlights what they do not want, both within and outside of the BDSM context. Good communication about kink practice and desires for scene content should therefore include a discussion on (a) acts that are consented to, (b) acts that a person does not consent to, and also (c) safe words. The last refers to words that can be used to end a scene if needed or to slow down the intensity of a scene. A color scheme is common: green means that everything is good and that the scene can continue; orange means that the intensity of the scene should be toned down; red means that the scene must end. Anyone involved in a scene regardless of their role can use safe words. This means that although one person might be dominant, the submissive person still has a formalized influence over the scene. If the scene involves play that hinders verbal communication, such as using a gag, the people involved usually agree on physical cues, like a hand gesture or dropping a handheld object.

Aside from discussing acts, it is also useful to discuss what kind of feelings and emotions you want to explore in a scene. Examples might be sexual frustration, powerlessness, being wanted, despair, and so forth. I would encourage anyone interested in BDSM play to reflect on the following: (1) What kind of feelings and emotions do you want to be the recipient of? (2) What kind of feelings and emotions do you want to be immersed in? (3) What kind of feelings and emotions do you want to express to others in the scene? Agreeing on acts is good, but there are important qualitative differences in how acts are performed that profoundly impact the emotional dynamic of a scene.

The more specific you can be about your preferences and wants, the better the prerequisites are for a mutually satisfying scene. Moreover, preferences can shift depending on the day and partner involved. For me, having someone consent to a specific scene is incredibly powerful and results in a mixture of feelings like great joy, gratitude, pride, and responsibility. After all, consent is a gift of the kind that can never be taken or demanded, only voluntarily given. As such, consent is an act of trust that should always be treated with great care.

It is also worth noting that in an early stage of exploration of any given kink, it will be hard to say with certainty what kinds of acts are enjoyable and what are not. On her YouTube channel, Midori explained that when someone has no previous practical experience, it is possible to consent to exploration with an unknown outcome (Midori, 2022). Regardless of how much research one might do, it is impossible to know what something new will feel like when practiced. It is also important to acknowledge that this goes for anyone involved in a new activity regardless of which role they have in a scene.

Replacing dominance and submission with collaborative power play

In addition to explicit communication about preferences, BDSM contributes with a possibility to create a comparatively clear agreement with regard to social roles. I find that the added clarity alleviates a lot of the social anxiety that I otherwise feel in contexts where I am to seamlessly "find" my role and understand the roles of others through processes of social exchange that I cannot understand (cf Boucher, 2018; Pearson & Hodgetts, 2023; Pliskin, 2022; Price, 2022). At the same time, I have still experienced a lot of confusion due to conflicting content in established BDSM terminology because different BDSM practitioners might use the same terms for describing different things.

In BDSM, most scenes revolve around a dynamic of what is referred to as dominance and submission. A person who acts dominant during a scene is often referred to as a "Dom/me" or dominant, and one who acts submissively during a scene is often referred to as a "sub" or submissive. People who like to change roles between scenes or during a scene are usually referred to as being S/switch. In addition to the roles involved, the terms also refer to being in certain mental states of dominating or submitting in the scene, such as Domspace and subspace. Sometimes, the terms *Top* and *bottom* are used interchangeably with

Dom and *sub*, and other times to specifically mark practice that does not involve mental or psychological dominance (Goerlich, 2021).

Although these roles – Dominant and submissive – might appear rather clear, the role distribution of being Dominant or submissive has been profoundly confusing to me and something that I have needed to work on with partners. This way of marking these roles fits poorly with what the roles actually entail from a more pragmatic point of view, as both roles involve acts of leading and following. It also does not reflect neurodivergent or queer ways of doing BDSM.

In reality, being a Dom/me or sub necessitates more complex ranges of behavior. For example, a sub needs to have a high level of attention to bodily health during intense mental strain; they must be able to process intense pain and/or pleasure while in an altered state of mind. A sub also needs to engage in responsive signaling – that is, convey how they are impacted by acts performed by the Dom/me. Similarly, being a Dom/me involves a lot of receptiveness and cooperative skills, not just decision-making. During a scene, a Dom/me is expected to be capable of seamlessly switching between initiative, direction, and interpretation based on the signals they are getting from the sub. A Dom/me also needs to remember a large amount of information about the sub they want to engage in a scene with. These are far more advanced tasks than simple decision-making.

I believe that rather than adequately capturing the real role distribution during a scene, the terminology for these roles fills a fantasy function for some BDSM practitioners because it represents the illusion that they want to create. For me as an autist, however, the contradiction between the marking of the terms and the activities and mental states that they actually involve have made me hesitant to use them. I believe that my autiqueer standpoint allows me to see and experience these contradictions more readily than people who are at home with neuroconventional and heteronormative sexual practice.

Although heteronormativity is still part of the broader BDSM community (Jones, 2020), there are plenty of countercommunities in which norm-breaking BDSM practitioners can find support for their perspectives, needs, and desires (Bauer, 2021; Liang, 2022; Speciale & Khambatta, 2020). For example, these countercommunities offer richer and more nuanced perspectives on the power dynamic at play between a Dom and a sub (Bauer, 2021; Liang, 2022; Speciale & Khambatta, 2020). Like many critical BDSM practitioners, I strongly reject the notion that one person in a scene is "in power", while one other person is "without power" or have "surrendered their power". For me, this means that I consider BDSM to be a *collaborative power play* rather than Dominance and submission. Therefore, I believe that it is much more correct to describe a BDSM scene as a temporally constructed role play that alters normal power dynamics.

Similarly, one can play around with terminology for roles if the Dom/me and sub or Top and bottom does not fit. There is a plethora of words used to designate various roles: servant, owner, rigger, rope bunny, puppy, handler, goddess, power bottom, and service Top, just to name a few. Although there is not enough room in this chapter to explore all of these, the important takeaway is that there are many different roles and relationships that can be explored. More than that, the terminology for roles within BDSM play is not fixed, meaning that it is possible to explore and develop new terminology for social roles and relationships beyond what already exists.

Self-reflection and aftercare

Apart from communication about kinks before a scene, sharing introspection and self-reflection about what the scene felt like is a normalized part of aftercare within the broader BDSM culture. Aftercare opens doors for the practice of marking acts and experiences from a place of embodied knowledge outside the neuroconventional and heteronormative narrator's reach. Aftercare and post-scene reflection can thus be an empowering way to create autiqueer counternarratives of sexuality and sexual practice.

At the same time, many descriptions of aftercare within the BDSM community focus on the immediate period following a scene, often about one to two hours. This narrow time frame might not be enough for processing and expressing experiences in the realms of the altered mental states described previously, nor does it necessarily accommodate queer and neurodivergent ways of perceiving time and processing experiences (Bertilsdotter Rosqvist et al., 2023; Samuels, 2017). Broadly speaking, creating counternarratives that reflect autiqueer embodied experiences can be both intellectually and cognitively challenging (see, e.g., Jackson-Perry et al., 2020).

For my own part, I have found that I enjoy physical contact and cuddling as part of my immediate aftercare. This usually includes a very generalized verbal description about how the scene felt, but I cannot always give a detailed account of my experiences. When this is the case, I have used written feedback a few days later when I have had adequate time to process my experience. This written feedback has always been highly appreciated by my partners; they describe that they get both a lot of affirmation as well as useful information for future scenes.

Sexuality and an autistic sensory processing style: Implications for communication

In a sexual context, an autistic person's sensory processing impacts what is perceived as enjoyable (Grey et al., 2021). Because each autistic person has their individual sensory profile, there are not any generalizable sensory preferences. Although most would agree that it is normal that sexual sensory preferences vary somewhat between individuals, the narrator has marked many acts that often align with a neurotypical sensory processing style as "universally good". Unfortunately, these acts include many forms of sensory stimuli that can be directly harmful for many autistic people. Some examples are eye contact, which might feel intimidating and uncomfortable for an autistic person rather than good, and so-called sensual touch which might feel painful. Autistic people might also thoroughly enjoy sensory input otherwise marked as non-sexual. The narrator's marking of sensory processing and sensory experiences in a sexual context is strictly ableist at its core. Although the BDSM scene is open for different sensory processing styles and experiences, my experience is that many people still tend to treat the sensory stimuli marked by the narrator as "universally good" as acts that do not necessarily call for a discussion ahead of time.

There are no generalizable sensory preferences for autistic people, no grand narrative that fits most autistic people's sensory preferences, and no universal set of practices, so-called safe cards, that likely work for most autistic people (Boucher, 2018; Bertilsdotter Rosqvist & Jackson-Perry, 2020; Grey et al., 2021). From an autiqueer point of view, I would instead like to propose a shift of the norms and practices that regard sensory preferences. Such a shift to accommodate autiqueer needs would be to replace notions of a "universally good" sensory input enjoyable for those with a specific kind of body, with norms that emphasize that such preferences are highly variable between individuals. Experienced BDSM practitioners will usually straightforwardly ask if there are acts that a potential play partner finds directly off-putting; this is an excellent opening for this kind of conversation. As neurodivergent practitioners, we should also actively work to create space for these kinds of conversations by asking these questions ourselves. Asking what a partner feels like doing today never gets old and will likely result in a more authentic and enjoyable BDSM practice for all.

Developing a terminology for BDSM practices that align with autiqueer experiences

Sensory relief and sensory direction

In the BDSM community, there is an openness to the exploration of sensory experiences marked by the narrator as "bad" or "nonsexual". When it comes to how sensory processing works, however, this openness still relies heavily on neuroconventional norms (Pearson & Hodgetts, 2023). This can be observed in much of the language around sensory play. For example, the concept "sensory deprivation" is often used to describe the practices of blindfolding a person or dampening their hearing with ear plugs or similar. Calling these practices "deprivation" emphasizes that some kind of loss is taking place. However, for hypo- and hyper-reactive autistic people, this kind of language practice does not adequately capture how such experiences are felt. A more relevant terminology that I have come to use and that is rooted in my own autistic sensory processing style is *sensory relief* and *sensory direction*.

A clear example of *sensory relief* in my own practice is the removal of sight. As I am easily overwhelmed by visual sensory input, such practices do not feel anything like the deprivation conventional BDSM language use implies. Instead, I experience the deep sense of relief and relaxation of "getting a break" from the visual input that is often painful. It also means that I am temporarily relieved of the responsibilities that accompany sight, as my partner assumes the responsibility to pay attention to and interpret visual impressions relevant to safety.

In a related way, play where sensory impressions are suppressed or minimized also functions as *sensory direction*. For me as an autistic person, this means that if one type of sensory input to which I am hypersensitive, such as sight or hearing, is removed, I can experience other parts of the scene more fully. I would not describe this as enhancing other senses, which is a narrative that many neurotypicals use. Instead, my experience is that the suppression of a hyper-reactive sensory input frees up cognitive processing space to more fully explore other sensory input. Other sensory input does not become more intense per se but more accessible.

In addition, the exploration of many sensory impressions can also be a kind of *stimming*. I am very fond of certain textures, temperatures, materials, smells, and sounds. In a neuroconventional interpretative framework, these are marked as fetishism. A useful concept to mark the difference between fetishism and autistic sensory pleasure was recently presented by researchers Pearson and Hodgetts (2023) who instead call this *sensory joy*. While the behaviors might appear similar on the surface, the drivers behind stimming for sensory joy and fetishism are different. Fetishism is usually conceptualized as the desire to derive sexual pleasure from an object or a body part that is not conventionally marked as sexual. Stimming for sensory joy in a BDSM context, on the other hand, is something that helps autistic people to self-regulate and destress, regardless of whether that object/texture/smell/visual input is culturally constructed as sexual or not. The experience of stimming for sensory joy in a sexual context also combines sexual pleasure with the satisfaction of stimming.

Painful pleasures

From my autiqueer position, I find it meaningful to conceptually separate pain from hurt, where pain is a physical sensation as any other and where hurt refers to sensory input and situations that cause actual harm. While pain is a welcomed and highly appreciated practice within the BDSM community, it is often described in a way that mirrors the narrator's marking of the concepts as mutually exclusive or opposites. This can be seen in the widespread usage of phrases such as "being thrown between pain and pleasure" or of "being in the borderland between pain and pleasure" within the BDSM community.

My own bodily experience tells me something very different about physical pain and physical pleasure. It firmly rejects the notion that pain and pleasure are mutually exclusive or opposite inputs. Instead, I find that physical pain usually enhances physical pleasure through the added hormonal pain response. Physical pleasure also can increase pain tolerance. These are examples of the sensory input of pain and pleasure as two bodily experiences that are interactive rather than oppositional. Needless to say, this does not apply universally to all kinds of pain or all kinds of pleasure, and no sensory experience universally feels the same. As mentioned previously in this chapter, a safe context and an altered state of mind are prerequisites for being able to harmonize such sensory inputs. In addition, the combination of pain and pleasure often results in a feeling that is distinctly its own. This feeling merges these two kinds of bodily input in a way that I would describe as synergistic: it is more than merely the sum of its parts. For me, this is a feeling that simultaneously encompasses bliss, satisfaction, arousal, and calm. Moreover, it is not necessarily the case that pain stimuli needs to be combined with pleasure to produce pleasurable sensations. In the BDSM community, the concept *plainsure* is used to describe the pleasure that can be derived solely from physical pain through different kinds of impact play.

In her study, Boucher (2018) drew parallels between stimming and impact play. Like stims, impact play involves repetitive movement, and stims that involve physical pain have been observed to help some autistic people self-regulate. An autistic need to regulate through impact play and masochism are two examples of needs that are not given an outlet in everyday life. The BDSM community might be more accessible in terms of normalizing and accommodating autistic sensory needs. At the same time, having a different sensory profile as an autistic person might also mean that preferences need to be clearly stated.

I know that there are types of play that seem to cause most other people pain, but give me intense pleasure and vice versa. A term used in the queer BDSM community that I have grown quite fond of is *funishment* (see, e.g., the podcast *Queer Sex Ed* and workshop at the event "Queer Rope" at Karada House Spring 2023). The term is often but not exclusively used when referring to types of impact play that induce feelings of happiness, silliness, joy, and pleasure in the responding participant. Funishment, often contrasted with punishment, usually involves a lighthearted mood rather than a serious and strict kind of scene. This concept helps to break away from stereotypical ideas about what kind of moods and feelings "should be" involved in a scene that involves physical pain. It opens up for so-called atypical responses to experiences of pain, such as laughter and enjoyment, all possible parts of an autistic person's alternate sensory profile.

Shibari as a form of stimming

In Shibari, ropes are used to restrict freedom of movement. It thereby falls under the broader umbrella of bondage practices. Rope is a versatile tool that can be used for anything from tying someone's hands in a double column tie to a full body suspension. Using Shibari for suspension places special demands on binding the body in a stable fashion; the rope must be able to bear weight without injuring the person who is tied up.

Within the BDSM community, Shibari has been popularized by photographs shared via BDSM platforms and social media. The photographs depict a specific form of Shibari that takes place under specific circumstances, often embedded in a heteronormative, racist, fatphobic, and neurotypical gaze (Haraway, 1988; Jones, 2020; Lee, 2022; McDermott, 2022). The person doing the tying is usually a man, and the person being tied is almost exclusively a woman. The woman being tied is usually white, young, and thin. She is usually photographed from angles that make her look younger and thinner than she actually is (Jones, 2020; Lee, 2022). Much like in the overall BDSM community, there are feminist, anti-racist, anti-ableist, and queer countercultures within the Shibari scene that challenge the heteronormative visual storytelling (Jones, 2020; Lee, 2022).

As an autiqueer practitioner of Shibari, the dominant imagery described above does not reflect my experiences of tying or being tied, nor does it reflect my motivations. One of my primary motivations for being tied is that feeling the pressure from the ropes on my body is a form of stimming. My personal experience echoes the limited research on autism and BDSM, where researchers have sometimes drawn parallels between practices of Shibari and how some autistic people might use weighted blankets and the like as a stim (Boucher, 2018; Jones, 2020). The pain of the ropes cutting into the skin makes me happy and relaxed, as does the restriction of breathing that comes from being tightly tied across the ribs, waist, and stomach. In restrictive bindings, I can also create more pressure and pain if I want to – for example, by trying to straighten out a leg in a futomomo.[2] Like many autistic people, I sometimes struggle with pro-prioception – the ability to feel where my body is and where my body ends. The intense and often painful physical sensation of the Shibari ropes helps me become firmly rooted in body and my bodily limits.

Another driving force of mine is the subversive deconstruction of hetero-normative beauty standards that Shibari makes possible. In contrast to the smooth and even skin that dominates photographic depictions of Shibari (Jones, 2020; Lee, 2022), the ropes often cut into soft tissue and create folds during real play. Additionally, the way subcutaneous fat – for example, on thighs – is compressed by the ropes reinforces the visibility of irregularities, such as scars and cellulite. Discoloration of limbs from a temporal lack of blood circulation is common. In addition, the fact that the body is under the combined strain of pain, limited breathing possibilities, and possibly a position that is inherently challenging to hold (like in predicament play) means that the person who is tied up often sweats a lot as a result of the hormonal impact. I find myself deeply drawn to this "uglification" of the body because I long to experience authentic and unadjusted bodily responses that unapologetically manifest as a counter-practice to the heteronormative beauty ideals that dominate the Shibari scene. My experiences are very similar to those described by fat activist Lee (2022) in her autoethnographic visual and textual exploration of Shibari, where she describes finding beauty in what the dominating fatphobic visual narratives of the Shibari scene will not show.

Final reflections

Writing this chapter from an autobiographical perspective is like no other scientific work I have ever done. Using my own embodied experience as a material, I have been able to dig deep into the intersection of autism, BDSM, and queerness from an insider perspective. Putting my thoughts, feelings, and practices into words has provided me with the opportunity to tune in with myself, my partners, and my personal history. Through the application of scientific theory and previous research, I came to see my experiences from new angles and perspectives, making this a transformative research process on a personal level. Here at the end point of this process, I hope that this chapter can be a springboard for others on their own unique, subversive, and sex-positive explorations of BDSM, wherever that may lead them.

Notes

1 When used to described men during the Viking age, the term had strong negative and homophobic connotations, something it lacked when used about women. Some within the contemporary LGBTQ+ community have recently begun to reclaim the concept for male homosexuality.
2 A leg tie where the calf is folded back and tightly tied to the thigh.

References

Ambler, J. K., Lee, E. M., Klement, K. R., Loewald, T., Comber, E. M., Hanson, S. A., Cutler, B., Cutler, N., & Sagarin, B. J. (2017). Consensual BDSM facilitates role-specific altered states of consciousness: A preliminary study. *Psychology of Consciousness: Theory, Research, and Practice*, 4(1), 75–91. https://doi.org/10.1037/cns0000097.

Bauer, R. (2021). Queering consent: Negotiating critical consent in les-bi-trans-queer BDSM contexts. *Sexualities*, 24(5–6), 767–783. https://doi.org/10.1177/136346072097390.

Bertilsdotter Rosqvist, H., & Jackson-Perry, D. (2020). Not doing it properly? (Re)producing and resisting knowledge through narratives of autistic sexualities. *Sexuality and Disability*, 39, 327–344. doi:10.1007/s11195-11020-09624-09625.

Bertilsdotter Rosqvist, H., Nygren, A., & O'Donoghue, S. (2023). Moving through a textual space autistically. *Journal of Medical Humanities*. Advance online publication. https://doi.org/10.1007/s10912-023-09797-y.

Boucher, N. R. (2018). *Relationships between characteristics of autism spectrum disorder and BDSM behaviors*. Honor thesis, Ball State University. http://cardinalscholar.bsu.edu/handle/20.500.14291/201533.

Carlström, C. (2018). BDSM – the antithesis of good Swedish sex? *Sexualities*, 22(7–8), 1164–1181. https://doi.org/10.1177/136346071876964.

Carlström C. (2019). BDSM, becoming and the flows of desire. *Culture, Health & Sexuality*, 21(4), 404–415. doi:10.1080/13691058.2018.1485969.

Goerlich, S. (2021). *The leather couch: Clinical practice with kinky clients*. Routledge.

Goffman, E. (1963). *Stigma: Notes on the management of spoiled identity*. Touchstone.

Greenberg, S. E. (2019). Divine kink: A consideration of the evidence for BDSM as spiritual ritual. *International Journal of Transpersonal Studies*, 38(1), 220–235. https://doi.org/10.24972/ijts.2019.38.1.220.

Grey, S., Kirby, A. V., & Graham Holmes, L. (2021). Autistic narratives of sensory features, sexuality, and relationships. *Autism in Adulthood: Challenges and Management*, 3(3), 238–246. doi:10.1089/aut.2020.0049.

Haraway, D. (1988). Situated knowledges: The science question in feminism and the privilege of partial perspective. *Feminist Studies*, 14(3), 575–599. https://doi.org/10.2307/3178066.

Jackson-Perry, D., Bertilsdotter Rosqvist, H., Kourti, M., & Layton Annable, J. (2020). Sensory strangers: Travels in normative sensory worlds. In H. Bertilsdotter Rosqvist, N. Chown, & A. Stenning (Eds.), *Neurodiversity studies: A new critical paradigm* (pp. 125–140). Routledge.

Jansen, E., & Bancroft, J. (2023). The dual control model of sexual response: A scoping review, 2009–2022. *Journal of Sex Research*, 1–21. Advance online publication. doi:10.1080/00224499.2023.2219247.

Jones, Z. (2020). *Pleasure, community, and marginalization in rope bondage: A qualitative investigation into a BDSM subculture* [Doctoral thesis, Carleton University]. https://doi.org/10.22215/etd/2020-14247.

Kapp, S. K., Steward, R., Crane, L., Elliott, D., Elphick, C., Pellicano, E., & Russell, G. (2019). "People should be allowed to do what they like": Autistic adults' views and experiences of stimming. *Autism*, 23(7), 1782–1792. doi:10.1177/1362361319829628.

Klement, K. R., Lee, E. M., Ambler, J. K., Hanson, S. A., Comber, E., Wietting, D., Wagner, M. F., Burns, V. R., Cutler, B., Cutler, N., Reid, E., & Sagarin, B. J. (2017). Extreme rituals in a BDSM context: The physiological and psychological effects of the "dance of souls." *Culture, Health & Sexuality*, 19(4), 453–469. https://doi.org/10.1080/13691058.2016.1234648.

Kulick, D. (2005). Four hundred thousand Swedish perverts. *GLQ: A Journal of Lesbian and Gay Studies*, 11(2), 205–235.

Lee, J. (2022). Removing the armor: Art, the fat body and vulnerability. *Fat Studies: An Interdisciplinary Journal of Body Weight and Society*, 12(3), 527–542. https://doi.org/10.1080/21604851.2022.2046329.

LGBTQIA+ wiki. (2023). *Autiqueer*. https://www.lgbtqia.wiki/wiki/Autiqueer.

Liang, M. (2022). Playing with power: Kink, race, and desire. *Sexualities*, 25(4), 381–405. https://doi.org/10.1177/136346072096406.

McCall, L. (2005). Intersectional complexity. *Signs*, 30(3), 1771–1800. https://doi.org/10.1086/426800.

McDermott, C. (2022). Theorising the neurotypical gaze: Autistic love and relationships in *The Bridge* (Bron/Broen 2011–2018). *Medical Humanities*, 48(1), 51–62. doi:10.1136/medhum-2020–011906.

McDonnell, A., & Milton, D. (2014). Going with the flow: Reconsidering "repetitive behaviour" through the concept of "flow states." In G. Jones and E. Hurley (Eds.), *Good autism practice: Autism, happiness and wellbeing* (pp. 38–47). BILD.

Mead, G. H. (1934). *Mind, self, and society from the standpoint of a social behaviorist.* University of Chicago Press.

Midori. (2022). *Consent dojo w/Midori – Ep.1: Practical, Realistic & Joy Centered Consent.* https://www.youtube.com/watch?v=egPIPQRCABs.

Mueller, M. (2018). If all acts of love and pleasure are her rituals, what about BDSM? Feminist culture wars in contemporary paganism. *Theology & Sexuality*, 24(1), 39–52. https://doi.org/10.1080/13558358.2017.1339930.

Murray, D., Lesser, M., & Lawson, W. (2005). Attention, monotropism and the diagnostic criteria for autism. *Autism*, 9(2), 139–156. https://doi.org/10.1177/1362361305051398.

Pearson, A., & Hodgetts, S. (2023). "Comforting, reassuring, and . . . hot": A qualitative exploration of engaging in BDSM and kink from the perspective of autistic adults. *Autism in Adulthood*, 6(1). https://doi.org/10.1089/aut.2022.0103.

Pliskin, A. E. (2022). Autism, sexuality, and BDSM. *Ought: The Journal of Autistic Culture*, 4(1), 70–91. doi:10.9707/2833-1508.1107.

Price, D. (2022). *Unmasking autism: The power of embracing our hidden neurodiversity*. Octopus Publishing Group.

Price, N. (2019). *The Viking way: Magic and mind in late iron age Scandinavia* (2nd ed.). Oxbow Books.

Samuels, E. (2017). Six ways of looking at crip time. *Disability Studies Quarterly*, 37(3). https://doi.org/10.18061/dsq.v37i3.5824.

Speciale, M., & Khambatta, D. (2020). Kinky & queer: Exploring the experiences of LGBTQ + individuals who practice BDSM. *Journal of LGBT Issues in Counseling*, 14(4), 341–361. https://doi.org/10.1080/15538605.2020.1827476.

Turley, E. L. (2016). "Like nothing I've ever felt before": Understanding consensual BDSM as embodied experience. *Psychology & Sexuality*, 7(2), 149–162. https://doi.org/10.1080/19419899.2015.1135181.

7

AUTISTIC IDENTITY AS A SPRINGBOARD INTO EXPLORING QUEERNESS, EMBODIMENT, AND RELATIONALITY

Anna Day and Meaghan Krazinski

Introduction

This chapter reflects on disidentifying from neuro- and heteronormativity by exploring neurodivergence, queerness, embodiment, and relationality which we view through a process of unmasking and becoming. We conceptualise relationality broadly, both as "connection" with others and ourselves. We draw parallels between explorations of unmasking and gender/queerness as they intersect with our neurodivergence as a process of locating our modes of existence.[1] These "are precarious. They emerge as they are needed and then, like actual occasions, they perish" (Manning, 2016, p. 90). Modes of existence defy neuro- and heteronormativity by our examination of (un) masking neurodivergence and connection with others, as we find our "belief in the world" (Deleuze, 1989, 1972). By this we mean a refusal to "follow the world as given. A belief in the world is about crafting the condition to encounter the world differently each time" (Manning, 2016, p. 93). Writing the chapter led us to encounter the world differently; we hope reading it does the same for our readers.

What is a mask and the multiplicities of unmasking

Pearson and Rose (2023) summarise current understandings of Autistic masking across four conceptualizations: camouflaging (Hull et al., 2017), compensation (Livingston et al., 2020), adaptive morphing (Lawson, 2020), and transactional impression management (Ai et al., 2022). They note that some masking processes are more conscious than others and involve various levels of predetermined performativity. Importantly, Pearson and Rose (2023) draw on Livingston et al. (2020) to note that masking may even be a selection of

DOI: 10.4324/9781003440154-10

environments wherein one is more likely to blend in. Masks we wear by necessity or conditioning often are about safety; "practising non-autism" (Yergeau, 2018) through masking is one of these strategies. Masking (consciously or unconsciously) impacts our interaction with the world (what we present) and how others respond to us (e.g., mis-attunement is inevitable when others can only see our mask, not our internal experiences of Autistic identity; Pearson & Rose, 2021). Masking protects while simultaneously exhausts, drains, and burdens. Our experience of the world when we engage with it as "masked" may reinforce our mask and teach us that this is how we *should* engage with it. We highlight that living unmasked is a privilege; it may be unsafe to do so (Hartman et al., 2023). Sarenius (2022) describes and makes three types of masks to explore masking as a "constant of seeking and becoming". We use these different masks (Soft, Spiky,[2] Stratification) as a heuristic to explore unmasking. Yergeau (2018) writes, "I have spent most of my life practising non-autism" (p. 90): instead, let's practice being openly and flagrantly Autistic.

Analytical framework

This chapter uses rhizomatic becoming (Deleuze & Guattari, 1988) as an analytical framework as we explore gender identity, embodiment, and unmasking. Milton (2017) suggests that

> Autistic ways of being can be seen as being constructed as "rhizomatic": a psychologic system that has no parameters, no hierarchy nor status, but seemingly endless "connections" in which constructions of Autistic self and identity may be shaped by "rhizomatic memory."
>
> *(Pearson & Rose, 2023)*

Rhizomatic becoming, reminiscent of Autistic perceptions, is a process of unmasking and expressing our Autistic selves.

Becoming is fluid (Carlström, 2019). Moving from a position of "being" to "becoming" opens the possibility for change, transformation, and creative potential (e.g., in embracing different identities than others have prescribed for us). As related to gender divergence, it is crucial to position gender as "always to come" (Linstead & Pullen 2006, p. 1292), "something one *becomes* rather than something one *is* (Cordoba, 2022, p. xiii). The conceptualisation of an ever-moving self (where some aspects of identity become an integral part of "who I am" and others are fluid, expressed through the lived body [Desmond, 2023]) echoes our experiences of exploring multiple identities.

"Always to come" might be figured in the imagination but does not necessarily imply a preconceived idea that can be foreseen as a finished product. Cordoba (2022) described that a crucial part of gender becoming was exploration of embodiment and gender expression (e.g., indexing a nonbinary identity through fluctuating aesthetics such as clothing, hairstyles, makeup; [Morrison, 2023]).

We conceptualise embodiment as "both a *state* (corporeality) and a *process* (becoming aware of and identified with myself as corporeal" (Totton, 2015, p. 57, emphases original).

We include a focus on shifting embodiment as part of our becoming (e.g., changing external appearance or getting ink). These can act as "a tool, a process of exploring ourselves. It is adventure, discovery, surprises, changes . . . a beginning, a transformation, an ending, and anything else" (Rehor & Schiffman, 2022, p. 11). We suggest that ink and kink can be structures for unmasking as both are a process of noticing and negotiating what is in the differential between the felt world and the abstraction of linguistics of identity. We argue both ink and kink are a practice of bodying (Manning, 2020) and therefore becoming and unmasking. Manning (2020) employs bodying as a verb, pointing out the stakes of individuation: the policing of bodies "denies bodies of their potential transitions, of their becomings, imposing an identity on them that cannot be assimilated" (p. 219). As implied by Sarenius's (2022) masks, shifting embodiment can be simultaneously part of our becoming and unmasking. Getting tattooed and engaging in kink[3] relies on a reciprocal process of becoming: first, a negotiation, wherein the potential for a new identity emerges, then a relational expression based on deep connection and trust: a concrete way in which to experience the "felt sense of the other person, and the other's felt sense of me" (Totton, 2015, p. 32).

In this negotiation, some aspects of becoming depend on relationship and recognition. Until then, we can be suffocated by our mask and not even recognise its existence let alone name it: "Until the situation is right for meaning to become *more itself* in the special way that language allows, it remains unformulated. The act of formulation, that is, takes place only when meaning is 'ready' to become more than it has been; and to be ready it must percolate for as long as it takes" (Stern, 2019, p. 7).

Approach

Quoting Deleuze and Guattari (1987), Linstead and Pullen (2006) suggest that gender identity is

> constant becoming, a constant journey which must start and end in the middle because "a rhizome has no beginning and no end: it is always in the middle, between things, interbeing, intermezzo" (p. 25). As Adkins (2015) explains, a rhizome is non-hierarchical, instead its connections are lateral, unpredictable, it creates the new but without linearity, with no guarantee of what will be created. Any of the rhizome's connections can be cut, disconnected, reformed, always leading to new possible connections. This is to say, becomings are not straightforward, and ours is no exception. This chapter and its style is rhizomatic – it changed during its writing and is not

the same chapter as originally conceived. We had not anticipated the chapter would itself be part of our becoming; and yet, as we allowed ourselves to exist in the "chaotic realm of knowing and unknowing."

(Halberstam, 2011, p. 2)

Darting forward and back in what we dared and felt safe to say, the chapter located its own becoming. We purposefully present an account that holds complexity in its reading[4] to reflect the nature of rhizomes which pursue "connections that transform it, creates something new. A rhizome has no up and down, right or left, it is always in the middle" (Adkins, 2015, p. 24).

Using an autoethnographic approach, we reflect on the processes of loosening the masks. These emerge through explorations of Autistic and gender identity, embodiment, and relationality. The nature of autoethnography involves constant questioning and unveiling (Hughes & Pennington, 2017), which we liken to unmasking. We adopt autoethnological voices with a collective "One of Us" (Francis & Hey, 2009) to stress our joint presence (Bertilsdotter Rosqvist, Nygren, & O'Donoghue, 2024). We hold the tension between creating autoethnographic writing in *our* communication style – that is, we both enjoy and also rely on – using the words of others, be that from books, films, and so forth in our everyday lives (echolalia[5]) versus what is *expected by the academy* – that is, not to "overuse" quotations. Deleuze and Guattari (1988) contrast "performance" to "competence", and here we trouble the necessity for Autistic people to have unceasingly to orient ourselves toward "performing" neurotypical competence per neurotypical norms (pp. 12–13).[6] We contend there is value in thinking about writing with competence as a particular type of performance. Rather than always seeking to reassure our imagined neurotypical audience of our competence, what if instead we unmask and allow writing to serve as an embodied process, "an intensive trait starts working for itself" (Deleuze & Guattari, 1988, p. 13)?

Therefore, inspired by neuroqueering (Walker, 2021),[7] we reject neuronormative ideals of linearity in writing and choose *deliberately* to queer academic convention and use our own language, using quotations to make our point as we would do per our natural communication. We intend our writing to be nonlinear to reflect Deleuze and Guattari's representation of becoming as being rhizomatic. Our writing style is a mimetic "word collage": a "play of images" that "shakes loose" and extricates itself from the "dominant competence of the teacher's language" (Deleuze & Guattari, 1988, p. 15), reterritorialising, to create our own piece, becoming a process of (neuro)queering neurotypical and academic convention and becomes performative itself of the process of unmasking. Put simply, welcome to our unmasked thinking. We ask that you, dear reader, (be)come with us.

Becoming unmasked

What's in a name? Exploring language, becoming, and unmasking

We suggest that whereas masks are "worn" at an individual level (Ai et al., 2022), it is impressed on us, reflecting neuronormativity, heteronormativity, social injustice, and so forth. It is one of the masks *we* may wear, but it is created *within* the system in which we exist (Radulski, 2022). In this sense, the mask becomes a joint artwork, except the creators themselves are limited by their resources and vantage points, directed by rules, norms, and influences of which they may not even be aware. We see this mask operating at the level of what Sarenius (2022) calls the "stratification mask." It is about gaze: looking and being looked at, subject and object, and societal positioning. This mask requires a reevaluation of social and behavioral rules across contexts, which are bound up with other systems placed on us such as gender and race (Sarenius, 2022). Even while this mask may seem gridded and less malleable, it still has portals to becoming: as Deleuze and Guattari (1988) write, "Accounting and bureaucracy proceed by tracings; they can begin to burgeon nonetheless, throwing out rhizome stems" (p. 15). These are made of endless webs and connections, unique to the individual, but also one of possibility: each connection has the potential to be made into a new form, to form new (re)connections. However, one has to touch one's face or at least catch a glimpse of the mask in the mirror to unmask.

Given the mask is a joint artwork, coming out can be about surroundings that produce knowledge – community, connections, and privileges to do so. Epistemic injustice relates to social practices informing how knowledge is created and maintained (Fricker, 2007). Hermeneutic injustice shapes the tools one possesses to explain their experience (Fricker, 2007). Giving words to the types of masks we wear is an epistemic intervention to loosen and uncover the mask itself. As we discuss in later sections, kink can be a structure wherein the stratification mask becomes explicitly named. We note here that nonkinky relationships are often full of implied limits and dynamics, deployed nonconsensually, and in ways that sediment the layers of dominant society and compound vulnerability rather than peel them back or rework them. Core practices of kink/BDSM run counter to this, centering "negotiating and implementing consensual exchanges of movement, of authority, of sensation" (Goerlich, 2021, p. 74). Instead of the mask being tacitly weaponized in unspoken, nonconsensual ways of everyday life, an explicitly negotiated Dominant/submissive dynamic makes the nature of the relationship clear and explicit. Masks, once melted into the skin, can be taken off, and instead, a costume can be created. At the same time, the context is central, not only for forming and experiencing gender, sexuality, and relationality but also as a context of "sense making" (intelligibility/tellability; cf Bergenmar, 2016). Kink can become a launch point for controlling, safely exploring, or reimagining the scene in which these roles play out. In other words, a means by which to explore new languages that carry one into embodied experiences of relational agency. Is it any wonder that Autistic people, whose natural embodiment is often scrutinised, would find relief in new creative structures reclaiming control over the process of exploration of their bodies? Our individual journeys weave in and out of embodiment and language, with language opening avenues to navigate a redefined embodiment, and this newfound expressive capacity then rippling into the realms of our broader identity.

> Before I understood myself as Autistic, I shrugged thinking most words were empty and could not reflect inner experience. I then realised gender and sexuality interacted with my inheritance[8] (Ahmed, 2006) of my neurology and embodiment. Aspects of self, more legible to neurotypicality, were "pulled to the table" and others smothered into receding. The latent orientations inside, like autism, were no less real because they were obscured from the dominant view. It was in understanding my sensory world as valid and not a pathology, that I realised words were not always something put on us but something we also may reach for. That is not to say I am that label solely, but simply that the use of one label can help to show us the use of another. Once I could name Autistic identity (and its tensions), I could then claim and come out to other aspects of self.
>
> *(One of Us)*

Autistic identification is categorical and therefore can bring the baggage of identity politics. However, Autistic people continue to shape what this looks like in ways that directly attempt to dismantle the diagnostic gaze via the language of its own mechanisms. Furthermore, formal identification[9] can foster continuing exploration of being Autistic, crossing into an examination of gender identities/sexual preferences. Part of our becoming and (un)masking is having access to the language through which to understand and communicate our gender, our neurodivergence, and so on. How do we locate ourselves without words or other reference points through which to orient ourselves? Formal identification of Autistic identity can be an origin story moment, a linguistic container with which to take the mask apart. This, of course, depends on *how* the Autistic person has their Autistic identity confirmed. For many Autistic people, the dominant, deficit-laden rhetoric surrounding "diagnosis" and deficit means that

> they may have to cope with heavily loaded and stigmatising accounts of their nature, which . . . means that the identity offered can provide a harmful and personally damaging framework for interacting with the world that is a false picture than can damage both other people's perceptions of an actual person and that person's own idea of self. (Hobson, 2011, cited in Murray, 2023, p. 38). As Bernadi (2023) observes, an autism

"diagnosis" is "consecrated by the medical authority of the individual producing it; a document upon which a new identity exists, and it is forged."
(p. 115)

However, there are different ways to approach formal identification of
Autistic identity that do not mean repeating rhetoric of deficiency and deficit, based on collaborative exploration of whether someone's experiences
align with the Autistic way of being (see Hartman et al., 2023 for a detailed
guide to conducting neuroaffirmative, respectful identification of Autistic
identity in adults).

Following identification, the process of Autistic becoming moves in different
directions, moving inward and back in time, while also unfolding through trial
and error, exploration, and playfulness. Discovery of Autistic experience can
provide a new frame within which to understand oneself. Locating Autistic
identity can orient while simultaneously disorienting as we readjust our stories
("If we know where we are when we turn this way or that way, then we are
orientated. We have our bearings. We know what to do to get to this place or
that place" [Ahmed, 2006, p. 1]).

Orientation is ever shifting and becoming, and relationship with Autistic
identity shifts over time. The dominant, deficit-laden rhetoric surrounding
"diagnosis" means that the identity offered can provide a harmful and personally damaging framework for interacting with the world that is a false
picture than can damage both other people's perceptions of an actual person
and that person's own idea of self (Hobson, 2011, cited in Murray, 2023, p.
38). Orientation involves disentangling an Autistic sense of self from the
epistemic infection that occurs when neuro-normative assumptions and privilege driving deficit-based knowledge around Autistic experience is internalised by Autistic people, becoming a "non-autistic storying" of their own
experiences because they may not have had access to non-pathologising
concepts and language to form an Autistic storying (Bertilsdotter Rosqvist
& Nygren, 2023). Furthermore, testimonial injustice manifests uniquely for
Autistic people, in which masking and passing play a role: Yergeau (2018)
writes that the sharing of Autistic identity is often followed by ellipsis, in
which . . . is implied, "an unspoken invitation to question, interrogate, elaborate, and/or theorise that disclosure" (p. 142).

As a cisgender passing pansexual autosexual demisexual person mostly
focused on day-to-day survival, I allowed the default to be projected onto
me because my illegible Autistic self was constantly fighting burnout,
allowing no energy for anything else. Growing up, I did not understand
categories. How does someone know if they are gay or straight? "I would
know if you were gay", they said, attempting to "reassure" me of my enti-
tlement to neurotypical cisheteronormative white inheritances.[10] It
remained arbitrary to me – I respected these identities were important to

many, but to me, they did not capture the nuance needed. But I assumed there was something flawed with my perception. This epistemic infection grew under my mask forming complicity in my own erasure. Masking to survive leads us to assume that everyone else, too, is masking.

(One of Us)

Bumiller (2008), in her call to feminist disability studies to attend to the neurodiversity movement, wrote, "From the perspective of neurodiversity activists, sexual identity is often seen as irrelevant rather than socially significant," while at the same time noting the coalition between the trans rights and neurodiversity movements. Eight years later, Davidson and Tamas (2016) turned to the idea of the "ghost" to explain the way Autistic people often innately perceive the performance of gender and the way it can haunt us, manipulate us, animate us, rally others for us, or put a target on our backs when we fail to perform it (p. 61). Gender seems like the ghost everyone is hunting. Perhaps, it is that Autistic people are especially attuned to the falsity of this abstraction.[11] Jackson-Perry (2020) builds on Halberstam (2011) to discuss an "autistic art of failure" as a "particularly creative way of unknowing an imperfect system" (p. 224) of gender and sexuality, in which "under certain circumstances failing, losing, forgetting, unmaking, undoing, unbecoming, not knowing may in fact offer more creative, more cooperative, more surprising ways of being in the world" (Halberstam, 2011, p. 2). Navigating a labyrinth of identity complexities, we may inherit neurotypical cisheteronormative expectations. This echoes the broader narratives of many neurodivergent people, where the masking of autism and gender intertwine as an unquestioned survival expectation. Some may acknowledge the prevalence of queerness, and even affirm it but feel questioning its suppression to be an impossibility. If this strikes us as fascinating or untenable, we may turn it into a passion and strong identification; but if not, we may shrug.[12]

Unmasking will make us bump into categories and social contexts; it requires calculation and tactics, and given the society we live in, this usually means language in some form. Masking gives access to certain realms of neurotypical society, while at the same time damaging and taking a toll. Narayanan (2024) suggests that sometimes a hyper-adaptation is an impairment when it takes a toll that devalues or degrades its subject later on. Applied to masking, this notion complicates the idea of impairment as often discussed in the social model of disability by shifting the focus away from questions of access to societal resources via taking on a neurotypical shell but instead finding the barrier in the ways one may be stopped from expressing oneself. Sarenius (2022) conceptualised the stratification mask to understand this aspect of un/masking, naming it operates on the level of navigating society, cultural intersections, and social contexts. This mask is one of an airier, looser, hollower form in which you can see the person behind, trapped in a cage of their own making . . . an endless web of unidentified and identified social norms, overlapping personalities and mirrors. Every situation and person has their own appropriate mask formed. . . . You need to unplug the cultural conditioning of societal norms and behavioural expectations and be able to look at the individual behind the mask.

(pp. 22–23)

Being able to name ourselves as queer/nonbinary can offer new possibilities for constructing identities not predicated on neuro- or heteronormative assumptions and to start lifting the mask. At the same time, there are experiences (e.g., naming our relation to our body as we explore our embodiment – how we feel *in* our bodies that have interoceptive or proprioceptive differences) that defy words and yet too often we have "no choice but to use words to describe a kind of experience that is defined precisely by the fact that there is often not words for it" (Stern, 2019, p. 99). This can hinder explorations of our embodiment and can consolidate our masks. How do we make connections with others in exploring these issues when connection too often relies on words, and we do not have the words to describe ourselves to ourselves, let alone to others?

> The closest language I have to describe my way of being is nonbinary, but even this is constraining – my identity defined in terms of what it is not – that is, not binary. I prefer to use neuroqueer, "working to dismantle the binary categories that restrict all of us, and throw the boxes in the recycling bin where they belong" (Maheshwari-Aplin, 2021, cited in Totton, 2023, p. 160). I want to look androgynous, queer. While having explored nonbinary identity for some time, I used to feel "OK" presenting femme. Then I deliberately shifted my embodiment because I needed to look androgynous[13] (both to be consistent with my sense of self but – and in no means do I suggest this is the case for all nonbinary people – because I could not bear to look feminine any longer: "One *will* not, *can*not be this person, because when one was, life was not bearable" (Stern, 2009, p. 176, italics in the original). Presenting externally as myself (i.e., androgynous) reflects what I feel, what I am, but I know it is also partly a mask to protect myself. I don't want to write those words, and yet if I don't, I am masking. And then I'm lost trying to figure out the complexities of masking, unmasking, remasking. It's a head fuck".
>
> *(One of Us)*

Counterintuitively, some masks help to hold space to unmask. Becoming is related to both the act of witnessing and being witnessed (Cosantino, 2022). One of Us has intentionally used only "Dr." as a title *because* it gives no gender-based clues, serving as a linguistic shift in challenging the gender-based discrimination and inequalities embedded in binary, gendered titled language. Cordoba (2022) frames his study of nonbinary gender identity using linguistic becoming that works at the micro (individual) level and involves reassessing the language used to self-describe (e.g., titles and pronouns). He conceptualises gender as a constant, unpredictable, and fluid process of emergences, shifting, (re)assessment, and (re)configuration and names the importance of any theory of gender considering personal and material embodiment as well as linguistic performativity, and how these may interact with the social world. Many of Cordoba's (2022) nonbinary Autistic participants challenged gender stereotypes from early age, "eventually able to challenge the restrictions when they grew up and discovered new ways of describing their identity" (p. 59).

Words may not be *our* first language, and yet we are surrounded by neuronormative privileging of language, even when language simply cannot convey the complexity of what needs to be conveyed.[14] Sarenius (2022) creates a "soft mask" made of wrappings of crochet to represent the feelings of everyday embodiment and imitation of neurotypical gestures and communication that are ever-shifting, contextual, and exhausting (p. 15). Too often, without words that defend our right to embodiment, we remain smothered in the "soft" mask. What exists is a "*possibility* of a meaning" (Stern, 2019, p. 114, emphasis original) in which the "the meaning may very well be there – but the language is not" (Stern, 2019, p. 115). Let us queer the idea that we must use language as signifiers to "become" nonbinary and so forth. Language is only one part of the process; it creates "part of the meaning we can sense, but language has not yet finished" (Stern, 2019, p. 113). It takes time to find a *language*[15] (and this we suggest is not limited to words but may include our felt sensations, our embodiment, and what it feels like to exist within a flesh suit). Jackson-Perry et al. (2020) highlighted the limits of language in conveying Autistic experience, pointing out that we may be silenced by being unable to find a "shareable" language, that we may have our own "language" that others do not understand ("It's frustrating when only one person in the world speaks your language and everybody else can only communicate with you through your second, third, fourth etc. language but not your mother tongue" [Jackson-Perry et al., 2020, pp. 129–130]). Limiting *language* to words only can serve to entrap us within our masks and prohibit the exploration of queerness. Stern (2019) suggests that if "we cannot quite form the meaning, it is because we cannot quite yet be the person who would be expressed through that meaning" (Stern, 2019, p. 114). But what if the meanings that are offered to us through neuro- and heteronormative dominance of language do not offer us the *right* meaning that makes sense to our Autistic bodyminds?[16] Are we allowed to take off the soft mask without constantly naming what we are doing in preexisting categories?

Embodied connections: Unmasking through ink and kink as interactive interfaces

Unmasking is not a singular event or process but nonlinear and cyclical. Exploring Autistic identity and embodiment is an ever-shifting rhizome of connecting, (un)connecting, (re)connecting because we have many parts. We show certain aspects of ourselves to particular people in different contexts. . . . Like learning a new language, moving into a new way of being is not an event but a process: it takes time, consistent practice, and has a cumulative effect.

(Lyne, 2023, p. 52)

Unmasking one area can help locate the epistemic tools we lack to unmask in another: Bornstein (2022) reported that for some queer/trans Autistic participants, gender and neurodivergent identity development were parallel processes of internal/external realisation. Some deconstructed their cis, neurotypical masks as their friendship circle became more queer and Autistic. Gender and neurodivergence can be cocreated and intersecting. Whereas for others, neither neurodivergence nor gender identity were located as happening "first". One participant drew explicit connections between coming out and unmasking, remarking that gender exploration facilitated neurology explorations: "As I unmasked my gender, I realised that I was neurodiverse or autistic. . . . As one gender layer has unravelled, I feel like neurodiverse layers unravel as well" (Bornstein, 2022, p. 90; whilst neurodivergent would be the correct term here, we have kept to neurodiverse as this was the participant's original words). In either direction, it often is borne first from our embodiment: expanding connection to our bodies through exploring gender expression, allowing our bodies to unmask their Autistic embodiment in how we move (e.g., no longer suppressing stims, and as we gesture toward in this section, exploring kink as part of sexual expression or getting inked).

Getting inked or exploring kink are ongoing interactive processes. Exploring our embodiment is an ongoing process; it is

always provisional and ongoing, something that we are both doing and having done to us (Totton, 2015, p. 75). Embodiment is relational – it is through our bodies that we encounter and engage with the world (Merleau-Ponty, 1945/1962).[17]

(Totton, 2015, p. xvi)

Variations in bodily form mean ontological interactions with the world are different for different bodies (Turley, 2016). Merleau-Ponty suggests that the body is not itself an instrument but a form of expression, a making visible of our intentions (1964, p. 5, cited in Ahmed, 2006). Likewise, gender, as well as our neurology permeates our whole life experience. As Nicholson and Morgan (2023) write, "Whether or not our gender-reframe involves medical steps to alter aspects of our physicality, we can still find ourselves assigning new meaning to our bodies. This new meaning can have important consequences on how we want to use our bodies, how we want them to be touched, and how we want them to be understood" (Nicholson & Morgan, 2023, p. 111).

The self emerges both from and of the interaction between person and environment, not static but in perpetual motion, both enduring and momentary (Desmond, 2023). If we allow "gender to be recognised rather as something we *all experience, make sense of and communicate* then we are in the territory where gender is something that everyone can own for themselves" (Nicholson & Morgan, 2023, p. 109, emphasis original). Cordoba (2022) describes a range of gender embodiments by nonbinary participants (e.g., femme, androgynous, masculine, genderfuck). The definition of these varied by individual, contextual, and situational factors, being modulated by levels of comfort and safety. Many participants described that "their gender becomings emerged from a need to feel comfortable in their own embodied and linguistic experiences and as such was both an individual as well as a social process" (p. 76). (It seems as though some masks allow us to be more of who we are.) These crucial explorations in embodiment and gender expression can include indexing a nonbinary identity through fluctuating aesthetics such as clothing, hairstyles, and makeup (Morrison, 2023). In this context, both ink and kink emerge as powerful practices to (re)claim agency as we navigate a path that involves exercising our ability to both refuse and consent, acting as "languages in between", masking spoken communication. (Note: The weaving "in and out" of embodiment and language is a version of *non*consensual role play that starts early on in life.) Instead of taking on the roles and categories that have been prescribed by neurotypical society, we question them. Refuse them. Negotiate them. Invent our own.

> Ink is a state of ever becoming; a process of meaning making. It is embodiment as joy, grief, power, and vulnerability depending on the piece; "an ongoing process of becoming embodied, more and more" (Totton, 2015, p. 9). And so, I get more and more ink as I fit into place with myself. It is queering my body – my body as art, the "practice of freedom" (Munoz, 1999, p. 21). My tattoos are stories. Others are welcome to read them, but the meaning is for me, connection and expression to myself. Getting ink is in some ways a vulnerable process because I choose to surrender my body to the artist to make their canvas. And yet it is where I am at my strongest because each tattoo is becoming ever more me. Fuck it to convention. Art is expression and my ink is my art that I choose to wear. The artist I trust to convert my words into art, that's connection, creation together, the ultimate trust. No control. Connection and beauty.
>
> *(One of Us)*

Shifting our embodiment via the process of being inked makes clear the processes of explicitly negotiated consent of what is being done to one's body by another person in a process that allows us to inhabit our own bodies more deeply. Relinquishing control when feeling safe is a form of control that allows healing. Likewise, kink is a process that involves explicit negotiation of consent, providing a means to shift our embodiment and enabling us to inhabit our own bodies more profoundly and discover them in ways that emphasise gender as desired or decoupled from preconceived notions of gender. Both ink and kink enable exploration of the meaning of our body and what we do with it and facilitate the unmasking process and blur the "in and out" of language and embodiment. Both provide interoceptive input from the inside (e.g., via the experience of pain) and proprioceptive input from the outside (e.g., the Dom/me inflicting pain; the sensation of the tattoo needle). Both ink and kink enable us to be more present in our bodies when we are in control of the situation. This is important when many Autistic people have interoceptive and proprioceptive differences (i.e., the internal and external aspects of our bodies can feel unclear): "the intensity of pain sensations make us aware of our bodily surfaces, and points to the *dynamic nature of surfacing itself* (turning in, turning away, moving towards, moving away). When we can more acutely feel where 'I end and you begin,' we can do more with that, move more with that, become into that, or reject it. As I find the container that is my body, through processing new and more specific intensities, I can also find relief in that focusing as a form of monotropic pleasure. Such intensity may impress upon the surface of bodies through negation; the surface is felt when something is felt 'against' it. . . . Pain involves the violation or transgression of the border between inside and outside, and it is through this transgression that I feel the border in the first place" (Ahmed, 2014, p. 27, emphasis original. Through this reading, kink or ink becomes an Autistic "playground" for connection and sensory exploration or may become a portal to a flow state (Csikszentmihalyi, 1991), one of being completely focused and immersed with intense concentration on the present, loss of reflective self-consciousness, and distortion of temporal experience (Shahbaz & Chirinos, 2017). A flow state can be deeply healing and is often achieved through direct sensorial engagement with the world and provides relief from verbal exhaustion associated with masking and navigating a neurotypical world.

Unmasking Autistic connections: Love languages and nonhuman bonds

Not only can we shift away from neurotypical linguistic interfacing as a practice of masking by kink and ink but also by reclaiming and neuroqueering linguistics themselves as a practice of embodiment and connection to Autistic voice. This is akin to Manning's (2020) minor sociality which "edges into the force that unmoors expectations about the relationscapes that compose us. It speaks from the corners. From the ledges and edges of experience still taking form" (p. 227). Non-normative communication (i.e., embracing all forms of communication, be it spoken or written word, through kink or ink, by gesture, etc.) centers and affirms a neuroqueer relationality, and practicing this can be a neuroqueering of relationality. This means a decentering of linear verbal speech and normative turn taking, as well as a queering of time in the exchange. A neuroqueering of communication may include a privileging of touch and stimming as communication, an embracing of circuitous or overlapping speech, and space for everyday nonspoken communication through body language and so forth. The possibilities are infinite and multisensory. "New relationscapes will always require new concepts, or at least new ways of creating conceptual passwords" (Manning, 2020, p. 230) These interactions can be a way of affirmation and unmasking/becoming but are personal, contextual, and sometimes even ephemeral.

> Autistic love languages include many ways to say I love you. Did you know that? Sometimes it means I may interrupt you because I am getting so excited to share. It can include squeezing hands to a code-like rhythm. Sharing a stim. Finger dancing. Nuzzling. Echoing. Making up your own language.
>
> *(One of Us)*

Normative expectations and preoccupations with how one categorises acts of care may render Autistic relationalities and intersubjectivities illegible, begging the question how much is masking and how much is neurotypical epistemic ignorance that is unable to notice what is obvious to us? A familiar meme in the neurodivergent community interrupts this by naming a form of neurodivergent care. The meme originates with Myth (@neurowonderful) (2021) who suggests "five neurodivergent love languages" that include info dumping, parallel play, support swapping, "Please crush my soul back into my body", and "I found this cool rock/button/leaf/etc. and I thought you would like it". "Please crush my soul back into my body" is a move in which one person's body weight is used to apply deep pressure to another's body. Some may struggle to understand how this is not inherently sexual or romantic.[18] Preoccupations with this question removes opportunities to build on neurodivergent knowing about the complexity of the sensual and the sensory and build on deep understanding of what free embodiment and relational care feels like. On an everyday level, suppressing these relationalities to wait for permission for the proper neurotypical category to ascribe them to signals compliance with neoliberal norms.

Neuroqueer relationalities that do not participate in the production of these systems are often rendered forgotten or insignificant (Griffin, 2022). Before being coded as neurodivergent or named as such, a neurotypical view of one body lying atop another would likely be seen as sexual or romantic; instead of the primary function of this which is to provide a profound expression of embodied care does not have to be sexual, though for some, it might be. When we unmask, we are able to stop worrying about whether a particular movement falls into prescribed neurotypical categories. What is the line between naming the attention style of monotropic flows and fetishes? This is the topic for another chapter, or maybe it is a delineation we no longer need. As Bertilsdotter Rosqvist and Nygren (2024) write, sometimes delineating between sex and "not sex" is a very neurotypical exercise. Sometimes unmasking means we can stop worrying about the names for things and find relief in our own embodiment and a way of relating to others.

Autistic relationality is not only unique in the ways in which it untangles neurotypical categorizing but also in the object of attention and the quality or intensity of relationship. Unmasking in this way not only means we are able to stop regulating how we move but what we are allowed to relate to (and therefore value), as well as how we are allowed to feel, grieve, and love. We can unmask by reactivating the relations within us to nonhumans as precious and significant. Autistic people are more likely to value relationships with nonhumans, including those of the imagination or media.

> As a child, I loved a ripped pleather chair. The day we had to get rid of it, it was like a death. I wailed as the new chair was brought in. What would become of this being that I had such a strong relationship with? (It would be cast off into the dump, they said.) Discarded?! I was granted one extra night to spend with the chair to say goodbye. Yet it was communicated that I had to adapt. We cannot hold on to objects as friends. It is not "real" or "important" enough. There is no space to publicly grieve either. What happens to our emotional expression when we are asked at an early age to hide the loss of our best friends?
>
> *(One of Us)*

Peeling off our masks

Waletich (2023) writes,

> You are tired of no one seeing you behind it, so you put it down. You may be elated to be seen, and relieved of the heavy weight of the shield, but those rocks hurt. . . . Your awareness is not shielded.
>
> *(p. 54)*

Unmasking opens new possibilities in our lives and advocates for the rights of future Autistic people. However, it is not always possible and does not come without risk: "Possibility does not always feel good. Getting into trouble can be costly, and painful" (Ahmed, 2015, p. 185). Sarenius (2022) developed the "spiky mask" to conceptualise the ways constant overwhelm are embodied and painful realities for many Autistic people:

> As time goes by you start to melt, to lose the original form set out for you. You don't get to choose whether you melt all over the place or if you get blown off and get to stiffen again. It all depends on the surrounding factors.

Unmasking our neurology, sexuality, gender expression, or sexual preferences is not an argument for pretending we always control these surrounding factors and how unmasking is going to go for us (or you). Unmasking is hard – it may be authentic but also painful and vulnerable. As Ahmed (2015) writes "A feminist and queer politics of trouble might require that we share the costs of getting into trouble; that we find ways to support others in the project of creating what Butler calls 'liveable lives'" (p. 185). We join Neves and Davies (2023) in stressing that we are "not advocating for toxic positivity and denying the very real struggles many of us face daily. It is about acknowledging the pain, looking after ourselves, and aspiring to survive *and* thrive" (p. 4, emphasis original). We all wear the spiky mask and find it melting from time to time, but coming out (whether as Autistic or queer) is an "important part of identity formation which cannot be done alone." As Sarenius (2022) notes, it is sometimes about our surroundings: "Most models of identity formation acknowledge the importance of finding belonging, finding others who are like you" (Russell, 2023, p. 65). From a place of embodiment and neuroqueering of communication, finding "others like you" may not be in more static endeavors of membership to affinity groups, or in declaring your identity on social media but instead in practices of becoming that are continually reinscribed (that include recognition by *both* the human and the nonhuman).

Conclusion: Embracing different ways of being

Before we locate ourselves in the world, we may feel like we are endlessly floating underwater. Weathering storms of neuronormative assumptions and compulsory cisheteronormativity, we grasp at whatever lifeline is cast, even though they are tethered to high-cost stakes roped to calcified identities. Paddling, masking, trying to perform neurotypicality for survival, but in doing so, we limit our vantage point. We have neglected tensions around gender interiority and are stuck with constant dissonance that mirrors our sensory experience of neurotypical spaces as much as our gender embodiment, resigning to projections others place on us. If we pointed out forms of incoherent, oppressive aspects of arbitrary binary genderings, we were often dismissed or told we "are too literal". Thus begins the silencing and deprivation of epistemic resources for Autistic ways of understanding gender and sexuality. We cannot develop our own vocabularies from false pretenses. So we start again, reconnecting the rhizome here. Just as our beginning the process of unmasking was an ending, this ending is also a beginning: "What we call the beginning is often the end. And to make an end is to make a beginning. The end is where we start from" (Eliot, 1943). We look in the mirror and take the mask off again.

Following Carlström (2019), we conceptualise exploring modes of exploring embodiment including that of ink or kink as part of becoming (emerging from and within both explorations of Autistic and queer identity). By queering our appearance, we manifest our internal queerness. Absorbing our queerness, allowing it to absorb us is to "allow something to make an appearance. This appearance is a bringing forth, where something that *was* background *becomes* foreground (Ahmed, 2014, p. 37). Shifting embodiment can mean tattoos or hairstyle (foreground), or it can be a process that begets a shift in the valence, away from the mask and toward the body becoming.

Embodiment is embedded in and creates a relational context, both with regard to our own relationship with our bodies and with others and how they respond to our (shifting) embodiments. Embodiment is not static but "always provisional and ongoing" (Totton, 2015, p. 75). As we consider (shifting) embodiments, we heed the advice of Totton (2015) to heed to the body as *object* (something we have), *subject* (something we are), and *process* (something we become). Shifting embodiment involves shifting what we embody in relation to (from neurotypical ideas of the human) and how we communicate with other bodies. Instead of forcing ourselves to use language in the normative ways (though, as noted above, we recognize sometimes these are anchors of translation that we need as we signpost to others on the journey), we can neuroqueer communication in creative echoes that move in and out of verbal speech as necessary, be that by shifting embodiment, through touch, sensory connection, and so forth. There are infinite ways in which to become and loosen the mask.

Our becomings included finding and embracing queer joy, "unapologetically embracing who we are, what we identify with, what we stand for and what brings meaning to our lives" (Neves & Davies, 2023, p. 2). We do not seek to feel tolerated but to turn sideways to new possibilities because

> being tolerated implies that the cis-het society "accommodates" us. We are not seeking approval or to be tolerated and deemed acceptable by the majority. Queer Joy is about pridefully stepping into our power and asserting *we are Here*. No justification, explanation or apology needed.
>
> *(Neves & Davies, 2023, p. 3)*

Perhaps always living on the boundaries of idealised forms of neuronormativity freed us to find other ways of being on the edges. We have increasingly become neuroqueer and neuroqueered, engaging with "neurodivergence and queerness, and the intersections and synergies of those potentials" (Walker, 2021, p. 175). Exploring our Autistic identities and identifying as queer/neuroqueer stems from a position that "minds and embodiments [are] fluid and customizable, as canvases for ongoing creative experimentation" (Walker & Raymaker, 2020, p. 5). As we reorient framings of neurology and gender, relationships with ourselves and the world shifts, this can "be experienced as a kind of *fitting into place*" (Nicholson & Morgan, 2023, p. 116, emphasis original) since "if you have a queerer way of understanding yourself, you are also likely to have queerer ways of being to understand others" (Nicholson & Morgan, 2023, p. 114). Becoming never ends: our exploration of unmasking, examining our queerness, embodiment is ever fluid. There is no right way or a wrong way. There are different ways. Different ways of being. Different ways of approaching our place in the world. In the words of 13th-century Rumi:

> Out beyond ideas
> Of wrongdoing and rightdoing
> There is a field
> I'll meet you there

Notes

1 Here, we also hold in mind Sullivan's (1940/1953) notion of modes of experience, the parataxic and the syntaxic. The parataxic refers to experience that remains private "even to oneself. . . . One cannot articulate the meanings, even in one's own mind" (Stern, 2019, p. 2). In contrast, the syntaxic could be known or "public" in the sense that the "meanings of one's own experiences [can] become knowable to oneself. That is, one can reflect on one's own experience only to the extent that the experience is organised in syntaxic mode" (Stern, 2019, p. 4).

2 Made from hot glue with the mouth closed shut, covered in spikes: "influenced by BDSM culture as well as the popular metal band Slipknot's iconic performance outfits. The spikes try to create a distance to the outside like hedgehogs' aggressive protective method, sheltering the person within from further external stimuli" (Sarenius, 2022, p. 20).

3 We highlight the central role of consent in kink as with all sexual activity and refer the reader to Intermission on Consent for full discussion about consent and in relation to consent within a kink context.

4 In writing about his writing approach, Totton (2015) states, "Alongside a strong desire to write simply and clearly, I have an equally strong desire to be inexplicit and hard to follow" (p. xxvii).

5 "For the first time ever I was able / To break out of non-communicative echolalia / By using echolalia from a book / I told you I was Mrs. Who / The character who could only communicate / By quoting the words of others. / For a 12-year-old autistic kid / Who had never heard of autism or echolalia / I doubt anyone could have done better / Than we did that day". From *The Mind Bridge*, https://ameliabaggs.wordpress.com/, accessed 23 November 2023.

6 We do not refer to competence as a way of humanising Autistic people and recognising capabilities (which is, of course, something we fully support) but in the sense that this framing can be twisted and taken up to require Autistic people to mask and maintain the comfort of neurotypicality.

7 Defined as "engaging in practices intended to undo or subvert one's cultural conditioning and one's ingrained habits of neuro-normative and hetero-normative performance, with the aim of reclaiming one's capacity to give more full expression to one's uniquely weird potentials and inclinations" (Walker, 2021, p. 162).

8 Return on these investments of performing neurotypicality to access privilege are contingent on one's ability to *pass* as neurotypical. It is a raced and gendered prospect, feeding into ideas of neurotypicality and a version of cisgendered femininity defined by whiteness.

9 We consider formal identification a neurotypical tool that many Autistic people have reappropriated into a linguistic becoming, one that over time has moved past its own constraints. Increasingly, it moves away from functioning as a death sentence and instead as a defense mechanism that says to neurotypicality "Keep out".

10 It has been written about extensively how obsession and rigid adherence to hierarchy and social status is a characteristic of neurotypicality. Perhaps it is the way cisgenderism and heteronormativity are products of other oppressive systems of colonisation, that leads Autistic people, with our often more pronounced passion for justice, be more likely to interrogate them.

11 Autigender and gendervague are terms developed to express unique ways Autistic people may be unable to separate gender from their "Autisticness."

12 This is not universal across Autistic experiences.

13 "To queer the Self, one must look inwardly at the experiences that have shaped us, and then to the outward expression of those experiences" (Gray-Hammond, 2022, p. 99).

14 "The way my thoughts work creates some . . . problems for language. And it's not just that I haven't found the absolute best combination of words to translate my thoughts with. It's that on a fundamental level the thoughts don't translate" (Amelia

Baggs, "The Fireworks are Interesting," 5 March 2010, http://ballastexistenz.wordp
ress.com/.

15 "Knowing is incipient to the experience at hand, actively felt but often indecipherable
   in linguistic terms, alive only in its rhythms, in its hesitations, in its stuttering"
   (Manning, 2016, p. 37).

16 We use bodymind "because mental and physical processes not only affect each other
   but also give rise to each other—that is, because they tend to act as one, even though
   they are conventionally understood as two—it makes more sense to refer to them
   together, in a single term" (Price, 2015, p. 269). We also draw on Schalk's (2018)
   meaning of bodyminds, "requiring modes of analysis that take into account both the
   relationships between (dis)ability, race, and gender and the contexts in which these
   categories exist" (p. 3)

17 "If we explore embodiment, we encounter relationship; if we explore relationship,
   we encounter embodiment".

18 This is because often from a cisheteronormative neurotypical perspective, all embodiment is often feared to be sexualized or assumed to be romantic. Which is not to
   say it cannot ever be, but the way heteronormativity and neurotypicality are pre-
   occupied with coercive elements of sex as a binary (Is it? Or isn't it?) is equally
   rooted in definitions of sex as heteronormative penetrative sex being the only valid
   form of sexual expression.

References

Adkins, B. (2015). *Deleuze and Guattari's "A thousand plateaus": A critical introduction and guide*. Edinburgh University Press.

Ahmed, S. (2006). *Queer phenomenology: Orientations, objects, others*. Duke University Press.

Ahmed, S. (2014). *Willful subjects*. Duke University Press.

Ahmed, S. (2015). Being in trouble: In the company of Judith Butler. *Lambda Nordica*, 179–192.

Ai, W., Cunningham, W. A., & Lai, M. C. (2022). Reconsidering autistic "camouflaging" as transactional impression management. *Trends in Cognitive Sciences*, 26(8), 631–645. https://doi.org/10.1016/j.tics.2022.05.002.

Bergenmar, J. (2016). Translation and untellability: Autistic subjects in autobiographical discourse. *LIR*, 6, 60–77. https://ojs.ub.gu.se/index.php/LIRJ/article/view/3573.

Bernadi, F. (2023). Postponing humanity: Pathologizing autism, childhood and motherhood. In D. Milton & S. Ryan (Eds.), *The Routledge international handbook of critical autism studies* (pp. 106–121). Routledge.

Bertilsdotter Rosqvist, H., & Nygren, A. (2023). I am that name? Naming neurotypical imaginaries of the sole autist in autistic/autism fiction. *Canadian Journal of Disability Studies*, 12(1), 117–140. https://cjds.uwaterloo.ca/index.php/cjds/article/view/974.

Bertilsdotter Rosqvist, H., & Nygren, A. (2024). And I don't want you to show me: Resistance-writing autistic love-sexualities through text sharing practices. In H. Bertilsdotter Rosqvist, A. Day, & M. Krazinski (Eds.), *Living under a double rainbow: Exploring autistic genders, sexualities, and relationality*. Routledge.

Bertilsdotter Rosqvist, H., Nygren, A., & O'Donoghue, S. (2024). Moving through a textual space autistically. *Journal of Medical Humanities*, 45(1), 17–34. https://doi.org/10.1007/s10912-023-09797-y.

Bornstein, N. (2022). *"There is no cause, there is no effect": Experiences at the intersection of transgender and neurodivergent identities*. Master's thesis, University of Southern Maine. https://digitalcommons.usm.maine.edu/cgi/viewcontent.cgi?article=1428&context=etd.

Bumiller, K. (2008). Quirky citizens: Autism, gender, and reimagining disability. *Signs: Journal of Women in Culture and Society*, 33(4), 967–991. doi:10.1086/528848.

Carlström, C. (2019). BDSM, becoming and the flows of desire. *Culture, Health & Sexuality*, 21(4), 404–415. https://doi.org/10.1080/13691058.2018.1485969.

Cordoba, S. (2022). *Non-binary gender identities: The language of becoming*. Routledge.

Cosantino, J. (2022). The becoming: A mad trans oral history (re)telling. *Departures in Critical Qualitative Research*, 11(4), 42–60. https://doi.org/10.1525/dcqr.2022.11.4.42.

Csikszentmihalyi, M. (1991). *Flow: The psychology of optimal experience*. Harper Collins.

Davidson, J., & Tamas, S. (2016). Autism and the ghost of gender. *Emotion, Space and Society*, 19, 59–65. https://doi.org/10.1016/j.emospa.2015.09.009.

Deleuze, G. (1989). *Cinema 2: The time-image* (H. Tomlinson and R. Galeta, Trans.). University of Minnesota Press.

Deleuze, G., & Guattari, F. (1987/2012). *A thousand plateaus: Capitalism and schizophrenia*. Bloomsbury.

Deleuze, G., & Guattari, F. (1988). *A thousand plateaus: Capitalism and schizophrenia*. Athlone Press.

Desmond, B. (2023). LGBTQIA in rural Ireland. In A. Alman, J. Gillespie, & V. Kolmannskog (Eds.), *Queering gestalt therapy: An anthology on gender, sex, and relationship diversity in psychotherapy* (pp. 112–120). Routledge.

Eliot, T. S. (1943). *Little Gidding in four quartets*. Harcourt, Brace.

Francis, B. & Hey, V. (2009). Talking back to power: Snowballs in hell and the imperative of insisting on structural explanations. *Gender and Education*, 21(2), 225–232. https://doi.org/10.1080/09540250802680081.

Fricker, M. (2007). *Epistemic injustice: Power and the ethics of knowing*. Oxford University Press.

Goerlich, S. (2021). *The leather couch: Clinical practice with kinky clients*. Routledge.

Gray-Hammond, D. G. (2022). *The new normal: Autistic musings on the threat of a broken society*. Amazon.

Griffin, C. (2022). Relationalities of refusal: Neuroqueer disidentification and post-normative Approaches to narrative recognition. *South Atlantic Review*, 87(3), 89–110. https://doi.org/10.17613/6yfv-x618.

Halberstam, J. (2011). *The queer art of failure*. Duke University Press.

Hartman, D., O'Donnell-Killen, T., Doyle, J. K., Kavanagh, M., Day, A., & Azevedo, J. (2023). *The adult autism assessment handbook: A neurodiversity affirmative approach*. Jessica Kingsley.

Hobson, P. (2011). *The cradle of thought: Exploring the origins of thinking*. Pan Macmillan.

Hughes, S. A., & Pennington, J. L. (2017). *Autoethnography: Process, product, and possibility for critical social research*. Sage.

Hull, L., Petrides, K. V., Allison, C., Smith, P., Baron-Cohen, S., Lai, M. C., & Mandy, W. (2017). "Putting on my best normal": Social camouflaging in adults with autism spectrum conditions. *Journal of Autism and Developmental Disorders*, 47, 2519–2534. http://doi.org/10.1007/s10803-017-3166-5.

Jackson-Perry, D. (2020). The autistic art of failure? Unknowing imperfect systems of sexuality and gender. *Scandinavian Journal of Disability Research*, 22(1), 221–229. doi:10.16993/sjdr.634.

Jackson-Perry, D., Bertilsdotter Rosqvist, H., Layton Annable, J., & Kourti, M. (2020). Sensory strangers: Travels in normate sensory worlds. In H. Bertilsdotter Rosqvist, N. Chown, & A. Stenning (Eds.), *Neurodiversity studies: A new critical paradigm* (pp. 125–140). Routledge.

Lawson, W. B. (2020). Adaptive morphing and coping with social threat in autism: An autistic perspective. *Journal of Intellectual Disability – Diagnosis and Treatment*, 8(3), 519–526. https://doi.org/10.6000/2292-2598.2020.08.03.29.

Linstead, S., & Pullen, A. (2006). Gender as multiplicity: Desire, displacement, difference and dispersion. *Human Relations*, 59(9), 1287–1310. https://doi.org/10.1177/0018726706069772.

Livingston, L. A., Shah, P., Milner, V., et al. (2020). Quantifying compensatory strategies in adults with and without diagnosed autism. *Molecular Autism*, 11(15). https://doi.org/10.1186/s13229-019-0308-y.

Lopez, M. M. (2022). *Queering the body, collective identities through piercing and tattooing*. Master's thesis, San Francisco State University. http://hdl.handle.net/10211.3/203790.

Lyne, S. A. (2023). Working with sexual shame. In S. Neves & D. Davies (Eds.), *Erotically queer: A pink therapy guide for practitioners* (pp. 43–58). Routledge.

Manning, E. (2016). *The minor gesture*. Duke University Press.

Manning, E. (2020). *For a pragmatics of the useless*. Duke University Press.

Masheshwari-Aplin, P. (2021, July 14). *Being non-binary in the UK today*. [Blog.] https://www.stonewall.org.uk/about-us/news/being-non-binary-uk-today.

Merleau-Ponty, M. (1945/1962). *The phenomenology of perception* (C. Smith, Trans.). Routledge.

Milton, D. (2017). Autistic development, trauma, and personhood: Beyond the frame of the neoliberal individual. In T. Runswick-Cole, T. Curran, & K. Liddard (Eds.), *The Palgrave handbook of disabled children's studies* (pp. 461–476). Palgrave/Macmillan. https://doi.org/10.1057/978-1-137-54446-9-29.

Morrison, D. (2023). Queering relationships. In A. Alman, J. Gillespie, & V. Kolmannskog (Eds.), *Queering gestalt therapy: An anthology on gender, Sex, and relationship diversity in psychotherapy* (pp. 101–111). Routledge.

Munoz, J. E. (1999). The white to be angry: Vaginal Crème Davis's terrorist drag. In *Disidentifications: Queers of color and the performance of politics* (pp. 93–118). University of Minnesota Press.

Murray, D. (2023). Dimensions of difference. In D. Milton & S. Ryan (Eds.), *The Routledge international handbook of critical autism studies* (pp. 34–41). Routledge.

Myth [@neurowonderful]. (2021, May 27). *The five neurodivergent love languages: Info-dumping, parallel play, support swapping, please crush my soul back into my body, and "I found this cool rock/button/leaf/etc. and thought you would like it."* Twitter. https://twitter.com/neurowonderful/status/1398061897086226432.

Narayanan, Y. (2024). An ecofeminist politics of chicken ovulation: A socio-capitalist model of ability as farmed animal impairment. *Hypatia*, 1–21. doi:10.1017/hyp.2023.98.

Neves, S., & Davies, D. (Eds.). (2023). *Erotically queer: A pink therapy guide for practitioners*. Routledge.

Nicholson, S., & Morgan, E. (2023). Trans sex and relationships: A practitioners' dialogue. In S. Neves & D. Davies (Eds.), *Erotically queer: A pink therapy guide for practitioners* (pp. 108–122). Routledge.

Pearson, A., & Hodgetts, S. (2023). "Comforting, reassuring, and . . . hot": A qualitative exploration of engaging in bondage, discipline, domination, submission, sadism and (sado)masochism and kink from the perspective of autistic adults. *Autism in Adulthood*. Ahead of print. http://doi.org/10.1089/aut.2022.0103.

Pearson, A., & Rose, K. (2021). A conceptual analysis of autistic masking: Understanding the narrative of stigma and the illusion of choice. *Autism in Adulthood*, 3(1), 52–60. http://doi.org/10.1089/aut.2020.0043.

Pearson, A., & Rose, K. (2023). *Autistic masking: Understanding identity management and the role of stigma*. Pavilion.

Price, M. (2015). The bodymind problem and the possibilities of pain. *Hypatia*, 30(1), 268–284. https://doi.org/10.1111/hypa.12127.

Radulski, E. M. (2022). Conceptualising autistic masking, camouflaging, and neurotypical privilege: Towards a minority group model of neurodiversity. *Human Development*, 66(2), 113–127.

Rehor, J., & Schiffman, J. (2022). *Women and kink: Relationships, reasons, and stories*. Routledge.

Russell, J. (2023). Sex lives of asexuals. In S. Neves & D. Davies (Eds.), *Erotically queer: A pink therapy guide for practitioners* (pp. 59–74). Routledge.

Sarenius, A. (2022). *Masking: The constant state of seeking and becoming*. Bachelor's thesis, Aalto University Art Education. https://urn.fi/URN:NBN:fi:aalto-202209255698.

Schalk, S. (2018). *Bodyminds reimagined: (Dis)ability, race, and gender in Black women's speculative fiction*. Duke University Press.

Shahbaz, C., & Chirinos, P. (2017). *Becoming a kink aware therapist*. Routledge.

Stern, D. B. (2019). *The infinity of the unsaid: Unformulated experience, language and the nonverbal*. Routledge.

Sullivan, H. S. (1940/1953). *Conceptions of modern psychiatry*. Norton.

Totton, N, (2015). *Embodied relating: The ground of psychotherapy*. Routledge.

Totton, N. (2023). *Different bodies: Deconstructing normality*. PCCS Books.

Turley, E. L. (2016). "Like nothing I've ever felt before": Understanding consensual BDSM as embodied experience. *Psychology and Sexuality*, 7(2), 149–162.

Waletich, R. (2023). Experiment and phenomenology in treating gender dysphoria. In A. Alman, J. Gillespie, & V. Kolmannskog (Eds.), *Queering gestalt therapy: An anthology on gender, sex, and relationship diversity in psychotherapy* (pp. 46–61). Routledge.

Walker, N. (2021). *Neuroqueer heresies: Notes on the neurodiversity paradigm, autistic empowerment and postnormal possibilities*. Autonomous Press.

Walker, N., & Raymaker, D. (2020). Toward a neuroqueer future: An interview with Nick Walker. *Autism in Adulthood*, 1–6. https://doi.org/10.1089/aut.2020.29014.njw.

Yergeau, M. (2018). *Authoring autism: On rhetoric and neurological queerness*. Duke University Press.

PART III
Unlearning, Relearning

8

"WHAT WE ARE TAUGHT TO HIDE"

Kink as a Way to Explore Your Autistic Self

Helene Delilah and Hanna Bertilsdotter Rosqvist

Introduction[1,2]

> I can still feel that special feeling in my body. How it felt when I unlocked the door and went down that long staircase. The muffled and slightly echoing sound of my steps against the wooden stairs. The creaking of the heavy inner gate halfway down. The familiar, slightly confined scent that hits me when I open up the well-known, safe, and at the same time exciting LASH club space.
>
> *(Delilah)*

Delilah's deep connection to the club LASH, as described in her sensory recollection above, is complemented by her long-standing and influential presence in the Swedish queer kink community. From the mid-1990s, she has actively organised and engaged with this community, particularly in Stockholm, Sweden, but to some extent also around Europe. Serving as the president of club LASH,[3] she dedicated herself to creating a welcoming space for queer female, trans or nonbinary people exploring kink. This commitment seamlessly aligns with her extensive work in sexuality education at RFSU Stockholm (the Stockholm branch of the Swedish Association for Sexuality Education) since 2004, showcasing her enduring contributions to both personal and professional facets of the kink and queer communities. Hanna has been a member of the club LASH and for a brief period did voluntary work for the club.

Delilah was formally identified as Autistic in 2016 and six years later as an AD(H)Der. While coming to grips with her own neurodivergence, she could not help but notice how many neurodivergent people she has met over the years who identify as bi- or pansexual, trans or nonbinary, and who seem more open to multiple forms of relationships and practices outside heteronormative sexual scripts. This made her curious to further explore neurodivergent sexual experiences beyond heteronormativity, with a particular focus on kink. Kink, BDSM,[4]

DOI: 10.4324/9781003440154-12

and fetishism are somewhat fluid terms that can have slightly different meanings for different people. In this chapter, we will refer to kink as an umbrella term for all. Kink practices can be more and less intimate or connected to what is commonly thought of as sex. Kink can be like a "sensory playground" where the senses of the whole body, with the skin, smell, and taste, gets involved in the pleasure, in the different kinds of hot. It can be done together with one's own body or together with other bodies.

Price (2022) has argued that

> when Autistic people are at the reins of event planning, we can craft environments [such as kink gatherings] that are tailored to our sensory and social needs. In small, mask-free subcultures that are created and maintained by Autistic people, we get a glimpse of what a society that truly accepts neurodiversity might look like.
>
> *(p. 202)*

Based on a survey on BDSM practitioners, Boucher (2018) found that autistic BDSM practitioners were more likely than non-autistic BDSM practitioners to prefer activities associated with sensory stimuli. The importance of creating and finding safer spaces where we can explore our own and other people's bodies, sexual and sensory desires, and by doing so, find our people will be central in this chapter.

Sexual education for autistic people often simplifies neurotypical information but frequently overlooks support for autistic sensory and communication needs. Pliskin (2022) has argued for the importance of replacing models that pathologize sexual variety among neurodivergent people with those that empower us. This chapter builds on and adds to growing voices exploring the overlap of autism and kink through a sex-positive and neurodiversity-affirming perspective (cf Pliskin, 2022). Whereas previous research has emphasised more traditional sources of scholarship (Pliskin, 2022), this chapter emphasises community knowledge production and community theorising. We engage in a form of theorising described by autistic theorist Fergus Murray (2019) as being "drawn at least in part from internal observations." In this context, community theorising is delineated as theories is "drawn at least in part from internal observations" that emerge outside of academic settings, such as through mediums like podcasts, vlogs, and blogs. We will explore autistic kink (dis)pleasures, ways of communication, and strategies to manage challenges. We hope this chapter will inspire you to explore your own sexuality in a sex-positive and neurodiversity-affirming way.

Methods

Delilah's knowledge production process consists of different intermingling acts: exploring neurodivergent community sources outside of academia (podcasts, vlogs, blogs) on neurodivergent kink and sexuality, interviewing, and informal conversations with five kink community activists and friends on the topic (among them Hanna), preparing and doing lectures and workshops in the LGBTQ+/kink community on the topic, as well as doing a survey.

Since the participants in the interviews and informal conversations are autistic people whom Delilah knows from the Swedish kink community, the conversations quickly became very open-hearted. The data are rich with the participants' sexual experiences and needs. Using Pearson and Hodgetts's (2023) interview study on autistic people's experiences of BDSM as base, Delilah constructed a questionnaire. The 18-item questionnaire was adapted to fit a Swedish context and developed in relation to the insights from neurodivergent community sources outside of academia, the interviews and informal conversations and learnings from the lectures and workshops. Each question had both closed-answer options and a free-commentary space. The first section in the questionnaire concerned gender, sexual identity, age, number of years of kink practice, as well as type of kink practice. The second section focused on communication, aftercare, use of checklists, stimming in sexual situations, and experiences of meltdowns or shutdowns in sex/BDSM settings. This section offered brief explanations and related questions for a comprehensive understanding of various aspects of the subject. Participants were also encouraged to add concrete examples of their own in the free-commentary spaces. The survey elicited responses from 17 respondents. The respondents were recruited from Delilah's personal sphere and from the LGBTQ+ community during Delilah's lectures and workshops during the week of Stockholm Pride 2023.

Before participating, all participants (interviewees and respondents) were informed about the purpose of the study and that responses would be anonymous. They all consented to participate. The participants include women, trans, and nonbinary nonheterosexual people. Most are formally identified but some were self-identified as autistic. A third identified as autistic and two-thirds as AuDHDers. They were between 21–59 years old. All but one were identified as autistic as adults. Some participants had just one year of BDSM experience, but the majority had been involved in BDSM for several years. The majority of participants identified themselves as either submissive or switch. In the chapter, we have chosen to focus on two overall themes from the data: seeking out sensory pleasures and communication in kink settings.

In addition to being one of the five interviewees, Hanna has played a role in the writing process from the start, serving as a discussant and providing informal supervision on methods. In the later stages of the writing process as Delilah drafted the main content and results, Hanna transitioned from her initial roles as discussant/supervisor and data contributor to become a coauthor. In this capacity, Hanna revised the main draft and made contributions to the analyses. When discussing Delilah's experiences collectively, we will refer to her in the third person. When using "I," it indicates Delilah speaking in a first-person voice.

Seeking out sensory pleasures

> It is more enjoyable to live out with others with autism! More consensus from the beginning that things can feel extra wonderful or extra impossible, that it feels OK to ask about something three times. The knowledge that they will not look at me with a NT gaze but with a gaze at the same level. It's wonderful to be able to see yourself in others, both confirming and euphoric and healing. What we have been taught to hide can instead be hot to release, plus I like others who are equally nerdy.
>
> *(Participant)*

In this section we explore kink in relation to different types of autistic sensory pleasures, as different kinds of "hot to release", or what autistic blogger BeautiDivergent (2020) has referred to as "intense sensory-stimulating experience[s]".

Finding the right kind of hot sometimes means developing an expertise in "edging". Edging or sexual edge play is described by Bozelka (2021) as

> a masturbation technique whereby a masturbator of any gender holds off just before orgasm in order to intensify the eventual release or to leave oneself in a perpetual state of arousal, hovering at the edge of orgasm as long as possible. Edging prioritises deferred gratification.
>
> *(p. 174)*

In the setting of autistic sensory pleasures, edging is about finding a balance between too little and too much sensory input to find enough sensory input, sensory satisfaction. It is about exploring different intensities and degrees. For example, someone might be enjoying repetitive stroking and picking on certain types of textiles, like certain types of wool, linen, or silk fabric, but they get an even stronger degree of pleasure from skin contact with someone they are attracted to. Experiencing the pleasure of having skin contact with someone you are "skin compatible" with is described by one of the participants as being a "cat on catnip". To them, this means sensory hunger for skin contact, to touch, feel, smell, taste that person's skin.

Autistic blogger Thomas Henley (2023a) has described how he "hate[s] light touch, but find[s] heavy pressure relaxing". Seeking out autistic sensory pleasures is about exploring and experimenting with hyper-/hyposensitivity, sensory needs, and sensory regulation. This was expressed by one of the participants:

> One of my kinks is actually rope with a certain texture: I am quite a seeker who sees with my hands and with my nose, feels and smells all the time. It heightens my feeling and experience. I am very selective. There is no middle ground. It's either/or. Feel everything; pressure, heat, cold, smells. [I am] not actively looking for latex, but if someone has it on, I will want to feel it. [I] like semi-rigid natural materials. Scents: e.g., perfume scent can be too pungent. [I] don't like floral scents, but more spicscents. When something smells, I feel the taste of it – it is not always the same smell as "taste".
>
> *(Participant)*

One way to look for sensory pleasures is to think about your stimming. How do you stim? One of the participants says,

> I beep, moan and purr in pleasure. Ripping my partner's body, like a scratching post, and also my thighs, sheets, pillows, grass. Kneading and pushing myself and others in pleasure too – preferably with my nails.
>
> *(Participant)*

Stimming can be soothing and stimulating. Stimming may regulate, process, amplify, or suppress various inputs. Stimming is a short term for self-stimulatory behaviour. Stimming can be described as "a way to channel a lot of information into physical movement" (Kinkyboys, 2021) or a "self-regulatory mechanism" (Kapp et al., 2019). Stimming is closely related to seeking out sensory pleasures. Beeping, moaning, and purring can be seen as vocal stimming. Ripping and kneading can be seen as tactile stimming. Other common examples are whistling, humming, or singing rather than moaning during pleasure, or happily licking or chewing on your partner or on something.

Autistic blogger BeautiDivergent (2020) has stressed the need for more understanding and compassion for "sex stims" and "those of us that respond in a sexual way to carry out their stims". They write,

> I'm not a slut or someone out of control. I'm not even particularly promiscuous. I like sex. A. Lot. The act of sex stims provides a very intense sensory-stimulating experience. It engages the entire body. The proprioceptive repetition of thrusting. The vestibular input of heavy breathing and vocal exclamation of delight.

Similarly, autistic blogger Candice Christiansen (2021) notes that for some, stimming may include giving oral sex due to the tactile sensory pleasures of "how another person's genitals feel in their mouth". For others, giving oral sex may be sensorially repulsive due to taste, touch, and smell. Some may sensorially enjoy the sound of noises during sex, while others may find them sensorially repulsive. Candice Christiansen (2021) further notes,

> Masturbation could be a form of vestibular sensory seeking since it is a repetitive back and forth motion. It is also often a tactile sensory seeking behaviour that creates a sense of relaxation and proprioception in an autistic person's body. The repetitive movements can be incredibly soothing all the while creating a huge spike in dopamine via orgasm.

Some of the participants explicitly link their kink environments and practices to stimming (cf Pliskin, 2022, p. 73). Kink settings are described as spaces that "helps me to let go and be able to stim quite freely" (Participant). One participant noted,

I have come to realise that almost all BDSM can be seen as stimming! To explore and keep track of the ways I stim, I have started a stimming diary, where I write down my discoveries. I like to lick, suck, bite, squeeze, pinch, knead and give connective tissue massage to my partner.

(Participant)

Whereas some respondents had already considered their kink as a form of stimming, participation in the study prompted new perspectives on stimming for others:

I hadn't thought about this before today. The first thing I think of is that I love to bite my partners and always have. Definitely a stim for me. Other than that, nothing comes up right now but it is something I became very curious to delve into and explore.

(Participant)

Many participants described biting or scratching as a form of tactile stimming, often using these behaviors to regulate overstimulation during sexual arousal.

I bite when I come, either myself, a pillow, or my partner. If I am stuck and can't, I am easily overwhelmed.

(Participant)

Bringing up the importance of edging in the setting of sex stimming, one participant described exploring stimming orgasms during BDSM sex with a Dominant male autistic partner:

Some time ago I started to get a stimming orgasm with him. The stimming practices during sex kept getting more and more intense until I reach a certain point where I suddenly feel a great sensory joy and saturation. The sensory hunger usually moving me, urging me on, was suddenly satisfied. It was not a genital experience. It was more a sense of deep-seated sensory saturation. We soon learned that if we kept on having sex after this, the sensory saturation turned into an overload and soon enough a meltdown.

(Participant)

How do you present when you enjoy something? Perhaps you pinch or knead yourself or your partner because your hands need to go somewhere? Do you make sounds, use words, stim, or move your body in a certain way? How do you present if you dislike or are uncomfortable with something? Do you get silent and still? Perhaps you use hand signals? Could any of your reactions be confused with stimming, like if you use tapping out as a hand signal? Wouldn't you love to be able to stim more freely in sexual situations? Imagine it as a pent-up power within you, ready to be unleashed!

Kink as a space for resting

A recurring theme in the data was the perception of kink as a space for relaxation, where the participants released the everyday acts of self-control and self-management. Autistic people may experience this in both Dominant and submissive roles (cf Pliskin, 2022). Participants depicted kink as a supportive space when feeling overwhelmed, insecure, or exhausted. It serves as a means to shift from a mental to a physical state, providing a restful experience for some who can safely inhabit their bodies more fully in a kink setting. Additionally, a kink setting was highlighted as a space to address feelings of understimulation, whether mentally, physically, or both. Autistic Dominants may find satisfaction in guiding others in a way that feels optimal, while autistic submissives may value surrendering control to a Dominant partner.

Sub, Dom, top, or bottom spaces are commonly viewed in kink settings as altered states of consciousness (Ambler et al., 2017). In the case of autistic kinksters and fetishists, they can also be linked to autistic cognition, such as monotropic intense focused attention (Murray et al., 2005) or autistic flow states (McDonnell & Milton, 2014; Pliskin, 2018). Some of the participants described how a kink setting (or a fetish) allows them to focus on only one thing, such as receiving sensory input and thus being able to fully enjoy them. Kink settings were described as spaces where it is possible to feel close without the distraction of fans, bells, and one's own thoughts wandering off. This is expressed in the following:

> It becomes like blinders, I become focused on one thing. I can let go of thinking, worrying and guessing what I am expected to do, I just do as I am told. It feels like a warm heavy blanket all over me.
>
> *(Participant)*

Challenges of sensory overloads

Participants described stimming as an enjoyable form of sexual communication, using it to convey feelings and experiences of sensory input nonverbally in a kink setting. Simultaneously, trust plays a central role in a kink setting, providing a sense of safety to let go, cease masking, and stim freely (cf Kapp et al., 2019; Pearson & Rose, 2021). This trust in a kink setting facilitates exploration of one's own norms and practical understanding of what works best:

> I think that as an autistic person you learn by trying/experiencing yourself, not by listening to others. And there can be a gap between your theoretical and bodily knowledge; you can have a lot of understanding in theory but it does not work in practice for various reasons. You have to try something out a lot to gradually "get it into your body".
>
> *(Participant)*

The gap between a "theoretical" and "bodily" understanding may risk an overload that further may lead to a meltdown or shutdown as the person may not be aware of their early signs of overload. In a meltdown, the reaction is usually outward: screaming, crying, slamming doors, throwing things. It just bubbles up and can be difficult to stop. In the case of a shutdown, the reaction tends to be closure – we cannot talk, cannot move, we become seated or standing immobile. These breakdowns may look different on the surface, but what happens inside the person and the reasons behind them are often the same. Factors that can contribute to either a meltdown or a shutdown include but are not limited to social demands, frustration, embarrassment, challenges with communication, emotional triggers, and overwhelming sensory stimuli (Welch, 2023). The possibility of a meltdown/shutdown in a kink setting may create anxiety when it feels as if it cannot be escaped or when the space does not feel safe enough. It is important to understand that meltdowns are a reaction to a highly distressing situation or environment. Both can be compared to a reset. When we are at a reduced ability to process what is going on, we may struggle to communicate as we normally do, which can mean we go nonspeaking or struggle forming coherent sentences.

Some participants reflected on the difference in sensory input when it comes to input intensity and the possibilities to process the input in time and avoid overload. This is illustrated in the following:

> Calm and steady strokes work, but at a faster pace it becomes too much and I struggle to find time to process and start panic crying without control.
>
> *(Participant)*

> Spanking with the palm of a hand is fine, but spanking with birch twigs doesn't work because then I get sensory overload, probably because the pain is spread out over a more dispersed area.
>
> *(Participant)*

Shifting focus, deep breaths, checklists, and "yes and no questions" are some of the strategies shared by the participants to manage sensory input and avoid meltdowns/shutdowns from too much input intensity.

Some participants expressed an urge to understand why meltdowns/shutdowns happen and to learn how to create strategies to prevent them and, if possible, how to befriend them and share relevant information with their partner about how to act if and when it comes.

> When I get shutdowns, my unwilling mutism comes out and people need to ask yes and no questions and just talk about all sorts of things and when we have calmed down, we need to go straight to aftercare.

Sometimes I need to be spooned right away – I need to be the little spoon during these breakdowns as I often roll up into a ball when it happens. I need lots of validation and affirmation.

(Participant)

I'm pretty sure that when I go into little space[5] it's actually a half-baked version of a shutdown and that I then get stuck in it and become small.

(Participant)

At the same time as meltdowns/shutdowns are commonly described as something to be avoided, Thomas Henley (2022) has referred to happy meltdowns, triggered not only by socialising and sensory distress but surprisingly by overwhelming positive emotions. These meltdowns are described to involve confusion, talkativeness without a filter, uncontrollable smiling, difficulty transitioning out of social mode, and zero short-term memory. In line with this, one of the participants described a deliberate choice to risk a meltdown/shutdown as part of an edge play, where the edging toward a sensory overload may be part of the pleasure. This is contrasted to experiences of involuntary getting into a meltdown/shutdown in everyday life. This means that sensory overload is not always something to avoid. This complicates the neurotypical default of how "positive" and "negative" experiences are often framed as if they are not also highly personal, varied, and different across individuals. It depends on the setting and whether it is self-chosen or not.

I have memories of sessions that went wrong and where I "crashed" [got a meltdown] and how it was considered normal to crash when it gets too much as a sub. And it was sort of OK, especially with "milder" meltdowns (in my case I end up in a panic cry). There are even "scripts" for how it should be handled – that the Dominant cancels everything at once and give after care.

(Participant)

This self-chosen overload or edging toward sensory overload as part of the kink setting can be linked to traditions within the kink community of risk-aware consensual kink (RACK). RACK is used to frame and underline the importance of consent and mutual awareness about the potential risks in kink. The 4 Cs refer to caring, communication, (enthusiastic) consent, and caution (Williams et al., 2014). Part of this is the importance of clear communication, which is somewhat a signum and foundation for good kink practice (Kinkyboys, 2021).

> If someone experiences a meltdown or shutdown without prior information about their needs, there are a few things to keep in mind:
>
> - Stay with the person unless they give other directives, but make sure to give enough space to just breathe and reset.
> - Minimise possible stressors and triggers.
> - Talk in a calm, comforting voice to allow for slower processing.
> - Stick to yes-or-no questions and be prepared that it might not be possible to get answers at the moment. A nod or thumb up, thumb down may work if they are unable to speak.
> - Give time for settling down and recovery.

To prepare for future situations, consider asking about individual needs beforehand. If not done before, why not create your own meltdown map to understand how to prevent, manage, and recover from both meltdowns and shutdowns?

> ## MELTDOWN MAPPING IN A KINK CONTEXT
>
> - How do you recognise that you are about to get into a meltdown/shutdown?
> - What may lead you into a meltdown or shutdown?
> - What steps can be taken to prevent or overcome a meltdown or shutdown for you or your partner?
> - When and how is a good time to communicate about meltdowns/shutdowns for you?
> - Can you include information about meltdown/shutdowns in any kind of checklist?
> - What specific information about meltdowns/shutdowns do you believe is important for both you and others to be aware of?

Communication in the kink setting

> I get so much out of BDSM and kinks. It's an emotional relief and I can finally get a proper and crystal-clear structure between communication and action.
>
> *(Participant)*

> BDSM has a very clear way of regulating what should be included in a session. It becomes much easier to define and set boundaries for sexual activities you don't like.
>
> *(Participant)*

Clear communication came up as one of the main reasons why the participants found themselves drawn to kink. One does not have to second-guess what is expected of oneself; one will be told. Or one might be the one who sets the rules. Commonly, before entering a kink session, you communicate with a potential partner to find out if your kinks and preferred roles and expectations match at all. Some prefer to text, others, phone calls, and yet others want to zoom for a start. Beforehand, it is a good idea to agree on safe words, stop signals, and hand signals if one of you becomes nonspeaking.

> I have hand signals for when I'm overwhelmed, when I'm spaced out, I have a signal for when I'm OK, which I can use if I'm stimming a lot, or crying or if I can't or don't want to say something.
>
> *(Participant)*

When Delilah asked her participants about their thoughts on communication, they shared lots of well thought-out strategies. There were also voices saying that they would like to negotiate more or that they might have a greater need to communicate than they actually do. Some said they find it hard to talk beforehand and that they prefer to text, at least in the beginning. Some described how they have developed safety strategies to make sure the person they are meeting up with respects their boundaries and picks up on stop signals. The "traffic light system" was mentioned by several to be useful, where green usually stands for "I'm OK", yellow can mean something needs to change, and red means stop. Some described that they prefer not to speak at all during a session or only with very few words. Among ways of nonspeaking communication when speaking is difficult or impossible are to nod or shake your head, raising a hand, snapping your fingers three times for a break, double-tapping to ask for a check-in, repeated double tap to convey stop. In breath play, to push two or three times with force may mean yellow, and push away from the neck and pull with force may mean red.

In the midst of a session, you might become completely absorbed and miss asking direct questions or executing planned actions, possibly zoning out occasionally. Everyone involved is equally responsible for communicating and checking in with each other. It is never the sole responsibility of one person. Post session, you may still feel spaced out or too exhausted for discussions. If everything seems fine afterward, it is usually OK to postpone discussions. However, if there are challenging emotions, it is advisable to address them as soon as possible after allowing time to process your feelings and session experiences.

Another subject brought up by the participants is the need to get enough feedback from the submissive in order to feel secure in the role of Dominant or Top: for example, receiving specific information about what someone gets turned on by, if they want to continue, harder strokes, or perhaps at a slower pace? Any small detail that can be corrected? Just being told it is "OK" isn't enough. Pain scales can be one way to get around this. For example, the Dominant can ask the receiving part to rate the pain on a scale from 1 to 10, combined with agreeing on how high they wish to be pushed.

Several participants expressed a preference for literal communication. For example, one participant described how they wanted to be asked for consent often, even for small things like a pat or a hug. The risk of literal interpretation causing misunderstandings is also a thing that some of the participants reflect on.

> If someone says lie still, or shut the fuck up, then I do so, until something else is said. . . . Sometimes I have been asked after a while, are you OK? – Yes, but I was told to keep quiet. . . ? – I need to know when I can talk (or move) again, otherwise I will continue to carry out the last order until further notice!"
>
> *(Participant)*

A kink setting may be viewed as a potentially autistic-friendly space for communication and ways of being social. The participants described kink as enabling multiple choices when it comes to intimacy. For them, kink allowed them to find their own path and ways for intimacy and intimate communication including nonspeaking bodily communication between Dominant and submissive. Kink may also be a setting allowing being social with others in an interest-based way (Bertilsdotter Rosqvist, 2019), serving as a bridge to become intimate and engage in deeper social interaction with others without demands of being social in a neurotypical way. For example, one participant described how by studying Shibari (Japanese rope bondage) and practicing the technical skills on their own, they gained more confidence, just by trusting that their hands knew how to tie the ropes and perform a certain activity. Another participant described how they learned to actively express their wants and needs without expecting assumptions.

> It has helped me a lot to include my autism in negotiations about, for example, aftercare: To have a plan in advance. There will be chocolate. There will be a text message on day 2. Not being nervous that any of this will not happen. Also, I get completely overwhelmed as a submissive and can become non-speaking. Then I need yes-no questions, and to be able to stay until I come out of it myself and to hear nice things without having to answer anything.
>
> *(Participant)*

Some participants found satisfaction in the sense of discipline, while others went to great lengths to please their partners to avoid repercussions. For some, coping with harsh words and criticism can be challenging, making positive reinforcement and praise even more crucial.

- What are your communication needs? Before, during, after a session?
- What is your preferred way of communicating before and after a session – talking; irl, phone, Facetime/video chat, writing; text messages, chat, email?
- What is your preferred and alternative way of communicating during a session? Any specific words or actions such as hand signals? How do you or your partner communicate if one of you cannot or does not want to talk?

Cooling down, doing aftercare

Time and space for cognitive processing is central before, during, and after the session. For example, one participant described a need for a "longer time for warm-up and longer time for cool-down" and they worried that the other "will get restless because of this". Another participant expressed a need to be told "when it is time to leave". For example, in Kinkyboys podcast, the need and supporting that need is expressed as follows:

> When I am playing with someone I know is autistic and I'm Dominant; I like to integrate that to the end of the scene. To kind of winding it down gradually and end with putting on a blindfold to ease for the person. . . . To help them recenter themselves. It can be integrated in a sexy way! . . . Even the top may need a moment or two to "get back" to this reality. Good to know and to communicate beforehand, that "I will need some time to myself directly after we are done, to reconnect and recenter".
>
> *(Kinkyboys, 2021)*

When a session ends, there are different needs of aftercare as expressed in the quote above from Kinkyboys podcast. The need for a soft landing and connecting is something that was mentioned by many of the participants. But whereas some need lots of cuddles and closeness, others might prefer alone time for processing – for example, to sit under a blanket for a while – to even out and reset. For some, it is important to process the experience for a day or two before keeping in touch via text. As described by content creator Hayley Honeyman among others, the only way to know what actually works for you and your partner(s) is to ask and then communicate.

Unfortunately, eventually all those nice endorphins and oxytocin from the kink session will leave the body. Everything that felt so great disappears, and you might feel insecure, depressed, all alone, and vulnerable or perhaps bodily sensations such as coldness and fatigue. Within the kink community, this is referred to as a sub, Dom, top, or bottom drop.[6] Tops might experience massive guilt about their role in the scene even if they honored agreements and avoided harm successfully. For some, the drop may come the day after a great session. For others, the drop may come after two days. Yet others are not so affected at all. It is always advisable to check in on each other after a day or two. Most people appreciate and need to hear that they are worthy and appreciated for who they are and have been doing well. Stick to brief feedback rather than long conversations directly afterward. Be there for each other. Here are some participants' voices describing their views and needs of aftercare:

> I find it very difficult to know what I need in terms of aftercare, so it's something we're still experimenting with. My partners are usually allowed to try things out, so far it has mostly been about hydration and snacks, as well as physical closeness that is a bit more gentle.
>
> *(Participant)*

> Physical contact. Becoming a koala, ingesting drinks, and something with sugar usually. If something demeaning has been said, I need to hear the opposite. Hugs and cuddles until goodbye. The next day I like to have a check-in about how I thought the session went but sometimes not necessary or desired depending on how intense the session was.
>
> *(Participant)*

- What kind of aftercare do you need after kink practices?
- How did you come up with what you need?
- How and when do you usually communicate your aftercare needs?
- Is feedback usually part of your aftercare?
- If you get in touch afterward, how long afterward and in what way (meet up, talk on the phone, or texting)?

Using checklists

Most of the participants stated that they do not currently use any form checklist. However, half of them said that they would definitely benefit from having such list to use in the future, as it would make things easier.

> I would like to have a list to simplify things. My brain is usually not really there and then a list would be helpful. For me, it would be good to have a written list that can be used in all/most of the occasions. There is so much to keep track of, and so much is easily lost, because my focus might be somewhere else at the time, or because I struggle with timing sometimes. I have often thought that I should try to put together a useful list for myself, preferably one that can be both general and specific based on my own adaptation, but I think I need someone to help me out with that.
>
> *(Participant)*

Some participants recognized the potential convenience of having a checklist but expressed difficulty in finding the time, knowledge, or energy to create one. Others employed alternative approaches, such as sharing their yes-no-maybe list, discussing safe words and preferred communication methods. Additionally, some chose to reveal their preferences within an online kink community, using that platform as a way to indirectly convey their relevant interests. However, one participant noted,

> Verbal agreements always need to be written down for returning partners – if it's not written down, I don't remember it and then it doesn't exist.
>
> *(Participant)*

For some, creating checklists is part of their kink pleasure. For example, one participant explained that they

> love to create a checklist of things to include before the session starts. What my partner/s like, certain things that I want to include in the game and how to implement it. For example: One partner wants to be hit, then the question will be – with which tools? Which tools are interesting, scary, 'no way', afraid of but want to, good for punishment (if relevant), etc.? Where do you draw the line at too much pain? Where does the partner want to be hit? How do we land afterwards with aftercare if we have a long session of impact play? Should anything else be included? Does the partner want to be hit until they bleed or is it lighter marks they are looking for? How does the partner want to be treated while this is going on? And what do they want to experience, feel, and get out of the session, and what are their needs? But also what do I need and want out of it?
>
> *(Participant)*

These are relevant questions to ask yourself and others. And for once, the more details, the merrier and the more useful. To boost inspiration and creativity, try to put more focus on what you desire than on what you do not want to engage in.

- Do you incorporate checklists into your pre–kink session routine?
- If so, how frequently – sometimes, often, always, or rarely?
- Is it a standard practice for every occasion, specifically with new partners, or only when exploring something new?
- Is it a list you or your partner created, or did you discover it elsewhere?

Go create your own checklist

The participants' stories illustrated joys of unmasking and of acting out sensory pleasures together with other neurodivergent people, being in spaces allowing for different ways of cognitive processing and communication. Further building on the results of the study, we focus on practical recommendations in the final section on this chapter. To express one's needs effectively, the first step is to identify them. This can be challenging, particularly for those who lack experience or have not given it much thought. Perhaps the right questions have not been posed before? We believe that is a crucial aspect – asking numerous clear and specific questions and allowing room for reflection. It is OK if answering something not previously contemplated takes time. The more you ponder and discuss these aspects, the more intriguing it becomes. Some of the participants noted that participating in this study gave them an appreciated moment for self-reflection and hopefully even some inspiration to continue exploring themselves and others within this area. We hope the same goes for you who read this chapter. Therefore, we will end this chapter with a task for you: go create your own checklist!

To start or to have some guidance, here are some suggestions for questions to ask yourself and others. The following are only suggestions to inspire. It is up to you to pick out what is pertinent for you, your partners, and your sessions.

Let's start by exploring and creating your "Stimming Communication Profile" (Henley, 2023b).

Explore and create your own Stimming Communication Profile by asking yourself

- What do you communicate when you are bouncing (happy?), stomping feet (excited?), clapping hands (surprised?), chewing on something (focusing?), yawning or scratching (anxious?), mumbling (irritated?), or fidgeting (concentrating?)?
- Do you vary your stimming behaviors based on different situations and emotional states? For instance, do you stim differently when you are enjoying, feeling uncomfortable, anxious, tense, frustrated, or excited?
- Explore whether your stimming behaviors vary when you are experiencing arousal, understimulation, overstimulation, or satisfaction in a sexual context.
- How significant are external factors in determining whether and to what extent you engage in stimming during kink situations? For instance, does the familiarity with the individuals involved or the setting, such as a club space, influence your stimming behavior?

What senses would you like to involve? Prepare for and set the scene by thinking through and providing for your sensory needs:

- Body and touch: How do you like cuddles and caressing? Do you like to feel squeezed? What about scratching, biting, pinching, kneading? And slapping, whipping, spanking, flogging, caning? Impact play? On what parts of the body? Is it OK to leave marks or bruises? Temporary or permanent? Do you bruise easily? Any favorite or feared tools? Do you prefer blunt or sharp pain? How about sharp objects like pinwheels or knives?
- Taste – preferred tastes to go with the warm-up chat or for aftercare. Or if food play is at the table? Any food allergies?
- Bodily fluids, lubricants, and other squishy stuff – Is it OK to play around with and/or share body fluids like saliva, pussy juice, cum, blood, or urine? Do you like it wet and messy or not? Will it make you feel turned on or off? How about playing with food? If so, what kind of food and where on the body is OK?
- Smell – is there a certain scent or smell that turns you on or off? Does perfume or scented candles work for you, or will it rather give you a headache?
- Sound – any specific sounds that may be annoying or that makes you calm and open for what to come? What is your favorite music, songs, instruments, or no-nos? Preferred volume? Perhaps you like to just hear the surrounding sounds or prefer total silence with help of your favorite earplugs or headphones? If you are into spanking, does heavy sound increase your pleasure or not?
- Visual – do you prefer subdued lighting, colored lights, lava lamps, or the flicker of candles? Would you rather have no lights or be blindfolded to reduce visual input and thus enhance other sensory experiences? Is there a specific fetish object you need for visual focus or tactile comfort?
- Proprioception – the sense of body position, movement, and balance. Would you like to do activities such as swinging, hanging upside down, or feeling the pressure of your body against the ropes in a Shibari suspension session, or does this make you feel uncomfortable?

Finally, you may find the WH questions to be a useful tool:

- **Who** – who has been invited, who and how many are expected to participate?
- **What** – what can be expected to happen, before, during, after? What kind of event/club/social gathering? What are your soft and hard boundaries?
- **When** – what day and date, at what time? When is the session or event expected to end?
- **Where** – location, public/private? Address, distance, travel route to get there? Where do we meet up?
- **Why** – what is the intention or purpose of the session: powerplay, release through pain, sensory regulations, rope play, role play, edge play/pushing limits? Release of built-up tensions? Or for fun and/or pleasure or to simply explore together or get to know each other?

- **With what** – what do I need to bring, and what can I expect others to bring?
- **How** – how do we take care of each other? Is there a care plan/a safe system/risk assessment? Are there any physical or medical conditions that may be important to know about? This may include conditions like epilepsy, asthma, prior surgery, hemophilia, heart diseases, or specific medical treatments. If into discipline, power play, and shame games, consider what mental boundaries you might have. Have your preferred communication styles for the session been set (verbal/gestures)? Have you agreed on safe words/stop signals? How intense? Slow and sensual or pain oriented? For how long will the session or event last?

Notes

1 We wish to acknowledge the important commenting on earlier versions of this chapter by Ariel Pliskin and the editors.
2 As this chapter explores sexual activity, we acknowledge the importance of consent of all involved parties.
3 Club LASH, nowadays renamed as club Wish: https://www.clubwish.se/en/about-wish/.
4 Following a definition by Ali Hebert and Angela Weaver, BDSM refers to "a range of sexual preferences that generally relate to enjoyment of physical control, psychological control, and/or pain" (Merriam-Webster, n.d.).
5 "Little space" is a term used to describe the headspace or "frame of mind" an age regressor gets into that allows them to feel more youthful, childlike, or "little". It is the "mood" a submissive creates when they are acting and exploring their "little" side (DDLG playground).
6 By top drop and sub drop we mean a "crash" after the kink session has ended. It may be described as an "after-effect" by a particularly physically or emotionally exhausting session. See, for example, Magazine Demasque, n.d.

References

Ambler, J. K., Lee, E. M., Klement, K. R., Loewald, T., Comber, E. M., Hanson, S. A., Cutler, B., Cutler, N., & Sagarin, B. J. (2017). Consensual BDSM facilitates role-specific altered states of consciousness: A preliminary study. *Psychology of Consciousness: Theory, Research, and Practice*, 4(1), 75.

BeautiDivergent. (2020, November 12). Sex stims! (Just not too loud!). *BeautiDivergent* https://beautidivergent.wordpress.com/2020/11/12/sex-stims-just-not-too-loud/.

Bertilsdotter Rosqvist, H. (2019). Doing things together: Exploring meanings of different forms of sociality among autistic people in an autistic work space. *Alter*, 13(3), 168–178.

Boucher, N. B. (2018). *Relationships between characteristics of autism spectrum disorder and BDSM behaviors*. Honors thesis, Ball State University.

Bozelka, K. J. (2021). Nothing for nothing: Edging as filmic structure in the films of Jerry Douglas. *Porn Studies*, 8(2), 173–186.

Christiansen, C. (2021, April 14). The importance of stimming. *Candice Christiansen*. http://www.candicechristiansen.com/autism-blog/2021/4/14/theimportanceofstimming.

DDLG playground. What is DDLG? *DDLG playground*. https://ddlgplayground.com/blogs/the-playground/what-is-ddlg.

Henley, T. [@thomashenleyuk]. (2022, July 1). Happy meltdowns [video]. *Instagram*. https://www.instagram.com/p/CfcnixpNdXp/.

Henley, T. [@thomashenleyuk]. (2023a, March 15). Autism & intimacy [video]. *Instagram*. https://www.instagram.com/p/Cp0vwN6MDxH/?img_index=3.

Henley, T. [@thomashenleyuk]. (2023b, April 13). Stimming communication [video]. *Instagram*. https://www.instagram.com/p/Cq_Ae0RsP_F/?img_index=1.

Honeyman, H. [@hayley.honeyman]. (2023, July 14). *Have you established an aftercare routine yet?* [video]. *Instagram*. https://www.instagram.com/p/Cup7mSsAiG6/.

Kapp, S. K., Steward, R., Crane, L., Elliott, D., Elphick, C., Pellicano, E., & Russell, G. (2019). "People should be allowed to do what they like": Autistic adults' views and experiences of stimming. *Autism*, 23(7), 1782–1792.

Kinkyboys (Host). (2021, September). Kinky and autistic (no. 62). [Audio podcast episode]. *Kinkyboys Podcast*. https://open.spotify.com/episode/0rDRqWGiY2m5fXyjzuVPvj.

Magazine Demasque. (n.d.). Tops can drop too. *Magazine Demasque*. https://www. demasquemagazine.com/post/tops-can-drop-too. Downloaded 29 December 2023.

McDonnell, A., & Milton, D. (2014). *Going with the flow: Reconsidering "repetitive behaviour" through the concept of "flow states."* BILD.

Merriam-Webster. (n.d.). BDSM. *Merriam-Webster.com dictionary*. https://www.mer riam-webster.com/dictionary/BDSM. Retrieved 29 December 2023.

Murray, D., Lesser, M., & Lawson, W. (2005). Attention, monotropism and the diag-nostic criteria for autism. *Autism*, 9(2), 139–156.

Murray, F. (2019). Me and monotropism: A unified theory of autism. *The Psychologist*, 32, 44–49.

Pearson, A., & Hodgetts, S. (2023). "Comforting, reassuring, and . . . hot": A qualitative exploration of engaging in BDSM and kink from the perspective of autistic adults. *Autism in Adulthood*, 6(1). https://doi.org/10.1089/aut.2022.0103.

Pearson, A., & Rose, K. (2021). A conceptual analysis of autistic masking: Understanding the narrative of stigma and the illusion of choice. *Autism in Adulthood*, 3(1), 52–60.

Pliskin, A. E. (2018). Social and emotional intelligence (SEI) in BDSM. *Journal of Positive Sexuality*, 4(2), 48–55.

Pliskin, A. E. (2022). Autism, sexuality, and BDSM. *Ought: The Journal of Autistic Culture*, 4(1).

Price, D. (2022). *Unmasking autism: Discovering the new faces of neurodiversity*. Harmony.

Welch, C.(2023). Webinar – Understanding autistic burnout, inertia, meltdown, & shutdown (BIMS) with Dr. Welch. 30 May 2023. https://youtu.be/S_aM5sC1u28?si= Q4c_DgsE1Yurp_R3.

Williams, D. J., Thomas, J. N., Prior, E. E., & Christensen, M. C. (2014). From "SSC" and "RACK" to the "4Cs": Introducing a new framework for negotiating BDSM participation. *Electronic Journal of Human Sexuality*, 17(5), 1–10.

9

EXPLORING AUTISTIC ACCOUNTS OF SEXUALITY, INTIMACY, AND AUTHENTICITY

David Jackson-Perry

Introduction: A disorder of love, a disorder of self

The objects explored here – sexuality, intimacy, authenticity – all imply proximity: to others, to one's own experience, to a reflexive self. From the earliest days, however, autistic people have been conceptualised through *distance* on all these fronts, characterised in scientific literature and the popular imagination as deficient in or lacking social, affective, imaginative, and reflexive possibility, an "inability to attribute mental states to others and to oneself" (for discussion, see Dinishak & Akhtar, 2013, p. 110), and having a diminished or absent potential for empathy (for discussion, see Fletcher-Watson & Bird, 2020). The first published description of autism was – unpromisingly for intimate potential – titled "Autistic Disturbances of Affective Contact" (Kanner, 1943). The *Diagnostic and Statistical Manual* still defines autism through deficits in social-emotional reciprocity, in developing or understanding relationships, and in comprehending other people's interests or emotional worlds (APA, 2022). Autism has long been shaped as a "relational disorder that disrupts emotional interactions with others" (Davidson & Orsini, 2010, p. 131), long constructed as "a disorder of love" (Cascio, 2014, p. 309).

Unsurprisingly, then, early researchers perceived autistic people as "self-absorbed and lack[ing] the capacity to form relationships because their level of social and emotional development is obstructed by the characteristics of autism" (Elgar, 1985, p. 224). Considered uninterested in sexuality, the "deficits" supposedly inherent to autism were thought "to preclude meaningful sexual and intimate relationships" (Sala et al., 2020, p. 4133). The problem with autistic sexuality and intimacy was, in other words, autism.[1]

Although later research acknowledged that autistic people *do* have sexual and intimate interest, studies suffered from various flaws. First, even though there

DOI: 10.4324/9781003440154-13

have been some self-reported studies (e.g., Teti et al., 2019; Joyal et al., 2021; Barnett & Maticka-Tyndale, 2015), researchers largely solicited service providers or family members for information. Personally, asking my mom about my sexual life will provide little meaningful data regarding my intimate existence: interviewing family members or service providers about any person's sexuality is unlikely to provide information regarding the latter's private behavior or subjective experience of their intimate lives (Sala et al., 2020, p. 60). Indeed, interviewing third parties may result largely in discussion of "problematic behavior" – that is, behavior often perceived as causing problems to the third parties (Barnett & Maticka-Tyndale, 2015). This may contribute to the second flaw: reflecting broader autism research, the field is dominated by medical discourses positioning autism as "a list of deficits, impairments, limitations, and negatively valued deviations from behavioural norms" (Dinishak, 2016, p. 3). Although it is now acknowledged that autistic people are sexual and intimate beings, their intimate lives remain largely understood through "default comparison to sexual and neurological norms" (Bertilsdotter Rosqvist & Jackson-Perry, 2021), their sexual happenings measured against "neuroconventional and heteronormative vanilla sex" (see Mika Hagerlid's chapter in this volume).

By way of example, the literature consistently notes high levels of sexual and gender diversity among autistic people (Herrick & Datti, 2022; Strang & Fischbach, 2023), and research ponders how or why so many autistic people come to identify outside cisgender, heterosexual norms (Toft, 2023). To my knowledge – but not surprise – no research seeks to understand how or why autistic cisgender heterosexuals identify in this way: heterosexuality is apparently considered so self-evident that even *autistic* heterosexuality requires no explanation. Much literature thus positions "identities other than heterosexual and cisgender" as "contingent, mediated by social constraint, biological exceptionalism, or cognitive limitation" (Jackson-Perry, 2020, p. 222). An amalgam is made between assumed symptomatology and anything-but-cisgender heterosexuality, here as in other areas of disability (see Toft et al., 2020; Gill, 2015). For a brief, if bewildering, example, researchers lean on "rigidity and repetitive and obsessive behaviours" (van der Miesen et al., 2018, p. 145), "cognitive inflexibility inherent to ASD" (George & Stokes, 2018, p. 979), or "more rigid views" (Holt et al., 2016, p. 116) to explain autistic gender diversity. This is fascinating, given that autistic people are far more likely to identify *outside* sexual and gender norms than non-autistic peers: hidden behind what we "know" diagnostically, even *nonconformity* to normative notions of sexual and gender roles and behaviors is interpreted as inflexibility. This form of knowledge relies on the double assumption of autistic deficit and cisgender heterosexuality as the desirable norm from which deviation requires explanation: the two systems support each other. The "autism is the problem with autistic sexuality" discourse endures, and research still largely takes diagnostic criteria as the prism through which to explain autistic intimate happenings.

Probably the most pervasive theory in mainstream autism research, the "sheer force" of which "is difficult to ignore", is deficit in theory of mind (ToM) (Orsini, 2022, p. 10). ToM, robustly and repeatedly critiqued elsewhere (Fletcher-Watson & Bird, 2020; Gernsbacher & Yergeau, 2019), seeks to demonstrate and explain an assumed autistic inability to understand or take into consideration what someone else is thinking or feeling. Milton (2012, p. 884) reframes this as a "question of reciprocity and mutuality", a "Double Empathy Problem", proposing that social misunderstanding is bidirectional: if autistic people may have difficulty understanding non-autistic people, the opposite is equally true. Supporting this, Sala et al. (2020, p. 4140) note that "many autistic participants reported that their partner also being autistic, neurodivergent or having similar experiences such as social anxiety, was helpful in building understanding": "Social impairment" may then be less the problem than cross-neurotype communication. This disrupts a one-sided view positioning the problem within autistic individuals, in turn allowing a consideration of structural and social factors contributing to the complexity of navigating intimacy. Sala and colleagues (2020, p. 4140) note that "stigma and feelings of isolation . . . perpetuated by wider society" increase "social impairment through social exclusion". Further, while Joyal et al. (2021, pp. 1–2) acknowledge "difficulties in social cognition", their starting point includes the "institutional (e.g., insufficient sexual education), and societal (e.g., ableism assumptions, stigmatization, and exclusion) barriers" that complicate autistic intimate possibilities. This is one of relatively few self-reporting studies. As more autistic voices are heard, challenges to dominant readings of autism and ways in which neurodivergent people are "talking back" to biomedical conceptualisations of autism gain traction (Bertilsdotter Rosqvist & Jackson-Perry, 2021, p. 14). A move thus becomes possible from an individual, medical reading of autism toward a more social model: challenges may come as much from context as from any trait inherent to autistic people.

One underexamined trait "especially pertinent to autistic individuals" (Stark et al., 2021, p. 195) is "authenticity": "sincerity, truthfulness, originality, and the feeling and practice of being true to one's self or others" (Vannini & Franzese, 2008, p. 1621). Autistic people consistently score higher on items such as "expressing one's true self" or "authenticity" than non-autistic peers (Gillespie-Lynch et al., 2014; Kirchner et al., 2016). Conversely, research indicates that "the sociocognitive process of deception" (Ma et al., 2019, p. 3374) is costlier to autistic than non-autistic children: the former were eight times less likely to tell self-protective lies than the latter. Indeed, "authentic tendencies" may explain – as explanation appears necessary – the "over-representation" of diverse gender and sexual modalities among autistic people. Perhaps autistic people are not more likely to *be* other than cisgender and/or heterosexual: rather, non-autistic people may be *less able to bypass* those norms to arrive at an authentic expression of their own sexual and gender orientation or identity (Walsh & Jackson-Perry, 2021; see also Davidson & Tamas, 2016).

As well as some empirical, cognitive, and neurological indications supporting the notion that honesty is "a primary strength" in autistic people (Strunz et al., 2015, p. 4035) can be added that authenticity and its proxies have long been something of a marker of autistic identity, as witnessed by considerable online activity.[2]Main (2003), for example, parodies diagnostic criteria for "allistics", describing a group of people who "have difficulty with the difference between truth and falsity". Similarly, the Institute for the Study of the Neurologically Typical,[3] notes that "NTs find it difficult to communicate directly and have a much higher incidence of lying as compared to persons on the autistic spectrum". "Being authentic" has come to be a part of what "being autistic" means to many of those so identified.

However, it is still true to say that little is known qualitatively about autistic sexual and intimate experience – or, indeed, authenticity – from autistic perspectives. A gap in the literature persists of qualitative, in-depth research seeking to understand – through their own words and without recourse to assumptions of deficit – autistic experiences of these objects.

Methods

This chapter draws on and extends doctoral research (Jackson-Perry, 2023) exploring the barriers and opportunities experienced by autistic people in their intimate lives, using a framework of critical autism studies (CAS). CAS challenges deficit-based assumptions of autism, renders visible the power dynamics at play in autism discourse, encourages interdisciplinary research using inclusive and participatory methodologies, and considers both the cultural and biological factors that may "produce autism" (Orsini & Davidson, 2013; Woods et al., 2018).

Constructivist grounded theory, a systematic and inductive approach whereby the researcher "follows the data" rather than using predefined categories (Charmaz, 2014), was drawn on for data collection and analysis. Grounded theory is particularly appropriate for research in understudied areas (Chun Tie et al., 2019) and when seeking researcher accountability to those researched (Charmaz, 2014).

As Raymaker and Nicolaidis (2013, p. 176) note, "there is no single, formalized way to conduct participatory research". As a neurodivergent but non-autistic researcher working within CAS, participation was an important element of this research. A research advisory group (RAG) of nine autistic adults gave input into this study. Broader consultation included formal and informal community frequentation, an online survey (n = 567) into preferred participation methods and topics of interest concerning sexuality and intimacy, and a website where the RAG communicated and results were made available.[4]

Sixteen autistic participants, 22–54 years old with a variety of gender and sexual/affective[5] identities, were recruited via Twitter (the social media platform now called X). This resulted in 24 semi-directive interviews: seven participants completed a second interview and one a third. Confirming results from the online survey, most participants chose asynchronous written interviews, two Skype, and one instant messaging. Questions were sent in advance. Ethics approval was granted by the author's university ethics committee.

Findings

Two main themes emerged from participants' accounts – *Navigating the norm: Challenges to sexuality, intimacy, and authenticity* and *Reaching for resolution: Identifying and accessing authentic sexual and intimate experience.*

I have kept theory – which I leave for discussion – to a minimum, to allow participants' accounts to be "heard" without interruption. Similarly, I have organised these accounts for readability but have not provided sub-themes, rather structuring findings around particularly representative quotes, leaving the reader freer to draw their own conclusions. Participants' quotes are in italics.

TABLE 9.1 Interview participants: Country, age, diagnostic status, and sexual and gender identity

Name	Country	Age	Diagnosis/ self-ID	Diagnosis/ ID age	Sexual identification (participants' words)	Gender identification (participants' words)
Charlotte	UK	32	DX	32	Queer	Cis-woman
John	UK	32	DX	4	Neuro-queer/ Gray	Cis-male
Sara	UK	36	DX	33	Bisexual/ Polyamorous	Gender-queer
Charles	USA	42	DX	22	Hetero/Demi-ace	Cis-male
Finn	Australia	22	DX	19	Bisexual	Neutrois, AFAB
A	UK	23	DX	19	Asexual	Nonbinary
Beatrice	UK	25	DX	23	Bisexual	Cis-female
Julie	UK	30	DX	28	Lesbian	Woman
Mia	UK	40	Self-ID	40	Bisexual	Cis-female
Hazel	UK	23	DX	18	Heterosexual	Cis-female
Mike	Canada	54	DX	54	Hetero (?)	Male
James	UK	20	DX	14	Bisexual	Man
Gillian	UK	41	DX	38	Heterosexual	Female
Oliver	UK	27	DX	5	Pansexual	Cis-male
Karen	UK	47	DX	44	Lesbian	Nonbinary
Susan	UK	22	DX	14	Pansexual	Female

1 Navigating the norm: Challenges to sexuality, intimacy, and authenticity

This first theme sets the scene for participants' trajectories of sexuality, intimacy, and authenticity. The challenges faced are rarely posed by "being autistic". Disruption to intimate development is, rather, situated in the collision between difference – social, sexual, or cognitive – and peers and social structures that do not tolerate divergence from assumed norms.

> *I was made to feel a freak as a child (I was two years ahead of everyone else in school and still at the top of any class I applied myself, my mother died when I was 13, I lisped, I twitched, etc. [and of course, I'm autistic]).*
> (Charles)

The high-achieving (heterosexual) Charles got "*called 'faggot'*" and was regularly "*physically attacked at school*". His bullying seems related to both "autistic behaviors" and signs that peers read as indicating sexual identities requiring policing or punishing. Despite the apparently self-evident nature of "faggot", it is difficult to know whether participants are harassed for their perceived sexual orientation or whether this is in a sense an alibi: what is being punished, what needs suppressing, is perhaps difference more broadly.

The sense of being a "*late-bloomer*" (Charlotte) is recurrent. "*After puberty,*" says Hazel,

> [peers] *seemed to be interested in sex and intimacy all of a sudden. . . . I didn't really hit that part of puberty until age 16, which was strange because it was so much later, but prior to that I could just about manage holding hands or hugging people.*

Beatrice also felt that she was "*missing out*", noting that her peers all "*had some form of romantic relationship*", concluding, "*These feelings were so extreme that I regularly felt like I would rather die than be alone*".

Many participants "*never had an easy time with friends*" (Julie), limiting access to information about sexuality. As Susan says, "*I didn't really have friends from . . . 11 to 14 so I couldn't look to them for guidance* [about sexuality]": neither social norms nor sexuality education helped participants fill in the gaps.

> *A lot of my early experiences of sexuality and intimacy had caused me to clam up into accepting a confusing and distressing "normal" that it took a long time to unlearn.*
> (Beatrice)

The normative pressure on Beatrice's development, the need to "*unlearn*" her early conditioning illustrates a reflexivity and pragmatism common here. For

James, either *"the 'rules' of flirting or engagement"* were *"completely lost"* on him or ignored if they were *"heteronormative or otherwise nonsensical"*. Susan also analysed what makes polyamory an attractive option for her: it *"just makes sense practically speaking"*.

That autistic people may be less likely to conform to social norms than their non-autistic peers, as when Karen says *"I'm not somebody who ever really feels social pressures. I think being autistic we're . . . a bit immune to that"*, comes frequently into tension with pressure to *"do normal things"* (Susan) or be *"keen to follow social rules and behave appropriately"* (Charlotte).

Various interactional strategies are used to mitigate social pressures. One is to avoid contact altogether, as "A"[6] did following a "date":

> I suddenly felt like the expectations were different and things were going to happen that I didn't want or understand. I was too scared to actually talk to them about any of this. . . . Instead I . . . reduced contact and started avoiding them until they gave up.

Another interactional strategy is "camouflaging" or "masking",[7] social coping mechanisms whereby autistic people minimise "autistic behaviors"[8] while maximising those expected in non-autistic interactions, such as making eye contact. Participants referred to scripting, or playing roles, as they discuss navigating their social worlds. *"I'm occasionally capable,"* says James, *"of masking my struggles with small talk, but this is essentially a role I adopt like an actor"*. Scripting helps negotiate anxiogenic situations but has intimate downsides. Beatrice is interested in exploring her attraction to women, but her *"reliance . . . on scripts can make unscripted sex difficult"*. She goes on:

> If things go off script, I can get worried or frustrated, or go blank. This . . . is also why I have never had sex with someone who isn't a cis male. I really, really don't want to screw things up, misread signs, communicate poorly, and above all, make someone feel uncomfortable.

Far from lacking empathy, Beatrice seeks to mitigate others' discomfort. Hazel, who felt like a *"social anomaly"*, was *"hyperaware"* of the need to avoid doing anything that might aggravate that impression and *"avoided a lot of sexual related things because of that"*.

Heterosexuality was expected and (heteronormative) sex difficult to avoid. For Charlotte, for example, it was clear that she *"was 'supposed' to meet a nice boy and get married"*, and separation of sex and intimacy from desire, and its attachment to social expectations, was recurrent. Susan says, *"When I was 14 or 15 . . . I had my first 'boyfriend'. . . . I wasn't really interested in anything sexual then; I just knew it was a thing people liked and were supposed to do"*. For Beatrice, too, sex was not an expression of desire but something that "*should*" be done to "*make the guy happy*": nothing in sexuality and relationship education (SRE) was helpful in challenging this.

> The sex education I received gave me a grasp of the basics but wasn't terribly helpful for my sex life specifically.
>
> *(Charlotte)*

Teachers stuck to the "*basic mechanics*" (Mike) of heterosexual sex, leading to "*a lack of understanding and awareness of nonstandard orientations and relationships*" ("A"). All "A" learned about were

> *straight men and women getting into monogamous sexual-romantic relationships. . . . I'm not a man or a woman, I'm not straight, I'm not into sex, and I don't really understand monogamy or romance! So the types of relationships I might actually end up having happily – I never even knew they existed . . . or that there were other people in the world who felt the same way.*

Anything other than cisgender heterosexuality was unaddressed by SRE, which concentrated on monogamous, heterosexual intimate possibilities, rendering other expressions of sexuality invalid or invisible, and leaving participants without terms of reference with which to relate to and describe themselves. Indeed, participants' difficulty projecting themselves into an intimate future was common. For John, the hardest part about his intimate development "*was recognising the terms of reference for me to explore physical intimacy in the first place – I didn't know asexuality even existed*". Charlotte too "*was slow to explore* [her] *sexuality because queerness had not really been presented . . . as an option, and certainly not a neutral, normal one*".

Particularly for participants brought up as girls, discussion of pleasure was absent. As Beatrice writes,

> *That having an orgasm was something I was allowed to do . . . had never been explicitly said, and like most things in life, if it's not explicitly said I struggle to grasp that I am allowed to do something.*

Consent, a complex issue for participants, was also missing from SRE. It took Charlotte a long time to know that she "*was allowed to turn down guys who asked* [her] *out. . . . Even one lesson about that might have helped*". Beyond "*several experiences . . . on shaky ground, regarding consent, in that I was too drunk to consent*", Julie recalls situations where she "*didn't want it to happen but didn't know how to say no*", and elsewhere both Mia and Beatrice use identical words, with Beatrice thinking "*that what the other person wanted was what had to happen, for a very long time*":

I didn't have a voice. I was sexually assaulted. . . . I trusted far, far too easily. . . . I continually dated men several years older than me.

(Beatrice)

Lacking voice is common here, as are dating older men, sexual assault, and trusting people's intentions. Sara echoes Beatrice, remembering how she identified two relationships with older men as abusive, and "*relat*[ing] *this back to being autistic*", saying that she "*wasn't aware maybe of the designs that they had on* [her]".

Four participants suffered emotional, physical, or sexual parental and domestic (partner) abuse. Julie, because of "*inappropriate events that happened throughout* [her] *childhood . . . was always aware of* [herself] *as a sexual object*". She felt that "*kissing boys or having a boyfriend*" would bring acceptance by her peers, as "*it relied on* [her] *body, not* [her] *personality, which was generally deemed to be lacking*". This evolved into

desperate attempt(s) to be accepted by someone. . . . Adults would frequently have sex with me, often when I was too drunk or had taken [too many] drugs to consent.

Later, Julie had "*a relationship with a woman which was very abusive*". Mia also had an "*abusive ex . . . who made it . . . clear that being bisexual was not OK*" and by whom she "*was informed that no meant yes*".

The accumulation of parental and peer-led maltreatment left participants craving affection and intimacy and vulnerable to abuse as adults. The parental abuse Beatrice suffered led to "*existential loneliness* [kicking] *in really young*". Her sense of rejection led to recognition that "*the only option for love and support and closeness* [would come] *from outside of the family unit*". Sara also noted that the "*sense of alienation*" from her family impacted later relationships, which took as their starting point "*feeling unloved and not connected*".

2 Reaching for resolution: Identifying and accessing authentic sexual and intimate experience

The previous section described challenges participants identified in their intimate lives: this theme reflects processes through which resolution may be reached. The autistic or queer subjectivity that posed challenges to participants' peers and other actors earlier now brings opportunity for developing safe, meaningful, satisfying intimate lives. Running through this section is a need or an inclination for authenticity.

Concluding Sara's interview, I asked what the experience had been like for her. "*Fine, very positive*". However, after my repeated "checks" regarding her consent to participate, Sara responded more heatedly, "*I've given that written consent to you. . . . It's the fucking faffy neurotypical way of doing stuff basically. . . . If I say something, then I mean it, yeah?*"

Three-quarters of participants repeatedly referenced the importance of honesty and straightforwardness – proxies for authenticity – in opposition to neuroptypical "faffyness", politeness, or conformity, perceived as insincere. James's "*biggest personal challenge with sexuality and intimacy is a difficulty with (or disregard for) how you would conventionally approach people*". James continues, "*I struggle with the initial stages of conversation, like small talk, as it means I have to be dishonest with someone*". "A" "*can't really lie*", leaving them "*unlikely to end up in situations* [they are] *not happy with*", and John says, "*My honesty and largely unmasked autistic behaviour has at least kept me away from unwanted encounters in the past*".

Honesty positively impacted participants' intimate relationships. "A" has an "*instinct to tell people the truth*" about how they feel, with the result that "*the relationships* [they] *have are authentic*". Hazel's "*abruptness . . . helps* [her] *think about what* [she] *wants* [and] *to try and create that dialogue with* [her] *partner*", and Beatrice also says,

> I am very very good at speaking my mind and communicating and leveling with sexual partners. . . . If I am not met with the same openness, then I will drop them.

Authenticity is most possible with other autistic people. Previously, Oliver "*had to suppress a lot of* [himself] *so as to not make the other person too uncomfortable*". With his autistic partner, he writes, "*I was just me*". Finn too remarks, "*I find having sex with other autistics easier because I feel like I communicate better and don't have to worry about being perceived as 'weird'*", a sentiment echoed by "A":

> Communicating with other autistic people feels so much easier and more comfortable than with NT people – I learned how to have social relationships where feelings and expectations are explicit and spelled out without judgment.

Not being formally recognised as autistic through diagnosis is recurrently linked by participants with vulnerability to abuse and an inability to understand and express their sensory and intimate needs and desires: diagnosis, on the contrary, is an important step to intimate autonomy and well-being. Sara's words describing how diagnosis made "sense of past experience" is echoed by many participants throughout interviews:

> [Since diagnosis] I've been able to see my past experiences with a new lens and put words to them. Some of them are community words like "genderqueer" and "polyamorous"; some of them are clinical words like "sensory processing differences" or "autism", but I have been able to make sense of my experiences that I've had in the past.

Another step in seeking out authentic experience comes through identifying and frequenting similar others. For "A", whose major challenge had been "*a lack of understanding and awareness of nonstandard orientations and relationships*", the internet was "*magical*" in this regard:

> *The most useful counter . . . was making friends who are autistic, queer, trans, nonbinary, non-monogamous, etc. People who are weird in all the ways that I'm weird, and getting to form relationships with them and understand how they work . . . online friends are great, and can also become important in-person friends.*

The internet thus brought understanding of how "A's" "in-group" functions, the possibilities available *beyond* the heteronormative, non-autistic world, and access to community, online and face to face.

John met his husband and Charles met his wife on the internet. For Charlotte, "*probably the most sexually intimate relationship*" of her young adulthood

> *was . . . carried out mostly online. . . . We encouraged each other to try new things, including buying our first vibrators, trying them on the same night, and each reporting back on our experiences the next day.*

The internet functions as a counterweight to the limited intimate possibilities presented to participants growing up. Online, Finn "*discovered that the clitoris was above the vaginal opening, and under a hood*", found that their "*sexual proclivities were not just accepted, but shared*", and realised that they were not alone enjoying "*vaginal sex while identifying as transmasculine*". Mia "*continually felt wrong about* [herself] *and* [her] *sexual identity until very very late into adulthood*", when she discovered "*a lot of bi-positivity on Twitter . . . that . . . directed* [her] *towards bi-positive organisations*".

Participants often find themselves at the intersection of multiple minoritized positions: being autistic, being queer, and having interests perceived as being more specific than is expected. Much of John's life "*has been defined by . . . the people* [he] *met doing the things* [he] *loved*", and that "*was difficult in childhood*" where possibilities "*were mostly defined by your immediate geography*". With the internet, "*suddenly geography isn't a filter. Interests are the filter*", says John.

Intense interests (II)[9] may also fill the gaps of limited SRE. At 18, says Finn,

> *I started collecting sex toys. . . .* [They] *are very important for my sexual discovery, and I enjoy masturbating as a way to connect to my body. I used my blog as a way of investigating changes in my sexuality through periods of stress and new medications.*

From not knowing where her clitoris was and finding masturbation "*very exhausting*":

Masturbation has become enjoyable and important to me. . . . Hitting my specific pleasure spots makes everything much easier & more enjoyable, and the toys do most of the work for me.

Creating an environment where their *"sexual proclivities were not just accepted but shared"*, Finn also found *"a solid friendship group"* through her II in sex toys.

"Online fandom . . . the first time [Charlotte had] *ever seen erotic/sexual material . . . created with a female perspective in mind"*, helped her understand the *"feelings and experiences it was possible to have, how a sexual encounter might progress, and what kinds of sexual activities existed outside of PIV* [penis in vagina] *sex"*.

IIs also play roles within relationships. Hazel's are now *"a unifying experience"*, and she and her (autistic) partner *"teach each other about* [their IIs] *and spend time doing things around that interest"*. Elsewhere, Charlotte attests to a strikingly similar experience.

Mike powerfully evokes the erotic potential of his II in music:

I sit at the piano and improvise . . . whilst [my partner] *touches me, and kisses me. . . . This almost always leads to sex . . . and obviously plays into my world of music (sound) and touch, and is a very intimate experience. . . . My music is deeply involved in being intimate.*

One of John's interests is also music, which he used to understand sexuality and gender. Noting that *"pop singers"* do not have to conform to the same strict categories as other musicians, he goes on: *"Being neuro-queer is like taking that pop singer approach to things. . . . These labels are built for other people for other purposes that do not fit me"*. John concludes, *"As an autistic person I'm taking the pop singer approach in that regard to gender and sexual expression"*. His intimate and autistic identities are inseparable, his words evoking the labor that go into understanding his intimate positioning: in this, John was far from unique.

Once I began to acquire and apply language to describe my feelings and the things happening to me, I started allowing myself to develop my own desires and needs and eventually to express them.

(Beatrice)

For Beatrice and others, naming their intimate worlds required considerable emotional and cognitive labor. Many identify as variously situated in queer identities. However, autistic people – whatever their intimate orientations – may do similar labor around sexuality and sociality as neurotypical queer people do, without the advantages that belonging to queer communities may bring, as Gillian intuits when she says, *"I bet if I weren't heterosexual and had had girlfriends,* [identifying my desire] *would have been less of a problem as I could have learned from other women"*.

As Sara notes, *"People who are straight and vanilla*[10]*. . . don't . . . suddenly think . . . the word for what I'm doing is straight and I'm vanilla"*, echoed by Susan, regarding her polyamory: *"People all have an idea of the kind of relationship they want to have; they just don't think about it so explicitly, I guess"*. Participants demonstrate a similar reflexivity toward sexuality as to other areas: *"I like"*, says Beatrice, *"to think about things in detail before I do them, in all of life as in sex"*.

John's reflexivity around his asexuality taught him about himself and others:

> [Previously] *I assumed . . . that my experience was universal. . . . So I went through cognitive gymnastics to explain to myself why other people kept acting as if they wanted sex when I was so sure that no one really wanted it. I convinced myself that my teenage peers were just pretending to be attracted to people because they thought it's what adults did.*

John gradually gained a *"more accurate understanding of what other people feel"*, bringing *"more empathy for their different experiences"*. His understanding evolved through reflecting on his own intimate positioning. Autistic kids, like neurotypical peers, evolve, develop, and grow.

Discussion

Reading and listening to participants' accounts brought a strong sense of the powerful impact of normative intimate expectations and the creative ways they disregard, resist, or navigate them. Participants expressed both a hyperawareness of the need (and their "failure") to appear "normal", and a reflexive, pragmatic attitude: sexual and social expectations may be recognised and understood but lack sense or applicability to individuals' lives and so can be usefully disregarded. Throughout, we glimpse tension: a sometimes hyperconsciousness of social rules sits alongside the notion that autistic people are less susceptible than non-autistic peers *to* those rules. This reflexivity allows – or perhaps requires – participants to question social and sexual norms and "unlearn" earlier (hetero)normative policing and expectations.

Participants were acutely aware that heterosexuality is expected and had difficulty avoiding undesired (hetero)sexual encounters. Heterosexuality was experienced as "compulsory" (Rich, 2002) and other expressions of sexuality rendered invalid or invisible. Pressure to have heterosexual relationships and sexual experiences through social obligation rather than desire left participants vulnerable to abuse, atrophying their possibilities to project themselves into an authentic intimate future.

Many participants identified as variously situated in queer identities, making comparison to non-queer folk tenuous. However, autistic people – whatever their intimate orientations – may do similar labor around sociality as queer people do around sexuality, and the concept of neuroqueer (Walker, 2021) may be useful here. "Autistic people", says M. Remi Yergeau (2018, p. 92), "have long identified with or as the queer – whether by means of sexuality or gender identity, or . . . a queer asociality that fucks norms", and so "the sexuality and sensuality of people with ASD may indeed be read as queer, regardless of partner, activity, or intention" (Groner, 2012, p. 280). Charles, bullied as a "faggot" at school, is heterosexual, illustrating both that "autistic persons' deviance made visible, their embodied deviance, includes gender and sexual non-conformity" (Barnett, 2017, p. 1212) and that heteronormative expectations negatively impact even cisgender heterosexually identified individuals.

In the United Kingdom (most participants' country of residence), it is only recently that SRE has included "same-sex" relationships, and considerable uncertainty persists on the part of teachers as to what can be taught (Toft, 2023). Participants still, through considerable labor and reflexivity, came to understand their intimate orientations, albeit often later than they would have liked. "Naming", as Gayle Rubin (2011, p. 15) reminds us, "is a powerful tool"; without it, people are left with an isolating and stigmatised view of their intimate possibilities. The invisibility of alternative intimate orientations and punishment of divergence from intimate norms also hindered participants' possibilities to move toward what they felt to be authentic, intimate positioning.

The lack of discussion of consent in SRE is all the more worrying given both the high numbers of autistic people – particularly those raised as girls – reporting sexual victimisation and intimate maltreatment and the potential that sexual knowledge and education holds to mitigate this (Weir et al., 2021). Together with negative peer interactions limiting participants' access to potentially empowering information, as noted elsewhere (Kohn et al., 2023), findings illustrate how broader societal problems (a lack of discussion of anything but cisgender heterosexuality or of consent and pleasure) are exacerbated by other, more specific aspects of the social experiences of autistic participants (here, alienation from peers). Experiences among participants of victimization and alienation point to the prevalence and intensity of policing of sexual and behavioral norms. Fergus Murray calls this "Weirdmisia", or "hate for the weird".[11] What is being punished and regulated is behavior that threatens the norm; this perhaps points to commonality of experience and not the exceptionality that is generally applied to autistic people.

Participants countered "the fucking faffy neurotypical way of doing stuff" with "typically autistic" traits of honesty, openness, and straightforwardness (Gillespie-Lynch et al., 2014; Kirchner et al., 2016). The importance attached by participants to these qualities perhaps helps explain the suggested association between masking and mental health difficulties (Sedgewick et al., 2021). Although masking may be necessary, allowing a person to "hide in plain sight" in a hostile world, it is also a denial of personal self and a threat to autistic identity wherein honesty or authenticity are defining characteristics.

Non-autistic people's dishonesty and social conformity – a lack of clarity or a difficulty communicating straightforwardly and explicitly – was recurrently identified as problematic. Authenticity and its proxies were repeatedly refer-enced by participants as advantages in accessing and maintaining meaningful and satisfying intimate relationships and avoiding unwanted intimacy. Straightforwardness and the possibility to "be themselves" explain participants' preference for autistic friends, lovers, and sex partners, as noted elsewhere, with participants in Crompton et al.'s (2020, p. 1445) study particularly valuing relationships with other autistic people because they could "be their authentic, autistic self in their company".

Authenticity is also implicit regarding intense interests. Autistic psychologist Wenn Lawson (2021, p. 2424) notes that autistic people may display a "lack of guile", which requires them neither to engage in interests that they find, well, uninteresting, nor to try and convince others of the potential for gratification of their own interests. IIs – often pathologised in the literature through the "core deficit" of "repetitive and restrictive behaviours" (Jasim & Perry, 2023) – played a central role in identifying and maintaining satisfying intimate relationships, gaining information about sexual possibilities, and provided frameworks through which participants explored sociality and intimacy.

Conclusion and implications for practice

Despite what the literature would have us believe, participants' accounts illu-strated that "being autistic" was not the principal challenge they faced in their intimate lives, nor was "social intervention" the answer. On the contrary, rigid normative social and sexual attitudes and environments presented the weightiest problems. Elements of – often pathologised – autistic subjectivity offered a way through the *"confusing and distressing 'normal'"* that Beatrice described to then develop safe, authentic, and meaningful sexual and intimate lives.

Implications for practice

- Pellicano and Heyworth (2023, p. 4) note the "overemphasis on specific attributes of individuals as opposed to the broader contexts in which Autistic people live" when considering "intervention": "generally the broader context . . . creates the problematic response, not necessarily the behavior itself". The site of "intervention" cannot be limited to "autistic bodyminds" (Jackson-Perry et al., 2020, p. 125) but must include the "social bodymind". Findings clearly confirm the need to work on structural and societal (e.g., stigma and discrimination in various forms) levels.
- "Comprehensive and accurate sex education that addresses sexuality, inti-mate relationships, and gender identity diversity from a positive perspec-tive" (Dewinter et al., 2023, p. 4) is a necessity. However, SRE should also include more work around consent and pleasure.
- Practitioners need to use explicit language to describe both (a wide range of) intimate possibilities and promote pleasure and security.

Finally, it is clear through participants' accounts that far from requiring "correction", autistic subjectivities can provide a pathway to safe, meaningful, and pleasurable intimate lives. Intense interests, connecting with autistic and queer individuals and communities, a reflexive attitude to sexual and social norms, and a tendency for authentic interaction and experience represent solutions, not problems. The words of participants give a glimpse of what "neurodivergent modes of *flourishing*" – a concept from which deficit-based narratives have long excluded autistic individuals (Chapman & Carel, 2022, p. 8, italics added) – might look like. It is time for research and practice to move beyond statements of deficit, of purely individual intervention, of risk reduction, and to move toward the goal of a flourishing intimate autistic life, with the possibilities for pleasure, safety, authenticity, and interconnectivity that this implies.

Notes

1 I use both sexuality and intimacy: these might be object based, solitary, or sensory based, to name but a few modalities. I do not attempt a definition of either word to avoid any normative proscription.
2 For some examples, see https://neuroclastic.com/lies-are-painful/; https://autisticscienceperson.com/2021/05/17/be-honest-autistic-vs-neurotypical-honesty/.
3 http://web.archive.org/web/20101225092135/http://isnt.autistics.org/index.html
4 autismsexualityresearch.com
5 I differentiate between sexual and affective orientations as some participants identify as on the asexual spectrum.
6 Free to choose pseudonyms, this participant chose "A".
7 Lawson (2020) prefers "adaptive morphing", expressing the sometimes unconscious form this might take and avoiding implications of "deceit".
8 For example, stimming, self-regulatory or soothing behaviors like tapping or "hand-flapping".
9 Although the term "special interests" might be considered stigmatizing and authors such as Wood (2019) suggest other terminology such as "intense interests", participants here consistently used "special interests". I use both here.
10 A word used in kink communities to describe people and/or acts perceived as not being kinky.
11 https://oolong.medium.com/were-here-we-re-weird-get-used-to-it-26a5333fad30

References

APA. (2022). *Diagnostic and statistical manual of mental disorders* (5th ed. rev.). American Psychiatric Association.

Barnett, J. P. (2017). Intersectional harassment and deviant embodiment among autistic adults: (Dis)ability, gender and sexuality. *Culture, Health & Sexuality*, 19(11), 1210–1224.

Barnett, J. P., & Maticka-Tyndale, E. (2015). Qualitative exploration of sexual experiences among adults on the autism spectrum: Implications for sex education. *Perspectives on Sexual and Reproductive Health*, 47(4), 171–179.

Bertilsdotter Rosqvist, H., & Jackson-Perry, D. (2021). Not doing it properly? (Re)producing and resisting knowledge through narratives of autistic sexualities. *Sexuality and Disability*, 39(2), 327–344.

Cascio, M. A. (2014). New directions in the social study of the autism spectrum: A review essay. *Culture, Medicine, and Psychiatry*, 38, 306–311.

Chapman, R., & Carel, H. (2022). Neurodiversity, epistemic injustice, and the good human life. *Journal of Social Philosophy*, 53(4), 614–631.

Charmaz, K. (2014). *Constructing grounded theory* (2nd ed.). Sage.

Chun Tie, Y., Birks, M., & Francis, K. (2019). Grounded theory research: A design framework for novice researchers. *SAGE Open Medicine*, 7, 2050312118822927.

Crompton, C. J., Hallett, S., Ropar, D., Flynn, E., & Fletcher-Watson, S. (2020). "I never realised everybody felt as happy as I do when I am around autistic people": A thematic analysis of autistic adults' relationships with autistic and neurotypical friends and family. *Autism*, 24(6), 1438–1448.

Davidson, J., & Orsini, M. (2010). The place of emotions in critical autism studies. *Emotion, Space and Society*, 2(3), 131–133.

Davidson, J., & Orsini, M. (Eds.). (2013). *Worlds of autism: Across the spectrum of neurological difference*. University of Minnesota Press.

Davidson, J., & Tamas, S. (2016). Autism and the ghost of gender. *Emotion, Space and Society*, 19, 59–65.

Dewinter, J., Onaiwu, M. G., Massolo, M. L., Caplan, R., Van Beneden, E., Brörmann, N., & Van der Miesen, A. I. (2023). Recommendations for education, clinical practice, research, and policy on promoting well-being in autistic youth and adults through a positive focus on sexuality and gender diversity. *Autism*, 28(3), 770–779.

Dewinter, J., van der Miesen, A. I., & Holmes, L. G. (2020). INSAR special interest group report: Stakeholder perspectives on priorities for future research on autism, sexuality, and intimate relationships. *Autism Research*, 13(8), 1248–1257.

Dinishak, J. (2016). The deficit view and its critics. *Disability Studies Quarterly*, 36(4). https://dsq-sds.org/index.php/dsq/article/view/5236/4475.

Dinishak, J., & Akhtar, N. (2013). A critical examination of mindblindness as a metaphor for autism. *Child Development Perspectives*, 7(2), 110–114.

Elgar, S. (1985). Sex education and sexual awareness building for autistic children and youth: Some viewpoints and considerations: Response to the responses. *Journal of Autism and Developmental Disorders*, 15(2), 224–227.

Fletcher-Watson, S., & Bird, G. (2020). Autism and empathy: What are the real links? *Autism*, 24(1), 3–6.

Franzese, A. T. (2016). Authenticity: Perspectives and experiences. In *Authenticity in culture, self, and society* (pp. 103–118). Routledge.

George, R., & Stokes, M. A. (2018). Gender identity and sexual orientation in autism spectrum disorder. *Autism*, 22(8), 970–982.

Gernsbacher, M. A., & Yergeau, M. (2019). Empirical failures of the claim that autistic people lack a theory of mind. *Archives of Scientific Psychology*, 7(1), 102–118.

Gill, M. (2015). *Already doing it: Intellectual disability and sexual agency*. University of Minnesota Press.

Gillespie-Lynch, K., Kapp, S. K., Shane-Simpson, C., Smith, D. S., & Hutman, T. (2014). Intersections between the autism spectrum and the internet: Perceived benefits and preferred functions of computer-mediated communication. *Intellectual and Developmental Disabilities*, 52(6), 456–469.

Groner, R. (2012). Sex as "spock": Autism, sexuality, and autobiographical narrative. In R. McRuer & A. Mollow (Eds.), *Sex and disability* (pp. 262–281). Duke University Press.

Herrick, S. J., & Datti, P. A. (2022). Autism spectrum disorder and sexual minority identity: Sex education implications. *American Journal of Sexuality Education*, 17(2), 257–276.

Holt, V., Skagerberg, E., & Dunsford, M. (2016). Young people with features of gender dysphoria: Demographics and associated difficulties. *Clinical Child Psychology and Psychiatry*, 21(1), 108–118.

Jackson-Perry, D., Bertilsdotter Rosqvist, H., Annable, J. L., & Kourti, M. (2020). *Sensory strangers: travels in normate sensory worlds*. In Bertilsdotter Rosqvist, Hanna, Chown, Nick, and Stenning, Anna (eds) Neurodiversity Studies: A New Critical Paradigm. Routledge.

Jackson-Perry, D. (2020). The autistic art of failure: Unknowing imperfect systems of sexuality and gender. *Scandinavian Journal of Disability Research*, 22(1), 221–229.

Jackson-Perry, D. (2023). *Exploring autistic accounts of sexuality, intimacy, and authenticity*. Doctoral dissertation, Queen's University Belfast.

Jasim, S., & Perry, A. (2023). Repetitive and restricted behaviors and interests in autism spectrum disorder: Relation to individual characteristics and mental health problems. *BMC Psychiatry*, 23(1), 1–14.

Joyal, C. C., Carpentier, J., McKinnon, S., Normand, C. L., & Poulin, M. H. (2021). Sexual knowledge, desires, and experience of adolescents and young adults with an autism spectrum disorder: An exploratory study. *Frontiers in Psychiatry*, 12, 685256.

Kanner, L. (1943). Autistic disturbances of affective contact. *Nervous Child*, 2(3), 217–250.

Kirchner, J., Ruch, W., & Dziobek, I. (2016). Brief report: Character strengths in adults with autism spectrum disorder without intellectual impairment. *Journal of Autism and Developmental Disorders*, 46, 3330–3337.

Kohn, B. H., Vidal, P., Chiao, R., Pantalone, D. W., & Faja, S. (2023). Sexual knowledge, experiences, and pragmatic language in adults with and without autism: Implications for sex education. *Journal of Autism and Developmental Disorders*, 53(10), 3770–3786.

Lawson, W. B. (2020). Adaptive morphing and coping with social threat in autism: An autistic perspective. *Journal of Intellectual Disability—Diagnosis and Treatment*, 8(3), 519–526.

Lawson, W. B. (2021). Language, interests and autism: A tribute to Dr. Dinah Murray (1946–2021), an autism pioneer. *Autism*, 25(8), 2423–2425.

Ma, W., Sai, L., Tay, C., Du, Y., Jiang, J., & Ding, X. P. (2019). Children with autism spectrum disorder's lying is correlated with their working memory but not theory of mind. *Journal of Autism and Developmental Disorders*, 49, 3364–3375.

Main, A. (2003). *Allism: An introduction to a little-known condition*. http://fysh.org/~zefram/allism/allism_intro.txt.

Milton, D. (2012). So what exactly is autism? AET Competence Framework for the Department for Education. http://www.aettraininghubs.org.

Orsini, M. (2022). Who needs to (un)know? On the generative possibilities of ignorance for autistic futures. *International Journal of Qualitative Studies in Education*, 1–18. https://doi.org/10.1080/09518398.2022.2098399.

Orsini, M., & Davidson, J. (2013). Critical autism studies: Notes on an emerging field. In M. Orsini & J. Davidson (Eds.), *Worlds of autism: Across the spectrum of neurological difference*. University of Minnesota Press.

Pellicano, E., & Heyworth, M. (2023). The foundations of autistic flourishing. *Current Psychiatry Reports*, 25(9), 419–427.

Raymaker, D., & Nicolaidis, C. (2013). Participatory research with autistic communities: Shifting the system. In *Worlds of autism: Across the spectrum of neurological difference* (pp. 169–188). University of Minnesota Press. Rich, A. (2002). Compulsory heterosexuality and lesbian existence. In *Culture, society and sexuality* (pp. 199–225). Routledge.

Rubin, G. S. (2002). Thinking sex: Notes for a radical theory of the politics of sexuality. In *Culture, society and sexuality* (pp. 143–178). Routledge.

Rubin, G. S. (2011). Blood under the bridge: Reflections on "Thinking Sex." *GLQ: A Journal of Lesbian and Gay Studies*, 17(1), 15–48.

Sala, G., Hooley, M., & Stokes, M. A. (2020). Romantic intimacy in autism: A qualitative analysis. *Journal of Autism and Developmental Disorders*, 50, 4133–4147.

Sala, G., Pecora, L., Hooley, M., & Stokes, M. A. (2020). As diverse as the spectrum itself: Trends in sexuality, gender and autism. *Current Developmental Disorders Reports*, 7, 59–68.

Sedgewick, F., Hull, L., & Ellis, H. (2021). *Autism and masking: How and why people do it, and the impact it can have*. Jessica Kingsley.

Stark, E., Ali, D., Ayre, A., Schneider, N., Parveen, S., Marais, K., Holmes, N., & Pender, R. (2021). Coproduction with autistic adults: Reflections from the Authentistic Research Collective. *Autism in Adulthood*, 3(2), 195–203.

Strang, J. F., & Fischbach, A. L. (2023). A special issue of autism in adulthood dedicated to the intersection of autism and the broad LGBTQ+. *Autism in Adulthood*, 5(2).

Strunz, S., Westphal, L., Ritter, K., Heuser, I., Dziobek, I., & Roepke, S. (2015). Personality pathology of adults with autism spectrum disorder without accompanying intellectual impairment in comparison to adults with personality disorders. *Journal of Autism and Developmental Disorders*, 45, 4026–4038.

Teti, M., Cheak-Zamora, N., Bauerband, L. A., & Maurer-Batjer, A. (2019). A qualitative comparison of caregiver and youth with autism perceptions of sexuality and relationship experiences. *Journal of Developmental & Behavioral Pediatrics*, 40(1), 12–19.

Toft, A. (2023). Telling disabled and autistic sexuality stories: Reflecting upon the current research landscape and possible future developments. *Sexes*, 4(1), 102–117.

Toft, A., Franklin, A., & Langley, E. (2020). "You're not sure that you are gay yet": The perpetuation of the "phase" in the lives of young disabled LGBT+ people. *Sexualities*, 23(4), 516–529.

van der Miesen, A. I., de Vries, A. L., Steensma, T. D., & Hartman, C. A. (2018). Autistic symptoms in children and adolescents with gender dysphoria. *Journal of Autism and Developmental Disorders*, 48, 1537–1548.

Vannini, P., & Franzese, A. (2008). The authenticity of self: Conceptualization, personal experience, and practice. *Sociology Compass*, 2(5), 1621–1637.

Walker, N. (2021). *Neuroqueer heresies: Notes on the neurodiversity paradigm, autistic empowerment, and postnormal possibilities*. Autonomous Press.

Walsh, R., & Jackson-Perry, D. (2021). Autistic cognition and gender identity: Real struggles and imaginary deficits. In M. Kourti (Ed.), *Working with autistic transgender and non-binary people* (pp. 49–70). Jessica Kingsley.

Weir, E., Allison, C., & Baron-Cohen, S. (2021). The sexual health, orientation, and activity of autistic adolescents and adults. *Autism Research*, 14(11), 2342–2354.

Wood, R. (2019). *Inclusive education for autistic children*. Jessica Kingsley.

Woods, R., Milton, D., Arnold, L., & Graby, S. (2018). Redefining critical autism studies: A more inclusive interpretation. *Disability & Society*, 33(6), 974–979.

Yergeau, M. (2018). *Authoring autism*. Duke University Press.

10

AND I DON'T WANT YOU TO SHOW ME

Resistance Writing Autistic Love-Sexualities through Text Sharing Practices

Anna Nygren and Hanna Bertilsdotter Rosqvist

Introduction[1,2]

In this chapter, we will **reread** autistic acts of love. To reread is to work with countermemory as a method. Verónica Tello (2022) argues that countermemory is not (only) a means to register erased histories. It is a way of thinking non-dialectically, of adding and adding through hoarding. That is, to "make something out of what is already here – governed by feminist politics of maintenance, care and affirmative sabotage" (p. 400). We like **hoarding**. We like the **excess** of adding and adding. We like how countermemory makes it possible to transform the hurtful into something pleasurable, softening as it winds around. Rereading is an experience of resistance. Re-reading creates and maintains stimmy desires. Our re-reading is iterative and echolalic. It is stimmy in nature (Yergeau, 2018). It is repetitive. We circle round and around. We hope that the text will have a stimmy feel to it, and we invite you, the reader, to *become* with us as you *stim* with and perhaps *fuse* with us.

Become. Stim. Fuse. With us.

Steven Shore (2003) describes fusing thus:

> Whenever I get a very strong emotion and I am not clear as to where it comes from, I have to consider whether someone I am in communication with is displaying a similar emotion, which I am picking up from them. Sometimes I feel as if I am *fused* with that other person's emotions and can't separate myself.
>
> *(p. 37, emphasis added)*

In this chapter, we associate fusing with a sharing of experiences of the world. This is not intended *to show* (to teach) but *to share* (to co-experience). Co-experience

DOI: 10.4324/9781003440154-14

includes verbal and nonverbal sharing of experiences. In *A Room Called Earth* by autistic author Madeleine Ryan (2020), the neurodivergent I/Eye of the novel overcomes double empathy problems and achieves successful neuromixed communication, where the neurotypical man is able to "get the message". Getting the message is sharing the rhythm, accepting the invitation to share experiences with the I, to transcend the neurotypical gaze. It means to listen to different experiences rather than silencing or ignoring them, even if that means to let go of neuroconventions. It means to cry, to intimately and safely relate in a way inclusive of neurological differences. As the I notes,

> And I don't want to *teach* him about me, I want him to *experience* me.
> *(Ryan, 2020, p. 232, emphases added)*

Welcome to a moment of connection. This is an invitation to experience us. Again and again. We will be adding and adding experiences.

But first, some notes.

A note on names

A note on names, the collective writing process, and quoting ourselves: The quotes in this text referred to as coming from H/Anna come from a shared document that we worked with. Some quotes do actually belong to one of us specifically, but most of the quotes became part of a conversation where our voices were mixed up in each other's and where we melted together while quoting and requoting each other. In a way, we would like to refer to this as echo/lalic.

A note on theoretical frameworks

The chapter is built on a mosaic theoretical framework. Our main influences in the chapter are Damian Milton's **double empathy** problem, Catherine McDermott's theorizing the **neurotypical gaze**, and some **neuroqueer** theorizing of **temporality**. Milton (2012) defines the double empathy problem as "a disjuncture in reciprocity between two differently disposed social actors" (p. 884). In brief, this means that the more cognitive and socially different two people are, the more difficult it is for them to engage with each other socially, and clashes are to be expected. However, it is a mutual difficulty. It is not a problem located in one person, where the solution is to teach one person to become more like the other. Rather, a solution may be to recognize mutual communication difficulties and develop translation competence (cf Bertilsdotter Rosqvist et al., 2022). The double empathy problem is a common literary trope in fiction storying neuromixed encounters. However, as we will discuss in our analyses, depending on who is doing the storying, communication failures are either portrayed as a problem of autism or as a problem of difficult neuromixed communication.

Combining McDermott's sense of "the neurotypical gaze" and her investigation into "non-conventional love-acts" with neuroqueering Halberstam's notion of queer temporalities, we chose to dig deeper into the (many) different forms autistic love may take. This digging takes the shape of a collective reading of autistic fiction, where *sharing* **with each other** embodied experiences of reading is as important as the original text. The digging is a sensory, tactile act, chewing the words with hands and teeth and knees. It is boundary work as in a work with boundaries, crossing and soaking boundaries, layers upon layers **sticking** together. This means this text is several layers.

We describe our theoretical framework as a mosaic – that means, taking different old porcelain stuff, breaking them and piecing them together (we try to break them nonviolently), taking the patterns and colors that work for us, mixing and making new patterns. Then the text works with layers, with help from the mosaic. Think about it not as a floor or a flat surface of mosaic but a sculpture. Looking at it from different angles, the already mixed patterns are mixed again and again. Then try to touch the sculpture, adding yet another sensory pleasure to the analytic work.

Let's make a list! This text is

1) a literature study of fictional representations of autistic love;

A note on literature: We will use large and maybe confusing amounts of fiction and poetry to try to capture our love-sexual-textual experience and practice. This means we will not always explain the plots in length. Even though that might be frustrating, we also hope it will encourage further readings (maybe counter-readings of ours), and we also want to just show the narrative as not only one narrative but several, repeating, contradictory, oppressive, and emancipator narratives, like a field of texts.

2) a duo-autoethnographic account of our reading experiences of fictional representations of autistic love; and

3) a duo-autoethnographic account of our experiences of fictional representations of autistic love and our own relationships on the love-sex spectrum mirrored or twisted through this reading.

The neurotypical gaze

Combining the notion of the double empathy problem with feminist theorist Laura Mulvey's (1975) notion of the male gaze, McDermott has theorized the neurotypical gaze. As an illustration of the possibilities with the concept, she analyses the impact of the neurotypical gaze in the Nordic noir crime television series *The Bridge*. At the center of the series is the Swedish female police detective Saga Norén. In the third series, she has a Danish male detective, Henrik Sabroe, as her counterpart. Henrik is described on Wikipedia as someone "who understands her complex nature and accepts her for who she is." Thure Lindhardt, the actor playing Henrik says, "Henrik is a man who has lost everything, and he needs somebody like her who does not judge him." Saga is not explicitly written as autistic, but she has been coded as autistic due to "her emotionally detached tendencies and perception of the problems in the world around her" (Wikipedia, Saga Norén; cf Mullis, 2019). McDermott's analysis of *The Bridge* is an autistic rereading of non-autistic readings of Saga's expressions of love. McDermott argues that "neurotypical ways of loving are typically produced as the most socially legitimate, autistic love is not only figured as undesirable, it is often not even recognised as a form of love in the first place" (McDermott, 2022, p. 2). From here, McDermott goes on to theorize three aspects of "the neurotypical gaze". First, a neurotypical pleasure of looking at autism (p. 3). Second, a "fixing" of autism as a socially undesirable subject position (p. 3). And third, the neurotypical perspective has a primary inward focus (p. 1), "far more interested in examining and preserving the boundaries of normalcy than in gaining insight into autistic subjectivity and interiority" (p. 4). Invoking the term "neuroconventional", referring to "the norms and conventions of neurotypicality" (p. 5), McDermott shows how the neurotypical gaze "works to naturalise neuroconventional ideas about love and relationships" (p. 5) and, by this, "misses or altogether discounts the non-normative ways" (p. 5) neurodivergent people *do* connect with others, reflecting themes of the double empathy problem (Milton, 2012).

Going further than Milton, McDermott points toward the possibilities of autistic collective rereadings. With the support of different autistic spectators and commentators of the TV series, McDermott brings forth an alternative autistic reading. From this reading, an alternative (neuromixed) love story emerges and, perhaps more important, becomes possible to recognize. In this alternative love story, which shares characteristics with the neuromixed love story in *A Room Called Earth*, the neuromixed relationship between Saga and Henrik is, first, based both on "a mutual respect for one another" and an equality between partners – where both characters share "some distinctive atypicalities", expressions of cognitive difference, where none of the partners tries to alter each other's "way of being in the world" but rather offer support (p. 6). Second, McDermott brings forth alternative expressions of autistic love and autistic acts of love and care. Central in neuroconventional frameworks of love and care is verbal declarations of love. They are to be expressed with certain regularity, in the right way, and in the right context. In contrast, Saga's declaration of her love to Henrik "does not correspond with this framework of intelligibility or validity", making it "not as easy to read Saga's love acts as acts of love". However, McDermott (2022) directs the reader toward "other acts of care", or expressions of "non-conventional love acts", suggesting "not that Saga is incapable of love, but rather that perhaps a neurotypical audience might not recognise it." Among such other acts of care are Saga's intense interest in things of importance to Henrik and her motivation to resolve earlier arguments of theirs.

Neurodivergent temporalities

Difficulties of neuromixed communication are often portrayed in fiction and research as compounded by mismatches in time and pace, where neurodivergent temporality is represented as too slow or too fast compared to neurotypical temporality (cf Bertilsdotter Rosqvist et al., 2022). This illustrates parallels between neurodivergent temporality with queer temporality (cf Halberstam, 2003). Queer temporality contrasts with heteronormative temporality. Heteronormative temporality refers to dominant notions of development and lifeline that people are expected to follow, such as marrying a person of the "opposite" sex and having children within a certain age range.

Bringing together queer temporality with autistic theorizing, Jake Pyne (2021) posits trans- and autistic temporality in contrast to chrononormative temporality, arguing that "cripping trans time through autistic disruption offers a route of escape" (p. 345), thus pointing at how both neurodivergent and queer temporality intersects with and disrupts normative ideas of both time and subjecthood (Freeman, 2010, p. 3). To further build on Pyne, the tangling of neurodivergent and queer temporality in fiction may be illustrated by *The Kiss Quotient* by autistic author Helen Hoang (2018). In *The Kiss Quotient*, the central character is Stella, a wealthy autistic woman. Feeling pressure from her parents to find a life partner and start a family, Stella decides to hire Michael, a male escort, to teach her to navigate intimacy with others. The plot of the novel focuses on the development in the relationship, from an economic transaction, where Stella initially buys lessons in sex-love by Michael. Gradually the relationship turns into a love relationship, where a declaration of love ends the relationship as an economic transaction and turns it into an intimate relationship (and in the end marriage). In this way, the narrative in *The Kiss Quotient* is not disrupting either neuro- or heteronormative ideas of time and subjecthood. Rather, it is a story about a neuroqueer past (illustrating neuroqueer temporality as something to grow out of) turning into a hetero-/neuronormative happy ending (representing neurotypical, heterosexual adulthood as the only adulthood, the only acts of love). To neuroqueer acts of love, we need to reread it.

Rereading autistic love: To love whatever it may be solely for oneself

Let's start our rereading. In *The Kiss Quotient*, the picturing of neuromixed love-heterosexuality is central to the plot. The novel centers the dynamics of a neuromixed heterosexual intimate relationship between an explicitly named (cf McGrath, 2017) autistic and a non-autistic character. In the novel, the neurotypical partner (Michael) takes on a loving albeit caregiver role against the autistic partner (Stella). Stella's challenges with sensory issues during intimate encounters are portrayed as a reflection of her autistic traits. As the story unfolds, Michael gradually helps Stella learn to appreciate and enjoy sensory aspects of heterosexual experiences.

We will reread *The Kiss Quotient* with the help of another example of autism fiction, *Movement* by Nancy Fulda (2011), and an example of autistic poetry, *You Are Helping This Great World Explode* by Hannah Emerson (2021). *Movement* is a novel centered on the autistic, nonverbal dancer Hannah and her non-autistic family. During our rereading, we will contrast two different love concepts, building on different meanings of love acts. The love concept that is central for the plot in *The Kiss Quotient* is love as loving you (as a person-centered love). However, it is also centering the work of speech acts (Austin, 1975) or verbal declarations of love in intimate encounters. In line with McDermott's analyses of love in *The Bridge*, this form of love stresses a narrower meaning of acts of love, where the importance of saying "I love you" with certain regularity, in the right way, and in the right context is central. In Fulda and Emerson, another love concept is central: loving the world (or loving whatever it may be solely for oneself). This broadens the meanings of acts of love.

In the following exchanges, we reread acts of love:

> Is saying "I love you" really *The Love Act*? I know it is used. It is, yes. But so many love narratives show the love act as something less obvious. I think saying "I love you" could be a perfectly autistic way of expressing love. (But like, why repeat it, and why say it if you're not sure, and especially, why validate LOVE as a special kind of relationship at all?) I think the problem is the hierarchization of relationships, that declares friendship as of lesser value than romantic relationships. (A hierarchization related to concepts of heteronormative "relationship escalator" and "sexual scripts".) I think that is part of the problem with Hoang's novel. Hoang's sort of *Pretty Woman* story states that love is made not as an economic transaction. The main female autistic protagonist in *The Kiss Quotient*, Stella, buys lessons in love, but it cannot continue as that kind of transaction, that is not "right". (H/Anna)
>
> Oh God. I really can't understand what love IS. (And I don't want you to show me.) (H/Anna)
>
> I think about what Nancy Fulda (2011) writes in the novel *Movement* about loving the shoes, an extension of the body, loving the things, loving the world. I love the world more than I have ever loved a person. I love being alive. (That doesn't mean I don't sometimes want to die.) (H/Anna)

Hannah Emerson (2021) writes,

> yesyesyes. Loving the blue is loving mother
> earth yes yes. Please get that the triangle
> is the world bursting beginning life
> . . .
> Please get that you need
> to only explode

into yourself nothing
yes
yes
yes.

(pp. 10–12)

Emerson is autistic, but she writes poetry and not romance or crime stories. Is it a commercial thing? The love thing? The commercial love needs to be neuroconventional or needs to make the neurodivergent love acts to adapt to neurotypicality. Emerson's repetition of yesyesyes is more an expression of love to me than the verbal speech act "I love you". I want to read about a love for the world as a valid kind of love.

(H/Anna)

Reading Hoang's love story next to Emerson's poetry, it becomes obvious that Hoang's story is very much a *story*. It works with temporality, telling acts of love as actions taking place on a timeline, according to or differing from a neurotypical timeline. Love, it seems, through the novel, is developed through time. Importing Halberstam's notion of queer temporality and Milton's double empathy problem, this could be understood in terms of a clash between neurotypical temporality and neurodivergent temporality. An alternative to the neurotypical love timeline, might be the autistic repetition (yesyesyes) or the overwhelming all-at-once (cannot be finite, its dimension is that of the world). This accounts for a sort of alternative development, where love does not move forward (in a neurotypical sense of forwardness).

This text will continue to move without forwardness. It will circle round and round, dwelling, rocking back and forth. **Start and end again and again.***We are not sorry for that.*

Rereading autistic sex: And I don't want you to show me

Byers and Nichols (2019) have examined the engagement in online sexual activities among autistic adults, assessing through an online survey heir recent involvement in nonarousal (Information Seeking, Chatting), solitary-arousal (S-OSA), and partnered-arousal (P-OSA) online sexual activities, discussing their results in terms of their implications for sexuality education aimed at assisting autistic adults "to establish a healthy and meaningful sexuality". We ponder about the questions posed in the survey, whether my online sexual activities are nonarousal, solitary-arousal, or partnered-arousal, and whether my sexuality is a "healthy and meaningful sexuality" from a neurotypical point of perspective.

I don't want you to show me. However, we will start and end again and again with a story of neurotypical gazing at our "socio-sexual functioning" (Hancock et al., 2017). In this story, the main protagonist is the parent, professional, or researcher looking at me and showing me how to do it. It is about sex. How to do it.

> Having fewer opportunities for appropriate informal and formal sexual health education leaves them [autistic young people] at a double disadvantage from others [neurotypical young people] who are receiving this information from both of these avenues.
>
> *(Hancock et al., 2017, p. 1831)*

When we read research accounts about the need for "appropriate informal and formal sexual health education" (Hancock et al., 2017, p. 1831), we think about the neurotypical parental loving gaze. The most illustrative working of neurotypical parental loving gaze is research based on parental reports. Parental reports on autistic sexualities consists of parents (mainly mothers) storying their (mainly male) children's experiences of sexual attraction and interest in relationships and their own role in their children's sexual education, with the neurotypical researcher as target audience. Such parental narratives are commonly described as "fraught with tensions" (Pryde & Jahoda, 2018, p. 172). On the one hand, parents are pictured as "play[ing] a key role in supporting them [their children] with their developing sexuality". This acknowledges the want of the parents to support "their offspring's socio-sexual needs" and the want to provide "appropriate sex education" (Pryde & Jahoda, 2018, p. 166). On the other hand, parents express concerns about how "exposure to explicit materials could encourage inappropriate sexual behaviour" as well as "about who would love their sons when they grew up" (Pryde & Jahoda, 2018, p. 166). Similarly, Villamayo (2020) notes that from the professional perspective, "the active participation of the family is important" to the child's sexual development" (p. 34). At the same time, "both professionals and families find it complicated to address the topic, due to still existing taboos, the fears and the lack of information" (p. 34)

Let's start (again and again, again and again, again and again). Let's leave the neurotypical parental or professional gaze. Entering the neurodivergent gaze. In order to start and end this memory of research – to reread who is telling who – we need a countermemory. H/Anna is telling H/Anna about me.

> I prefer to tell you about me, and you to tell me about you, instead of my parents telling me about or looking at me. I wonder if my mother ever has been wondering about who would love her daughter when I grew up. I remember the biology teacher's awkwardness when she was supposed to in accordance with the Swedish sexual education learning objectives, teach us 14-year-olds, the biological aspects of heterosexual encounters. I wished that my biology teacher didn't have to. I felt so sorry for her to be in the awkwardness. I remember the feeling of going later to a professional educator at a local youth guidance center in smaller gender-segregated groups of peers to talk about contraceptives. I don't remember asking any questions. What I fantasized about didn't seem appropriate and I didn't need contraceptives.
>
> *(H/Anna)*

Back again to the neurotypical gaze. In research, Autistic girls are pictured as having more sexual and romantic experiences than autistic boys (Pecora et al., 2019; Graham Holmes et al., 2023). They (me) are less likely to have experienced "serious social or legal consequences" due to "socially inappropriate sexual behavior (e.g., masturbation in public and nonconsensual touching)" (Graham Holmes et al., 2023, p. 56). In contrast to neurotypical women, autistic women are sometimes represented as having less sexual desire, fewer sexual behaviors, and less sexual awareness (Bush, 2019; Pecora et al., 2019). Sometimes autistic women are represented as "exhibiting higher levels of sexual understanding" or as "subject to more adverse sexual experiences" than autistic men and neurotypical men and women (Pecora et al., 2016). In contrast to these depictions in research and following the countermemory from the visit to the local youth guidance center, H/Anna further reflects on their fantasies of age play at early teens. Age play may be part of sexual dominance-submission role-playing within a BDSM setting.[3] In this case, the desire results in a sense of isolation from same-aged, female-bodied peers (as pictured in the extract above) but also the sense of being welcomed and embraced when finding their way into the queer community.

At 14, I mainly fantasized about being sexually abused by a bit older boy, possibly an older relative. Some years later, I realized I was bisexual, submissive, and into BDSM. And I started to have a lot of sexual experiences with both female-bodied and male-bodied sexually dominant people. I was curious, sex became one of my many focused interests, and the queer community was supportive and nonjudgmental. I thought for a long time I was queer. Later on, I realized I am neuroqueer, or rather, I am doing neuroqueering.[4]

(H/Anna)

Sharing: To desire whatever it may be solely for oneself

Bush (2019) notes that "self-reported sexuality research among people with autism spectrum disorder (ASD) is small but growing" (p. 275). And I start thinking about what do we do when we write, "self-report" our own sexualities to each other? I report to you; you report to me. And I start to think about sexual experiences: what is autistic sexual experience? Below, I will start to tell you about my first orgasm. It was not what has been referred to in research accounts of autistic sexualities as "person-oriented sexual behaviours" (or "person-oriented sexual behaviours with obvious signs of arousal") but rather "some form of sexual behaviour" (Van Bourgondiera et al., 1997).

Drawing on the intensification of friendly writing, friendly as in friends with benefits, let's start with my first orgasm. I read/look at you. You read/look at me. Sharing the experience of senso-sexual desire whatever it may be solely for oneself.

The first time I got an orgasm through doing yoga, I was 17 and lying in a split position on the floor in my parent's living room. A song was playing: Passenger's "Let Her Go". I still can't hear that song without feeling a slight tingling feeling between my thighs. To be honest, I can't actually know that it was an orgasm since I had not had one before, nor have I had one after, I mean, not in the "regular" way. Not through sex with other people or through masturbation. Some might say I haven't really tried. I prefer to think I haven't been interested.

I have never enjoyed those few times I have had sex. Even though I've been attracted to the person (sometimes I haven't), the feeling of "nothing strange should be in my pussy" never disappears. This is a serious problem when it comes to gynecological pap test – I had to book a special appointment with an extra hour of therapy before I could stick the little metallic stick into my vagina (I had to do it myself because I burst into tears when the gynecologist tried to do it).

I think about it as hypersensitivity. The split orgasm touches my whole thighs, while the pussy touching is so closely connected to one tiny space, and that space feels penetrated as soon as it is touched.

(by me or by others)

Reading Helen Hoang's *The Kiss Quotient*, I feel so sad. There, the autistic main character, Stella, has never enjoyed sex. But when she meets the "right" guy (a male escort she hires to "teach her" sex and love), he "cures" her from her autistic sexual fussiness. Suddenly, she enjoys sex. Reading that, it feels like when people tell me, "You just haven't met the right one yet." And I want to say, "Yes, I have. I have my cat, and we have 'sex' when she lies in my lap and stims with the blanket". That is a sexual feeling. I don't mean to sexualize cute animals (or I do); I just want to say that it can be more than sex-sex.

I've learned to use my hypersensitivity. I can do stretching, quit publicly, and experience an orgasmic feeling when other people are watching and they do not know. My sexual zones are my whole body. I can super-lightly touch my skin, almost any part of the body, and feel this immense joy. When other people touch me, they are always too hard or too soft in their touch.

(H/Anna)

I like this.

Resistance-writing autistic love-sexualities through desire flows

Loiselle (2011) has complicated the concept of resistance and explored the ways girls' resistances are produced through "desire flows" (cf Deleuze & Guattari, 1987). Desire flows makes resistance a creative and productive force – that disrupts, exceed, (re)configure, and/or (re)code the concepts and words used to describe "reality" (Loiselle, 2011). In Loiselle's case, resistance is about working against the categorization of being "at risk". In this chapter, working with desire flows and resistance is about working against ideas of autistic people as dependent on care or teaching in somewhat violent ways by neurotypical partners, parents, or professionals. We need alternative approaches to articulate our experiences of love and sexuality that do not adopt perspectives influenced by neurotypical gazes.

Deleuze and Guattari (1987) write about the ruptures and the lines of flight, signaling processes of becoming – new possibilities and ways of being. We understand this as the act of resistance, the act of emotionally and affectively engaging in a work of resistance – be it ideas of girlhood or autism – create and become lines of flight and flows of desire.

> I think about Audre Lorde's writings on self-care. As an act of resistance. I think of self-care as desire, not only desiring the self but also, through the self, desiring the world. I think about reading the ambiguous depiction of femininity in Simone de Beauvoir's *The Second Sex* (1949) and writing-discussing it with a friend, getting the feeling that there is something uncanny in the feminine body, and the language about it. My friend says, "This is not feminism, not anymore". But my response to the text is writing a 20-page essay on Beauvoir's brutal but hidden lesbianism, and I *feel feel feel* so much from this resistance-writing. And I think about using things for one's own purposes, misinterpretations guiding my thinking, anger, and sadness, reshaping my actions, feeling the energy. Feeling the feelings as vibrations, as music.
>
> *(H/Anna)*

From teaching to sharing

In the first part of this section, we will reread another example of autistic fiction: *The Grasmere Cottage Mystery, Dead in the Garden* by autistic author Dahlia Donovan. The novel is the first book in the *Grasmere Cottage Mystery* trilogy described as "sweet gay romance" on the author's web page.[5] Similar to *The Kiss Quotient, The Grasmere Mystery* centers the dynamics of the intimate relationship between an explicitly named autistic (the professional musician Bishan) and a non-autistic character (the businessman Valor), and their relationship is similarly pictured as a caregiver-caretaker relationship challenged by the autistic character's challenges with sensory issues during intimate encounters. However, in contrast to *The Kiss Quotient* where the teaching of neuronormative, heterosexual pleasure is stressed as part of the relationship development (as a neurotypical curing), in *The Grasmere Mystery*, Bishan's sensory issues are described as something Valor needs to accept as part of him loving Bishan. However, Bishan's sensory issues are also framed as alternative sensory pleasures which partly is shared by the partners. In the following exchanges, we will ponder about this: about curing/teaching versus acceptance/sharing. About definitions of love. About being in neuromixed intimate relationships.

> Reading *The Grasmere Cottage Mystery*, I also feel sad. The autistic almost-main character is depicted as not "cured". A neurotypical curing is not part of the plot. The (kind) neurotypical partner accepts that Bishan doesn't want to be touched. Is that the alternative? The neurotypical partner could either "cure" or "be kind". The author, Donovan, is themselves (actually) autistic. I still feel their portrayal of autistic love is very normative. I think there is a gap between sensitivity and sexuality caused by the social norms around sex. What sex can be – and *of course* it could be said that sex could be anything, there are lots of kinks, but still, there is a certain idea about sex as something different from senses. I don't feel like that. I would have liked it if Bishan's music playing in Donovan's novel was written like a sexual experience because I think it is. I feel music like sex. Dancing like sex. I still often feel like I don't *understand* when I am "sexy" or doing "sexy stuff". I sometimes get messages on the internet from men who want to fuck me. I find that hilarious because they don't know what fuck means to me.
>
> *(H/Anna)*

> I think of the first time I was considered autistic by a partner. I was in the final stages of a longer (D/s, 24/7, non-monogamous) relationship. My Dominant partner at that time (who is a psychologist) had some time during the relationship concluded that I was not autistic but possibly an introvert, and more important, I was "teachable". A goal in our relationship, therefore, was about me being taught different things that I experienced challenging, aiming at making me a better submissive. Basically, I don't mind self-development, but in retrospect, I have realized that certain aspects of this training basically went against my own neurodivergence. Nearing the end of the old relationship, I developed another intimate relationship. In this, my new (Dominant) partner, who has a physical disability, declared that it was time for adjustments to be made to my neurodivergence. Rather than keep teaching me neurotypicality, she encouraged me to explore my neurodivergence. To unlearn what I had learned with the support of one Dominant partner and to relearn with the support of another.
>
> *(H/Anna)*

Being in love with ourselves

> Earlier this evening I couldn't figure out how to connect the new speaker system, so I'm listening to a Spice Girls CD, and relishing in the sound of the first album I ever bought, while dressing up like the kid I was when I bought it. I loved wearing Mum's kimonos and dancing in the mirror when I was a child. It's like I

knew I would be this person eventually and tonight she's so much fun. Oh my goddess, I can't think of anything better. It's the moment before the moment and I can breathe. Anything can happen from here, and I'm in love with myself.

(Ryan, 2020, pp. 33–34)

I very much recognize myself in Ryan's character. Her enjoyment of the world as precisely self-care, self-love.

(H/Anna)

Closer to the end now, we will move from teaching, to accepting, to sharing, to be in love with ourselves, to be in our enjoyment of the world. With the help of our readings of *A Room Called Earth* by Ryan (2020) and *Emily L* by Marguerite Duras (1987/2007), we will countermemory our self-love. Our self-love is sometimes to reread the moment before the moment where we can breathe, where we fuse.

I remember kissing her neck until she came. And I was so surprised that someone can get an orgasm by kisses on the neck. I went up in the fusing. Infected by her pleasure. Kissed her neck because I felt something that I usually think of not the other's actual perhaps "physical" experience but the "horniness". As if I can inhale the other's horniness through my skin, my mouth, to some extent smell.

(H/Anna)

During sex, I have never experienced fusing. In text, a hundred times. In text, I feel exhilaration – the intellectual and emotional in the text is like a sexual pleasure. (I once read Marguerite Duras's (1987/2007) book *Emily L* while riding a boat in a storm, thought it was like taking drugs – think of what Ryan's I in *A Room Called Earth* describe as she doesn't need to take drugs, she's already in the sensory fun.)

(H/Anna)

The air, the atmosphere between us that was so condensed, as we stood there. We just looked at each other. Don't remember if it was direct eye contact or if it was with flickering eyes. I could feel the intensity of the focus. When the focus is mutual, perfect, with everything you have (body, mind), you direct your focus toward the other and feel the other's focus directed toward yourself. I think we both began to tremble, breathing became heavier. But it was mostly like superficial signs. The important thing was that mutual focus. Being locked in a way, like a kind of mental bondage. Not being able/willing to get out of focus.

(H/Anna)

The idea of what sex and love *are* is internalized in our minds. This makes countermemorying a self-love act in itself. Our love-sexuality can never be "free" from the neurotypical gaze, but we can use countermemories to reread it. To get somewhere else.

> I think I get more orgasm-like feelings from texts. Kind of get off on the same text that gets off on sex (or in my case, stretch). I think about this in terms of NOT KNOWING the line between sex and non-sex. (Do neurotypicals truly know or believe in a/the difference, or is it simply constructed by some kind of neurotypical rules? Do they know they are simply constructions, constructing? Do they care that they essentialize and regulate and . . .) And that sexual or orgasmic pleasure for me is rarely related to attraction to another person.
>
> *(H/Anna)*

Last, we want to share an experience. This experience, also including several people, is Anna's translation work with Emerson's *You Are Helping This Great World Explode*. Reading the sensory part of Emerson's (2021) poetry:

> Please go to the triangle
> to find please find love there
>
> yes yes. Kiss the blue of our hearts
>
> yesyesyes. Loving the blue is loving mother
> earth yes yes. Please get that the triangle
> is the world bursting beginning life
> *(p. 10)*

> Please get that you need
> to only explode
> into yourself nothing
>
> yes
>
> yes
> yes.
> *(p. 12)*

Triggered the urge to write a Swedish version of the poems. The repetition of "yes" – which might even be similar to a quite neuroconventional orgasm feeling – became, in the reading of the whole poem, a sign of the text pushing the reader to a feeling of love for "the blue" and "mother earth" as well as an explosion, into oneself, nothing.

When reading, I feel the blue. The blue is not "feeling blue" as in "feeling sad" (though this sadness is part of the nothing-explosion too!). I feel the blue as the sea and the sky but also something more; I feel the color running through me, it fills me, I think a little of *Blue Is the Warmest Color* (2010) by Jul Maroh, which ties the blue to the queer and lesbian love. I think of mother earth, not as a stereotypical idea of nature as a female area or femininity as especially "natural" (but yes yes it is maybe part of it, I don't know), but I think of my mother and my love for my mother in all love I feel and I think of the earth, as a blue thing in my brains and my veins, and I *feel feelfeel*. The blue, the mother, the earth, is inside me, and it is exploding. *Yesyesyes*. So I wanted to try to continue the poem and I wrote a Swedish version, and when I was writing the Swedish version of Emerson's text, my own poetical desire could not be controlled and I continued to write. It became an extended translation.

I was in contact with the publicist and editor of Emerson's poetry, and they contacted Emerson, who read my translation (incomprehensible to a non-Swedish-reading person); the publisher wrote that Emerson, together with other people (including her mother), read and listened to my text, and Emerson answered my translation with a poem, *The Poetical as the First Language*. I got the email with the answer-poem in the middle of the night because of the time difference, and I was in bed, feeling feelings tingling my body, feeling like an orgasm, not in my pussy but in the back of my upper arms and the knees and the inside of my thighs. Was that a sexual feeling?

Notes

1 We wish to acknowledge the important commenting on earlier versions of this chapter by Ariel Pliskin and the editors.
2 As this chapter explores sexual activity, we acknowledge the importance of consent of all involved parties.
3 Ageplay or age play is commonly defined as "a form of roleplaying in which an individual acts or treats another as if they were a different age, sexual or non-sexually. Ageplay is roleplaying between adults, and involves consent from all parties." PARAPHILIA: Ageplay. https://arizonaforensics.com/top-ageplay/#:~:text=Ageplay%20or%20age%20play%20is,involves%20consent%20from%20all%20parties. Downloaded 11 September 2023.
4 As Walker (2021) originally conceived neuroqueer as a verb, as "neuroqueering as the practice of queering (subverting, defying, disrupting, liberating oneself from) neuronormativity and heteronormativity simultaneously" (p. 160).
5 https://dahliadonovan.com/grasmere-series/

References

Austin, J. L. (1975). *How to do things with words*. Oxford University Press.
Bertilsdotter Rosqvist, H., Hjorth, E., & Nygren A. (2022). Meeting up in broken word/times: Communication, temporality and pace in neuromixed writing. *Medical Humanities*, 49(3). doi:10.1136/medhum-2022-012384.

Bush, H. H. (2019). Dimensions of sexuality among young women, with and without autism, with predominantly sexual minority identities. *Sexuality and Disability*, 37(2), 275–292.

Byers, E. S., & Nichols, S. (2019). Prevalence and frequency of online sexual activity by adults with autism spectrum disorder. *Focus on Autism and Other Developmental Disabilities*, 34(3), 163–172.

de Beauvoir, S. (1949/2009). *The second sex* (C. Borde and S. Malovany-Chevallier, Trans.). Knopf.

Deleuze, G., & Guattari, F. (1987). *A thousand plateaus: Capitalism and schizophrenia* (B. Massumi, Trans.). University of Minnesota Press.

Donovan, D. (2018). *The Grasmere Cottage mystery, Dead in the garden*. Hot Tree Publishing.

Duras, M.(1987/2007). *Emily L*(S.Stridsberg, Trans.). Modernista.

Freeman, E. (2010). *Time binds: Queer temporalities, queer histories*. Duke University Press.

Fulda, N. (2011). Movement: A short story about autism in the future. *Asimov's Magazine*.

Hancock, G. I. P., Stokes, M. A., & Mesibov, G. B. (2017). Socio-sexual functioning in autism spectrum disorder: A systematic review and meta-analyses of existing literature. *Autism Research*, 10(11), 1823–1833.

Hoang, H. (2018). *The kiss quotient*. Corvus.

Holmes, L. G., Anderson, K., Sieber, G. S., & Shattuck, P. T.(2023). Sexual and reproductive health services for autistic young people in the United States: A conceptual model of utilization. *Perspectives on Sexual and Reproductive Health*, 55(1), 49–61.

Loiselle, E. (2011). *Resistance as desire: Reconfiguring the "at-risk girl" through critical, girl-centred participatory action research*. University of Victoria (Canada).

McDermott, C., (2022). Theorising the neurotypical gaze: Autistic love and relationships in The Bridge (Bron/Broen 2011–2018). *Medical Humanities*, 48, 51–62.

McGrath, J. (2017). *Naming adult autism: Culture, science, identity*. Rowman & Littlefield.

Milton, D. E. (2012). On the ontological status of autism: The "double empathy problem." *Disability & Society*, 27(6), 883–887.

Mullis, C. (2019). Reflection: Autistic-coded characters and fans in fandom. *Canadian Journal of Disability Studies*, 8, 147–156.

Mulvey, L. (1975). Visual pleasure and narrative cinema. *Screen*, 16(3), 6–18.

Pecora, L. A., Hancock, G. I., Mesibov, G. B., & Stokes, M. A. (2019). Characterising the sexuality and sexual experiences of autistic females. *Journal of Autism and Developmental Disorders*, 49(12), 4834–4846.

Pecora, L. A., Mesibov, G. B., & Stokes, M. A. (2016). Sexuality in high-functioning autism: A systematic review and meta-analysis. *Journal of Autism and Developmental Disorders*, 46(11), 3519–3556.

Pryde, R., & Jahoda, A. (2018). A qualitative study of mothers' experiences of supporting the sexual development of their sons with autism and an accompanying intellectual disability. *International Journal of Developmental Disabilities*, 64(3), 166–174.

Pyne, J. (2021). Autistic disruptions, trans temporalities: A narrative "trap door" in time. *South Atlantic Quarterly*, 120(2), 343–361.

Ryan, M. (2020). *A room called earth*. Penguin Books.

Shore, S. (2003). *Beyond the wall: Personal experiences with autism and Asperger syndrome* (2nd ed.). Autism Asperger Publishing.

Tello, V. (2022). Counter-memory and and-and: Aesthetics and temporalities for living together. *Memory Studies*, 15(2), 390–401.

Van Bourgondiera, M. E., Reichle, N. C., & Palmer, A. (1997). Sexual behavior in adults with autism. *Journal of Autism and Developmental Disorders*, 27(2), 113–125.

Villamayo, V. L. (2020). Sexual expression of people with ASD: Perception of education professionals (Expresión sexual de las personas con TEA: Percepción de los profesionales de la educación). *Siglo Cero*, 51(2), 33–53.

Walker, N. 2021. *Neuroqueer heresies: Notes on the neurodiversity paradigm, autistic empowerment, and postnormal possibilities*. Autonomous Press.

Yergeau, R. (2018). *Authoring autism: On rhetoric and neurological queerness*. Duke University Press.

11

BEARING WITNESS TO SEXUALITY

Therapy and Education Groups for Autistic Adults

Ariel E. Pliskin, Kim Fernald, Hanna Vaughn and E Merten[1]

Introduction

This chapter illustrates group therapy to support the sexual health of Autistic adults. Informed by research, sex positivity, peacemaking principles, the neurodiversity paradigm, and personal experience, these groups aim to overcome anti-Autistic ableism and build on participant strengths. This chapter contributes to the emerging literature on neurodiversity-affirming therapy (Chapman & Botha, 2023) and offers recommendations to professionals seeking to run similar programs.

This chapter provides a collection of informed intervention designs that could support Autistic sexuality in a neurodiversity-affirming fashion. The distinctions in the chapter between descriptions of our group, approaches we recommend, and predictions of what would be effective are more grammatical than substantive. We hope that readers will view such distinctions as different ways we phrase options for their consideration. Although our preliminary experiences were promising, we did not conclude a standard protocol or systematically evaluate the results. Rather, we adapted each course based on feedback from previous clients and engagement with the clients in the room. We hope this chapter will inspire more rigorous evaluation. Even though this chapter primarily phrases options in terms of psychotherapy groups, implications can be drawn for individual psychotherapy, other healing modalities, research, and the personal journeys of Autistic people. We hope that readers will use this chapter to inform services they offer as they adapt based on their competence, scope of practice, setting, and clients. We encourage providers to pursue additional training when necessary and discern when to collaborate or refer to other professionals.

DOI: 10.4324/9781003440154-15

Literature review

Reviewing representative examples of the literature on sex education and diagnostic criteria illustrates how anti-Autistic bias is interwoven with sex negativity. Similar to the general population, access to sexuality education for Autistic youth is lacking. When it does exist, it usually limits emphasis to reproductive anatomy and prevention of pregnancy and sexually transmitted infections (STIs) (Taverner, 2023).

Whereas adolescent sex education in the United States increasingly covers healthy relationships and consent, most research on improving consent practices involves university students. Given that sexual activity often begins during adolescence, it should be no surprise that the consent practices of young adults are lacking. Evaluating research on consent education, reviewers commented that programs that conceptualise consent violations as mere miscommunication may result in limited effectiveness because they fail to address the underlying power dynamics of gendered violence (Anderson & Whiston, 2005; Fenner, 2017). Given that Autistic people perceived as female are targeted by predators at much higher rates than Autistic males and non-Autistic women (Cazalis et al., 2022), to reduce sexual violence, education for all people should deconstruct heteronormativity, anti-Autistic bias, and other forms of prejudice.

Reviewing debates surrounding the evolution of diagnostic categories can help mental health providers and educators critically examine their attitudes and professional knowledge. Advocates of both sexual variety and neurodiversity must navigate dilemmas of definition. Categories originally used to label pathology are today redefined by community members as markers of pride. Psychiatric diagnoses in the United States are contained within the *Diagnostic and Statistical Manual* (DSM) published by the American Psychiatric Association (APA, 2022). Although inclusion in the DSM implies pathology in a way that does not align with the dignity of marginalised groups, diagnosis is often required to receive resources. Thus, at times advocates work to narrow official diagnostic criteria and, other times, to expand them.

Approximately four decades after activists succeeded in lobbying the APA to remove homosexuality from the DSM, a new generation of activists successfully convinced the APA to clarify that consensual sexual sadism and masochism are not inherently pathological. Before that, members of the BDSM community could be diagnosed with a paraphilic disorder, a category that also included nonconsensual sexual sadistic coercion and perpetration of childhood sexual abuse. The status of psychiatric disorder had negative consequences for consenting adults – for example, working against consensual BDSM practitioners in divorce custody hearings (Wright, 2018). Critics continue to contend that the way paraphilias are defined in the DSM overemphasises deviation from the culturally privileged status of penis-in-vagina sex at the expense of focusing on well-being, consent, and harm (Joyal, 2021).

While gay and sadomasochism advocates worked for the removal or narrowing of DSM criteria, Autistic advocates worked to broaden criteria (Kapp et al., 2019). Like transgender people, Autistic people have recognised that under the limitations of the medical model, formal identification is required to access accommodation, resources, and healthcare. Typifying the interwoven nature of sex negativity and ableism among researchers, Schöttle et al. (2017) linked higher rates of "paraphilia" to Autistic sensory sensitivity and "restrictive and repetitive movements". Reflecting normative bias against both neurodiversity and sexual variety, many interventions targeting Autistic sexuality have aimed to explicitly teach the "hidden curriculum" of dating, which Autistic people are presumed to miss (Gougeon, 2010), rather than empowering them to recognise scripts, critically assess them, and write their own.

Peacemaker and sex-positive tenets can help empower Autistic people to write their own scripts. The three Peacemaker Tenets are (1) not knowing, (2) bearing witness, and (3) taking action that emerges from bearing witness (Glassman, 1998). In the terminology of bearing witness, dominant systems impose rigid and prejudiced patterns of knowing. Not knowing thus involves becoming aware of and loosening social patterns of prejudice. While doing so, group members can become empowered to bear witness to the system as a whole and to their experiences within that system. Bearing witness to the system involves practices that increase sexual well-being by supporting Autistic clients to understand how they are marginalised by ableism, how their neurotype intersects with other social locations, how to empower themselves, and if they desire, how to contribute to intersectional justice. The social system involves both cultural and institutional aspects.

Cultural factors that impact Autistic people include the interwoven nature of neuronormativity and heteronormativity (Walker, 2021) as well as epistemic injustice (Chapman & Carel, 2022). Epistemic injustice is made up of hermeneutic and testimonial injustice (Fricker, 2007). The concept of hermeneutic injustice describes how our culture lacks the language for Autistic people to understand their own experiences. The concept of testimonial injustice highlights that Autistic voices have not been considered – for example, when the APA has defined autism. Lifelong experiences of these injustices contribute to Autistic people's challenges in understanding and expressing their inner worlds. The bearing witness practices in the chapter may offer an antidote to testimonial and hermeneutic injustice.

Learning about various identity labels and seeing what fits can help reduce shame and generate pride, while positive Autistic identity can help people accept themselves and convey to others information about needs and preferences. However, there are limits to the ability of any words to capture the complexities of reality. Michel Foucault, a "godparent" of queer theory (Barker & Scheele, 2016), said, "If identity is only a game, if it is only a procedure to have relations, social and sexual-pleasure relationships that create new friendships, it is useful" (Foucault, 1984, p. 166). At the same time, he warned, if people feel the need to discover and conform to some true inner essence, then identity can have a limiting impact similar to that of dominant heterosexual norms.

Media, another cultural factor, both reflects and shapes popular conceptions of people who occupy different social locations. Scholars look both at characters who are explicitly identified as Autistic and those who are "coded" Autistic (Mullis, 2019). For example, *The Big Bang Theory* portrays a stereotyped neurodivergent asexuality, as well as the expansion of stereotyped depictions over time to include young heterosexual cisgender males (Willey & Subramaniam, 2017). *Everything's Gonna Be Okay* expands representation by including early and late diagnosis, females and males, nonmonogamy, asexuality (in a nonstereotypical fashion), bisexuality and same-sex relationships, though it has limited representation of racial diversity (Mylo, 2022).

ARIEL'S STORY

Many of the adaptations to mindfulness and cognitive behavioral interventions in this chapter were inspired by a training I completed called Mental Health Therapy with the Autistic Client offered by the Autism Society of Greater Wisconsin (ASGW). My co-leaders and I added additional components inspired by other experiences including my training with Bernie Glassman in the Zen Peacemaker Order. Starting as the senior student of a Japanese Zen master, Roshi Bernie Glassman shifted over decades of teaching from emphasizing meditation to promoting diverse ways to experience the oneness and interconnectedness of life (Queen, 2012).

After Buddhism spread to non-Asian Europeans and Americans in the late 19th century, socially engaged Buddhism applied Eastern and Western religious and social thought to novel interpretations of tradition (Queen & King, 1996). Incorporating socially engaged Buddhism and social justice can address the way many mindfulness-based interventions emphasise individual factors without adequate consideration of systemic factors.

As an Autistic child, I was reprimanded for struggling to sit still in class or perform well in sports. A social worker provided me with cognitive behavioral therapy (CBT) that helped me challenge the internalised belief that I was inferior to others. Although the cognitive restructuring techniques of CBT were helpful, something was missing. Writing in my journal, I would get into arguments with myself and become frustrated with my inability to argue away stressful thoughts that I knew were irrational. I realised that countering rigid reason with more rigid reason was not enough.

After an unsuccessful first attempt into professional life in my early 20s, I vagabonded around South America, where I experimented with different ways of living, including various spiritual communities. Eager to deepen my contemplative practice, I entered training in Massachusetts to become a Zen Peacemaker minister (Pliskin, 2020). As I dived into Buddhism and yoga in supportive, inclusive communities, I learned to slow down and more fully feel my emotions. These practices allowed me to unpack stressful thoughts while compassionately bearing witness to the underlying feelings. Unlike my experience with CBT, I did not have to attempt to let go of the thoughts; the thoughts let go of me.

The Peacemaker training introduced me to communication techniques such as Nonviolent Communication (NVC; Rosenberg, 2015) and the Way of Council (Zimmerman & Coyle, 1996). Going through NVC lists of emotions helps me identify my feelings and reduce the risk of distancing myself from vulnerability through intellectual analysis. The Buddhist emphasis on not-knowing laid a foundation for shifts in my identity and relationships. Participating in BDSM,[2] dance, and tantra communities helped loosen the pressure I felt to act like a straight, neurotypical man.

These communities introduced me to ways of accessing greater embodiment while exploring more varied gender and sexuality expressions. We practiced sharing our safer sex practices, expressing desires, making requests, saying yes, and saying no. BDSM communities often adhere to standards summarised by mnemonics such as the four Cs of caring, consent, caution, and communication (Williams et al., 2014). By combining structured sexual health conversations with codes of conduct and community conversations about norms, we created environments that promoted growth and development. As I found joy and empowerment, my personal journey influenced my professional aspirations.

Our groups

Our programs were offered in the form of two groups courses, one primarily focused on bearing witness to the self and physical environment, and the other focused on bearing witness to other people and society. Each course ran for seven to ten weekly sessions of 1.5 hours. The final session of each course involved a participant evaluation that we used to modify subsequent rounds. We have offered both multiple times, and many participants returned. The default session format was as follows:

1) Guided Practice
2) Group Norms Review and Accommodation Check-in
3) Check-in circle: report progress on previous intention
4) Lesson
5) Activity or Discussion
6) Council circle: reflections about the session and setting a weekly intention

Facilitating these groups has been profoundly fulfilling. Members of our groups have reported feeling connected around topics regarding which they have always felt alone, feeling more comfortable being themselves without fear of being rejected, and letting go of the belief that they need to fix themselves. Participants reported relief from tension and stress, greater embodiment, and enhanced connection to their emotions.

Sex-positive principles

The following sections illustrate how groups offered by the authors have supported Autistic and other neurodivergent adults in developing sexual health including avoidance of risk, authentic expression, communication, consent, pleasure, and fulfillment. This chapter applies the following principles of sex positivity according to the Eight Dimension Model of the Center for Positive Sexuality (Pliskin, 2020; Williams et al., 2014). We hope readers will consider how these principles may apply to them.

1. *Peacemaking*: This chapter defines bearing witness to include both collective and individual peacemaking practices. Bearing witness includes mindfulness, though the term "bearing witness" highlights a systemic approach.
2. *Multiple ways of knowing*: Honoring different ways of knowing includes listening to neurodivergent voices, appreciating variety within Autistic voices, and incorporating various approaches to knowledge construction. For example, the experience of autism is understood as influenced by both biology and culture.
3. *Open, honest communication*: The preference of many Autistic people for direct, explicit language aligns well with the sex-positive principle of direct communication about sexual activity. The group introduces methods to support communication: The Way of Council involves a ritual start and end, a talking piece, and intentions to listen from the heart, speak from the heart, be lean of speech, and be spontaneous (Zimmerman & Coyle, 1996); Nonviolent Communication (NVC) specifies observations (distinguished from interpretations), emotions, needs (distinguished from strategies), and requests (distinguished from demands) (Rosenberg, 2015).
4. *Ethics*: The activities in this chapter aim to replace arbitrary norms that privilege dominant groups with norms of care, inclusion, authenticity, self-determination, and social justice. Emphasis is placed on the professional ethics of group leaders. Working with Autistic clients requires professionals to develop what we call neurocultural competence and humility. Neurocultural competence involves an understanding of Autistic neurology and awareness of the value of neurodiversity-affirming subcultures. Neurocultural humility involves self-examination to reduce the risk that the professional's inculturation with dominant norms of neurocognitive functioning will harm clients.
5. *Strengths, well-being, and happiness*: The standard medical model often views disability as impairment and emphasises personal coping skills to improve self-regulation and modify behavior. By contrast, the social model of disability may describe functional challenges as resulting from a lack of person-environment fit. As participants focus on strengths and reduce pressure to hide Autistic traits, they gain confidence in unmasking. Group leaders should keep in mind the benefits of unmasking and that masking is

an instinctual survival strategy, that unmasking takes time, and that unmasking is a privilege experienced within a supportive context (Hartman et al., 2023).

6. *The recognition that individual sexuality is unique and multifaceted*: Our groups reflect the belief that sexual health is closely related to both overall mental health and general well-being. We keep in mind the way that neurotype intersects with various sexual, gender, and other identities.

7. *Humanization*: Ableist approaches dehumanise Autistic people by neglecting to listen to their voices. By contrast, Autistic people are humanised when their goals are centered and their ways of being are understood and accommodated. Humanization involves customizing offerings. Before entering a group, leaders could collaboratively explore a given participant's fit. Concurrent individual therapy or other supports may help navigate challenges and integrate group lessons. All instructions should be offered as invitations and all activities should be optional.

8. *Application across all levels of social structure*: The following sections illustrate how group leaders could support the sexual health of Autistic people through bearing witness at various levels. The concentric circles in Figure 11.1 illustrate the areas covered in our groups as well as the structure of this chapter, starting with the highest level of social complexity and zooming in one level at a time to the individual self.

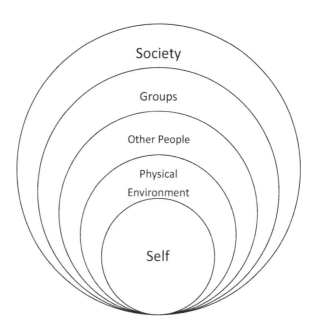

FIGURE 11.1 Levels of complexity from society to self. Bearing witness at each level supports participants in addressing their sexual health needs.

While this program frames dysregulation as systemic instead of merely individual, varying tools empower participants to choose personal, interactive, or collective strategies to meet their needs. Tatkin's (2018) four levels of nervous system regulation strategies align with the levels illustrated in Figure 11.1. Auto- and Self-Regulation take place at the Self Level, while External and Interactive Regulation take place at the Other People and Groups Levels:

a   Auto-Regulation ("It just happens")
b   Self-Regulation ("I do it")
c   External Regulation ("You do it")
d   Interactive Regulation ("We do it")

Bearing witness to various levels of complexity

Bear witness to society

Systems of power impact individual experiences, including sex. Marginalised groups often internalise disparaging messages and blame themselves for their struggles without adequately understanding the role of broader systems. To counteract that, we as group leaders introduced a shared terminology for social analysis and guided participants to explore the impact of social factors on their experience.

An intersectional analysis of power which includes neurotype follows the queer and feminist therapy tradition of exploring the impacts of marginalised and privileged social locations on the problems that lead clients to seek treatment (Constantinides et al., 2019; Tilsen, 2021; Worell & Remer, 2003). Given that an intersectional analysis would suggest that people with multiple marginalised identities may experience the harm of compounding oppressive forces (Crenshaw, 1989), group leaders should be sensitive to additional challenges faced by Autistic people of color, Autistic LGBTQ+ people, and Autistic women.

The Wheel of Power and Privilege has been used in therapy for at least two decades (Worell & Remer, 2003) and has been recently updated (e.g., Duckworth, 2020). This diagram not only illustrates the various identities that can exacerbate or mitigate the marginalization of neurodivergence but also invites exploration of how these identities interact with each other. For example, a white Autistic man may have his straightness or manhood questioned because of his neurodivergent ways of acting even though he is cisgender and heterosexual. Nonetheless, in many contexts, his white, cisgender, and heterosexual status may buffer him from discrimination experienced by Autistic people without those privileged identities. This is especially the case if he conforms to socially accepted images of maleness that are somewhat divergent without being too divergent, such as the successful geek chic tech professional (Willey & Subramaniam, 2017; Willey et al., 2015). People with privileged identities can also be harmed by limiting norms.

Activities

- **Identify social influences:** The Liberation Health Triangle (Martinez & Fleck-Henderson, 2014) invites clients to write a problem they would like to address at the center of a worksheet and then write personal, cultural, and institutional factors that influence their problem in boxes on each corner of a surrounding triangle.
- **Identify social location:** Locating themselves on a Wheel of Power and Privilege can help participants reflect on their marginalised and privileged identities. Appreciating the benefits and limitations of identity helps group leaders support participants in exploring established and emerging identities.
- **Analyze media:** Critically viewing media depictions of neurodivergence can help participants increase awareness about and critically evaluate dominant messages.
- **Social action:** Working for systemic change can be empowering. Participants may write an opinion piece for a media outlet, contact a government representative, or compile and distribute a work demonstrating what they have learned in the group (Duba et al., 2010).

Bear witness to groups

Bearing witness to groups addresses any group setting clients encounter, including the therapy group itself. Cultural norms and specific social interactions come together in various group settings. Groups can reinforce prejudiced patterns of knowing or support Autistic people to authentically bear witness to themselves and each other. Sex education classes or therapy groups may provide explicit messages about what is considered healthy and normal for sexuality, gender, and neurocognitive functioning. However, standards are also communicated in all types of social venues, including home, school, work, healthcare, and recreational settings. Reviewing past experiences can help group members understand what has shaped their degree of self-acceptance. A group leader may ask participants to reflect, Were past settings inclusive of sexual variety and neurodivergence? Were they supportive of Autistic flourishing? Were standards of consent and care emphasised more than conforming to heterosexuality? How about current settings?

To facilitate engagement, it may help group leaders to address the past negative experiences of group participants. For example, in the DEAR MAN Skill taught in dialectic and behavior therapy (DBT) groups, the A stands for "Appear confident, effective, and competent" and is described as follows: "Make good eye contact. No stammering, whispering, staring at the floor, retreating" (Linehan, 2015). This is a representative example of how neurodivergent people are pressured to mask. A neurodiversity-affirming group can offer space to process past experiences of pressure to mask.

Many groups involve a collaborative process in the formative stage in which participants contribute to a list of shared norms. Group leaders may contribute options such as "take space; make space", "everything is optional", and "accommodate diversity". Norms may include explicit reference to accommodating neurodivergent needs and discussion around how to respond if one person's needs conflict with someone else's. It is not enough to merely review the agreement to advocate at the start of the session; additional support may be necessary for participants to feel comfortable sharing differences and for that sharing to feel constructive.

Within the therapy group experience, participants can experience replacing oppressive assumed social norms with cocreated, consensual, explicit, and inclusive ones. Leaders play a distinct role in shaping participants' experience of the group. As group leaders, we draw connections between our explanation of standard therapist ethics (e.g., confidentiality, informed consent) and group content. We discuss why we disclose certain personal details or thoughts and not others. Given that the power imbalance between the group leaders and participants cannot be avoided, transparent discussion of that imbalance can help avoid harm. For therapists to share aspects of their own social location and community involvement has several benefits, including helping leaders and clients navigate shared community spaces without engaging in dual relationships (Constantinides et al., 2019; Worell & Remer, 2003). The literature on therapist cultural humility emphasises maintaining a stance of not-knowing and curiosity and stresses that openly acknowledging identity can be helpful in avoiding harm when the therapist has privileged identities that clients do not (Hepworth et al., 2023).

Lack of a supportive environment, lack of safety, being targeted by others, and stress can prohibit interest in sex or reduce sexual fulfillment. By contrast, many Autistic people find safety, connection, and belonging in communities organised around shared interests, including those centered on various fandoms (Fein, 2015; Price, 2022) or those centered on alternative sexuality (Pliskin, 2022). Autistic interests (further explored in the "Bear witness to self" section) that have the opportunity to thrive in the community may become serious leisure (Bertilsdotter Rosqvist, 2018). An example of an alternative sexuality community that meets the criteria for serious leisure is BDSM. Many BDSM practitioners meet the criteria for what researchers call serious leisure (Newmahr, 2010; Sprott & Williams, 2019), including sustained focus over several years, deepening skills, a community of practice, and durable benefits (Stebbins, 2010). BDSM is particularly associated with providing a clear structure of explicitly negotiated consent and increased relational fulfillment (Pliskin, 2018).

Activities

- **Map out influential groups and communities:** Creating an ecomap can help clients reflect on the past and current social settings (Hartman, 1995). Participants may be supported to evaluate the extent to which social settings reinforce neuronormative standards or support care, inclusion, and neurodivergent liberation. Participants who experience gaps in supportive community connection can be aided to pursue such connection.

- **Create supportive groups:** The therapy group may provide a corrective and supportive group experience. Skills developed in the group could be used in other settings.
- **Accommodation check-in:** We ask which elements of their personal choices, our group experience, and society at large have supported or challenged their well-being. We ask if there were instances in which they took individual steps to accommodate themselves and whether there are any needs the facilitators or the group could accommodate better.
- **Broaching:** Therapists transparently discuss the power dynamic between therapist and client and may share their locations within systems of power and privilege as well as parts of their ecomaps.

Bear witness to other people

Sex can be an activity in which not-knowing, bearing witness, and action unite between people in powerful ways. Autistic people report that explicit communication can help accommodate sensory needs and craft customised sexual activities beyond the normative emphasis on penis-and-vagina sex (Barnett & Maticka-Tyndale, 2015; Gray et al., 2021). To help individuals create a safe and supportive environment for partners to bear witness to each other during sexual activity, the group focuses on challenging cultural assumptions, practicing clear communication, articulating boundaries, and setting up the environment to meet sensory needs.

Talking about sexual desires and boundaries at a time when partners are not engaging in sexual activities can help people understand each other, clarify intentions, and enhance pleasure. This type of sexual negotiation allows partners to bear witness to each other. Each partner may also take personal time to prepare for a conversation by reviewing checklists of activities they would like to include. In tandem with the emotional exploration skills described in the "Bear witness to self" section, the NVC format for making requests (Rosenberg, 2015) can help participants ask for what they want.

Activities

- **Co-regulation:** In planning for sexual or kink play, people can plan to start with activities that regulate their nervous systems both individually and interactively.
- **Checklists:** Filling out checklists indicating interest in sexual and BDSM activities (Fulkerson, 2010; see chapter in this volume) and relationship types can help clarify how one wants to engage with others and result in feeling more empowered to share with potential or current sexual partners.

- **Making and responding to requests:** We teach the NVC structure for making requests (Rosenberg, 2015) as well as introduce additional tools specific to sexual negotiation such as the Three-Minute Game (Martin & Dalzen, 2021).

Bear witness to the physical environment

Autistic sensory sensitivity may contribute to pleasurable and transcendent sexual experiences or to distraction, discomfort, and pain. Given that mindfulness has been shown to aid sexual fulfillment (Barker, 2017; Brotto, 2022; Mize, 2015) and adapted mindfulness practice may be helpful for Autistic people (Cachia et al., 2016; Juliano et al., 2020; Kiep et al., 2015; Singh et al., 2011), supporting participants to develop mindfulness can likely enhance sexual satisfaction. Mindfulness is defined as paying attention to the present moment with a nonjudgmental, accepting, open, kind, and curious attitude (Shapiro et al., 2006). Sexuality educators and therapists who work with adults often teach clients how to incorporate mindfulness into physical intimacy through practices like Sensate Focus (Weiner & Avery-Clark, 2017), Sensate Touch (Fielding, 2021), and the Three-Minute Game (Martin & Dalzen, 2021). Given that being coerced to conform to neurotypical standards can be traumatic, Treleaven's (2018) adaptations of mindfulness for trauma survivors are relevant to working with Autistic clients.

Bearing witness to one's surroundings involves tuning into the five senses in a regulated fashion. There are many factors to keep in mind when introducing contemplative awareness practices. There is a risk of propping up the false narrative that marginalised people learning mindfulness are broken and need expert instructors to demonstrate the correct way of doing things. Further, introducing mindfulness techniques may constitute cultural appropriation when instructors neglect to acknowledge the cultures from which the practices emerge. Native American voices describe neurodecolonization as efforts to incorporate traditional and contemporary cultural practices into mindfulness instruction when working with marginalised groups (Yellow Bird, 2013). By a similar token, we work to recover, cultivate, and incorporate the innate wisdom of neurodivergent sensorimotor processing.

Autistic people stim to navigate three types of experience that may be overwhelming: sensory, cognitive, or affective (Kapp et al., 2019). These three factors correspond with common objects of mindfulness practice: senses, thoughts, and emotions. In addition to alleviating unpleasant experiences, Autistic people may stim proactively to pursue fulfillment, and stimming may result in deeply meaningful or transcendent experiences (Walker, 2021). Viewing the tenets of not-knowing, bearing witness, and taking action as co-emergent is especially beneficial for Autistic people who process information actively. A co-emergence conceptualization transcends dichotomies of being versus doing, perception versus response, and witnessing versus testifying.

There are many ways to practice mindfulness. Active stimming may be a more effective mindfulness practice for Autistic people than passive seated meditation. In a typical introduction to mindfulness, participants may be guided to settle into a "comfortable seated position", close their eyes, and listen. Autistic people may be slower to habituate toward unpleasant sensory stimuli or they may not habituate at all (Ward, 2019). Thus, many Autistic people will not easily find a comfortable seat. Silent seated meditation may work for some Autistic people at some times, but it may also remind them of being coerced or it may contribute to sensory overwhelm. White-knuckling one's way through sensory pain is not conducive to an open and accepting attitude.

Activities

- **Explore implications of sensory profile for physical intimacy:** Using a sensory evaluation from an occupational therapist or a tool such as the one in the *Neurodivergent Friendly Workbook of DBT Skills* (Wise, 2022), Autistic people can become empowered by identifying which senses they experience as hypo- or hypersensitive, the impact of those sensitivities on sex, and accommodations to better meet their sensory needs.
- **Free the stim:** Solo or partnered sex can be viewed as a potentially pleasurable experience of stimming. While intentionally practicing breath control or muscle relaxation are examples of self-regulation strategies, any of what Tatkin (2018) called "auto-regulation" strategies can also become a conscious self-regulation strategy. With that in mind, we support participants to reflect on whether they want to cultivate or modify existing stims and whether they may want to try new ones.
- **Guided attention:** Offer guided attention is practice designed to free participants from fears of performing incorrectly. Instead of asking them to sit still, we invite them to rock and swivel in their chairs with curiosity about how doing so feels in their bodies. We invite participants to pick up a fidget toy from the table and explore if they feel attraction or aversion to any tactile sensations on their fingers. Avoiding the tendency of some mindfulness training to default to encouraging participants to build tolerance for discomfort, we invite each participant to attempt one adjustment that would increase their comfort and ease.

Bear witness to yourself

Sex involves a mix of bearing witness to external and internal sensations. Previous sections addressed attending to sensory stimuli in the environment as well as the body, thoughts, and feelings of another person. This section addresses bearing witness to oneself. Navigating Autistic sensorimotor engagement can involve cultivating centeredness, presence, stability, and serenity (Walker, 2018). However, given unaccommodating sensory environments, trauma, and exposure to compliance-based behavioral interventions, Autistic people may struggle with interoception, or perception of internal body sensations. Difficulties understanding body signals can contribute to difficulties in identifying or naming emotions. Practices such as those within Mahler's (2019) Interoceptive Curriculum can help. Building interoception should aim to benefit the Autistic person rather than to meet neurotypical standards.

Mahler's Interoceptive Curriculum involves several components. Leaders may want to consider training or referral to complete a full program which may involve eight weekly sessions of 30 minutes (Hample et al., 2020). It is also possible that some interoceptive techniques could be incorporated into a group on sexuality. To build vocabulary, group leaders may ask participants to come up with as many descriptor words as possible to describe the internal experience of various specified body parts. Group leaders can add words that participants do not list such as "tight", "loose", "warm", "cold", "fidgety", and "still". To gain insight into how sensing the outside world can have an internal impact, a group leader may alter environmental factors (such as playing fast or slow music) as they invite participants to use words from the list to describe what they feel inside (Mahler, 2019).

Interventions from a variety of therapy modalities may treat Autistic thinking with prejudice and cause epistemic injury. For example, cognitive restructuring in CBT could compound how Autistic people are not afforded the right to accurately interpret their own experiences. A poorly informed therapist encouraging changing thoughts can invalidate Autistic clients. Whereas second-wave CBT focuses on modifying thoughts, third-wave CBT approaches that emphasise compassionately, accepting all thoughts can be more affirming for marginalised groups. It is also important to keep in mind that the experience of emotions for Autistic people may include phenomena such as synesthesia. For example, depending on emotional state, an Autistic person may see colors associated with sounds.

While applying cognitive restructuring to limiting beliefs can be helpful, developing flexible alternatives to binary thinking (Constantinides et al., 2019; Pliskin, 2020) avoids pitfalls. Resonant with narrative therapy (Laube, 1998; Cashin, 2008; Duba et al., 2010; Lopes et al., 2014; Monteiro, 2021), we work to help participants externalise harmful dominant discourses and facilitate the development of more authentic stories.

Monotropism refers to the tendency, common among Autistic people, to focus attentional resources on one thing to the exclusion of others (Murray, 2018). Monotropism may impact sex. Although more Autistic people identify as asexual than non-autistic people (Attanasio et al., 2022), most Autistic people are interested in sex and romance. Autistic people may have sex-related interests or may be so occupied with other things that they pay little attention to sex (Bertilsdotter Rosqvist & Jackson-Perry, 2021; Pliskin, 2022). The group supports clients in celebrating their interests and in understanding the impact of their attention on sex. Clients are empowered to channel monotropism toward fulfilling hyperfocus on fascinating topics or activities (Nowell et al., 2021) and away from getting stuck in anxious or depressive rumination or compulsion (Golan et al., 2022).

Building on foundational interoceptive work, we introduce the Window of Tolerance (Ogden et al., 2006; Treleaven, 2018) and facilitate an exploration of internal signs that let you know when you are within the window or when you are in a state of hyperarousal or hypoarousal. We introduce resources including a numeric scale to practice visually gauging where you are within the three zones. We support participants to reflect on stimuli that may push them out of the Window of Tolerance and techniques they could use to return (Treleaven, 2018).

Activities

- **Interoception:** Building vocabulary for sensations as well as building the ability to evoke, notice, describe, and interpret internal sensations can empower participants to recognise, care for, and advocate for their needs.
- **Explore emotions:** Clients may select from options on a list of emotion descriptor terms.
- **Expressive arts:** Emotions can be explored through creative expression.
- **Reconsidering limiting beliefs:** Internalised ableism can take the form of self-critical beliefs. Challenging such thoughts can increase self-acceptance and facilitate clarification of personal goals.
- **Monotropic attention:** Reflecting on the nature and patterns of attention can help create circumstances that direct attention toward fulfillment.
- **Nervous system:** Learning to recognise the signs of nervous system arousal can empower participants to care for and advocate for themselves. By learning which stimuli result in dysregulation, Autistic people can generate strategies for navigating challenging situations.

Conclusion

Adjacent to the pathology paradigm, overemphasis on the individual and neglect of the sociocultural perspective limited the justice and effectiveness of historic approaches to autism and sexuality. In contrast to the conceptualizations of biologically oriented physicians and the interventions of behavioral psychologists, the authors of this chapter draw from the person-in-environment and social justice perspectives of social work (Rogers, 2016). Researchers, parents, and health providers viewed sexual and neurodiversity as problematic deviations without awareness of their own cultural bias. By integrating individual and sociocultural perspectives and keeping in mind parallels between heteronormativity and neuronormativity, we hope to offer an approach that better supports Autistic thriving. Unpacking our own internalised ableism and improving our offerings is an ongoing process. We hope to sustain a conversation with our clients, with community leaders, with other service providers, and with researchers as we work for a more inclusive world. While our groups have been shaped by an autism-centered definition of neurodiversity, allistic clients have found them valuable. Listening to Autistic voices can offer innovative opportunities for all people.

Notes

1 Ariel wrote the first draft of this chapter and received guidance from their aunt Judit N. Moschkovich. Hanna Vaughn and E Merten helped with editing. The material in this chapter draws from two groups at Advance Psychotherapy Practice in western Massachusetts: a neurodivergent mindfulness group developed and led by Kim Fernald and Ariel Pliskin and a neurodivergent sexuality group developed and led by E Merten and Ariel Pliskin. The material additionally draws from a community presentation on BDSM and Autism developed and offered by Ariel Pliskin and Hanna Vaughn.
2 Bondage and discipline, dominance and submission, and sadomasochism

References

American Psychiatric Association. (2022). *Diagnostic and statistical manual of mental disorders* (5th ed., text rev.). American Psychiatric Association.

Anderson, L. A., & Whiston, S. C. (2005). Sexual assault education programs: A meta-analytic examination of their effectiveness. *Psychology of Women Quarterly*, 29(4), 374–388. https://doi.org/10.1111/j.1471–6402.2005.00237.x.

Attanasio, M., Masedu, F., Quattrini, F., Pino, M. C., Vagnetti, R., Valenti, M., & Mazza, M. (2022). Are autism spectrum disorder and asexuality connected? *Archives of Sexual Behavior*, 1–25.

Barker, M. (2017). Mindfulness in sex therapy. In Z. D. Peterson (Ed.), *The Wiley Handbook of Sex Therapy* (pp. 435–452). Wiley. https://doi.org/10.1002/9781118510384.ch27.

Barker, M.-J., & Scheele, J. (2016). *Queer: A graphic history*. Icon Books.

Barnett, J. P., & Maticka-Tyndale, E. (2015). Qualitative exploration of sexual experiences among adults on the autism spectrum: Implications for sex education. *Perspectives on Sexual and Reproductive Health*, 47(4), 171–179. https://doi.org/10.1363/47e5715.

Bertilsdotter Rosqvist, H. (2018). Exploring meanings of leisure among people with autism: "To have some fun on your own." *Research and Practice in Intellectual and Developmental Disabilities*, 5(1), 39–46. https://doi.org/10.1080/23297018.2017.1324737.

Bertilsdotter Rosqvist, H., & Jackson-Perry, D. (2021). Not doing it properly? (Re)producing and resisting knowledge through narratives of autistic sexualities. *Sexuality and Disability*, 39(2), 327–344. https://doi.org/10.1007/s11195–11020–09624–09625.

Bridges, J., & Glassman, B. (2014). *The dude and the Zen master*. Plume.

Brotto, L. A. (2022). *The better sex through mindfulness workbook: A guide to cultivating desire*. Greystone Books.

Cachia, R. L., Anderson, A., & Moore, D. W. (2016). Mindfulness in individuals with autism spectrum disorder: A systematic review and narrative analysis. *Review Journal of Autism and Developmental Disorders*, 3, 165–178.

Cashin, A. (2008). Narrative therapy: A psychotherapeutic approach in the treatment of adolescents with Asperger's disorder. *Journal of Child and Adolescent Psychiatric Nursing*, 21(1), 48–56. https://doi.org/10.1111/j.1744–6171.2008.00128.x.

Cazalis, F., Reyes, E., Leduc, S., & Gourion, D. (2022). Evidence that nine autistic women out of ten have been victims of sexual violence. *Frontiers in Behavioral Neuroscience*, 16, 852203. https://doi.org/10.3389/fnbeh.2022.852203.

Chapman, R., & Botha, M. (2023). Neurodivergence-informed therapy. *Developmental Medicine & Child Neurology*, 65(3), 310–317. https://doi.org/10.1111/dmcn.15384.

Chapman, R., & Carel, H. (2022). Neurodiversity, epistemic injustice, and the good human life. *Journal of Social Philosophy*, 53(4), 614–631. https://doi.org/10.1111/josp.12456.

Constantinides, D. M., Sennott, S. L., & Chandler, D. (2019). *Sex therapy with erotically marginalized clients: Nine principles of clinical support*. Routledge. https://doi.org/10.4324/9781315616780.

Crenshaw, K. (1989). Demarginalizing the intersection of race and sex: A Black feminist critique of antidiscrimination doctrine, feminist theory and antiracist politics. *University of Chicago Legal Forum*, 1989(1), article 8, 139–176.

Duba, J. D., Kindsvatter, A., & Priddy, C. J. (2010). Deconstructing the mirror's reflection: Narrative therapy groups for women dissatisfied with their body. *Adultspan Journal*, 9(2), article 4.

Duckworth, S. (2020). *Wheel of power/privilege* [Infographic]. https://www.flickr.com/photos/sylviaduckworth/50500299716/.

Fein, E. (2015). Making meaningful worlds: Role-playing subcultures and the autism spectrum. *Culture, Medicine, and Psychiatry*, 39(2), 299–321. https://doi.org/10.1007/s11013–11015–9443-x.

Fenner, L. (2017). Sexual consent as a scientific subject: A literature review. *American Journal of Sexuality Education*, 12(4), 451–471. https://doi.org/10.1080/15546128.2017.1393646.

Fielding, L. (2021). *Trans sex: Clinical approaches to trans sexualities and erotic embodiments*. Routledge.

Foucault, M. (1984). Michel Foucault, une interview: Sexe, pouvoir et la politique de l'identité. *The Advocate*, 7, 26–30.

Fricker, M. (2007). *Epistemic injustice: Power and the ethics of knowing*. Oxford University Press.

Fulkerson, A. (2010). *Bound by consent: Concepts of consent within the leather and bondage, domination, sadomasochism (BDSM) communities*. Wichita State University.

Glassman, B. (1998). *Bearing witness: A Zen master's lessons in making peace*. Bell Tower.

Golan, O., Haruvi-Lamdan, N., Laor, N., & Horesh, D. (2022). The comorbidity between autism spectrum disorder and post-traumatic stress disorder is mediated by brooding rumination. *Autism*, 26(2), 538–544. https://doi.org/10.1177/13623613211035240.

Gougeon, N. A. (2010). Sexuality and autism: A critical review of selected literature using a social-relational model of disability. *American Journal of Sexuality Education*, 5(4), 328–361. https://doi.org/10.1080/15546128.2010.527237.

Gray, S., Kirby, A. V., & Graham Holmes, L. (2021). Autistic narratives of sensory features, sexuality, and relationships. *Autism in Adulthood*, 3(3), 238–246. https://doi.org/10.1089/aut.2020.0049.

Hample, K., Mahler, K., & Amspacher, A. (2020). An interoception-based intervention for children with autism spectrum disorder: A pilot study. *Journal of Occupational Therapy, Schools, & Early Intervention*, 13(4), 339–352. https://doi.org/10.1080/19411243.2020.1743221.

Hartman, A. (1995). *Diagrammatic assessment of family relationships. Families in Society*, 76(2), 111–122.

Hartman, D., O'Donnell-Killen, T., Doyle, J. K., Kavanagh, M., Day, A., & Azevedo, J. (2023). *The adult autism assessment handbook: A neurodiversity affirmative approach*. Jessica Kingsley.

Hepworth, D. H., Vang, P. D., Blakey, J. M., Schwalbe, C., Evans, C. B. R., Rooney, R. H., Rooney, G. D., & Strom-Gottfried, K. (2023). *Direct social work practice: Theory and skills* (11th ed.). Cengage Learning.

Joyal, C. C. (2021). Problems and controversies with psychiatric diagnoses of paraphilia. In L. A. Craig (Ed.), *Sexual deviance* (pp. 91–116). Wiley. https://doi.org/10.1002/9781119771401.ch6.

Juliano, A. C., Alexander, A. O., DeLuca, J., & Genova, H. (2020). Feasibility of a school-based mindfulness program for improving inhibitory skills in children with autism spectrum disorder. *Research in Developmental Disabilities*, 101, 103641.

Kapp, S. K., Steward, R., Crane, L., Elliott, D., Elphick, C., Pellicano, E., & Russell, G. (2019). "People should be allowed to do what they like": Autistic adults' views and experiences of stimming. *Autism*, 23(7), 1782–1792. https://doi.org/10.1177/1362361319829628.

Kiep, M., Spek, A. A., & Hoeben, L. (2015). Mindfulness-based therapy in adults with an autism spectrum disorder: Do treatment effects last? *Mindfulness*, 6, 637–644.

Laube, J. J. (1998). Therapist role in narrative group psychotherapy. *Group*, 22(4), 227–244.

Linehan, M. (2015). *DBT skills training: Handouts and worksheets*. Guilford Press.

Lopes, R. T., Gonçalves, M. M., Machado, P. P. P., Sinai, D., Bento, T., & Salgado, J. (2014). Narrative therapy vs. cognitive-behavioral therapy for moderate depression: Empirical evidence from a controlled clinical trial. *Psychotherapy Research*, 24(6), 662–674. https://doi.org/10.1080/10503307.2013.874052.

Mahler, K. J. (2019). *The interoception curriculum: A step-by-step framework for developing mindful self-regulation*. Mahler Autism Services.

Martin, B., & Dalzen, R. (2021). *The art of receiving and giving: The wheel of consent*. Luminare Press.

Martinez, D. B., & Fleck-Henderson, A. (Eds.). (2014). *Social justice in clinical practice: A liberation health framework for social work*. Routledge.

Mize, S. J. S. (2015). A review of mindfulness-based sex therapy interventions for sexual desire and arousal difficulties: From research to practice. *Current Sexual Health Reports*, 7(2), 89–97. https://doi.org/10.1007/s11930–11015–0048–0048.

Monteiro, M. J. (2021). Narrative therapy and the autism spectrum: A model for clinicians. *Human Systems: Therapy, Culture and Attachments*, 1(2–3), 150–164. https://doi.org/10.1177/26344041211049763.

Mullis, C. (2019). Reflection: Autistic-coded characters and fans in fandom. *Canadian Journal of Disability Studies*, 8(2), 147–156. https://doi.org/10.15353/cjds.v8i2.495.

Murray, D. (2018). Monotropism – An interest based account of autism. In F. R. Volkmar (Ed.), *Encyclopedia of autism spectrum disorders* (pp. 1–3). Springer. https://doi.org/10.1007/978-1-4614-6435-8_102269-1.

Mylo, J. (2022). Everything's gonna be kinda queer: Autistic gender & sexuality in *Everything's gonna be okay*. *Ought: The Journal of Autistic Culture*, 4(1). https://doi.org/10.9707/2833–1508.1109.

Newmahr, S. (2010). Rethinking kink: Sadomasochism as serious leisure. *Qualitative Sociology*, 33(3), 313–331. https://doi.org/10.1007/s11133–11010–9158–9159.

Nowell, K. P., Bernardin, C. J., Brown, C., & Kanne, S. (2021). Characterization of special interests in autism spectrum disorder: A brief review and pilot study using the special interests survey. *Journal of Autism and Developmental Disorders*, 51(8), 2711–2724. https://doi.org/10.1007/s10803–10020–04743–04746.

Ogden, P., Minton, K., & Pain, C. (2006). *Trauma and the Body: A Sensorimotor Approach to Psychotherapy*. Norton.

Pliskin, A. E. (2022). Autism, sexuality, and BDSM. *Ought: The Journal of Autistic Culture*, 4(1). https://doi.org/10.9707/2833–1508.1107.

Pliskin, E. (2018). Social and emotional intelligence (SEI) in BDSM. *Journal of Positive Sexuality*, 4(2), 48–55. https://doi.org/10.51681/1.422.

Pliskin, E. (2020). Contributions to positive sexuality from the Zen Peacemakers. *Journal of Positive Sexuality*, 6(1), 24–32. https://doi.org/10.51681/1.612.

Price, D. (2022). *Unmasking autism: Discovering the new faces of neurodiversity*. Harmony Books.

Queen, C. S. (2012). *Engaged Buddhism in the west*. Simon and Schuster.

Queen, C. S., & King, S. B. (Eds.). (1996). *Engaged Buddhism: Buddhist liberation movements in Asia*. State University of New York Press.

Rogers, A. (2016). *Human behavior in the social environment* (4th ed.). Routledge.

Rosenberg, M. B. (2015). *Nonviolent communication: A language of life* (3rd ed.). PuddleDancer Press.

Schöttle, D., Briken, P., Tüscher, O., & Turner, D. (2017). Sexuality in autism: Hypersexual and paraphilic behavior in women and men with high-functioning autism spectrum disorder. *Dialogues in Clinical Neuroscience*, 19(4), 381–393. https://doi.org/10.31887/DCNS.2017.19.4/dschoettle.

Shapiro, S. L., Carlson, L. E., Astin, J. A., & Freedman, B. (2006). Mechanisms of mindfulness. *Journal of Clinical Psychology*, 62(3), 373–386. https://doi.org/10.1002/jclp.20237.

Singh, N. N., Lancioni, G. E., Singh, A. D., Winton, A. S., Singh, A. N., & Singh, J. (2011). Adolescents with Asperger syndrome can use a mindfulness-based strategy to control their aggressive behavior. *Research in Autism Spectrum Disorders*, 5(3), 1103–1109.

Sprott, R. A., & Williams, D. J. (2019). Is BDSM a sexual orientation or serious leisure? *Current Sexual Health Reports*, 11(2), 75–79. https://doi.org/10.1007/s11930–11019–00195-x.

Stebbins, R. (2010). The internet as a scientific tool for studying leisure activities: Exploratory internet data collection. *Leisure Studies*, 29(4), 469–475. https://doi.org/10.1080/02614367.2010.506649.

Tatkin, S. (2018). *We do: Saying yes to a relationship of depth, true connection, and enduring love*. Sounds True.

Taverner, W. J. (2023). *Sex education research: A look between the sheets*. Routledge. https://doi.org/10.4324/9781003189787.

Tilsen, J. (2021). *Queering your therapy practice*. Routledge. https://doi.org/10.4324/9781003011477.

Treleaven, D. A. (2018). *Trauma-sensitive mindfulness: Practices for safe and transformative healing*. Norton.

Walker, N. (2018). Somatics and autistic embodiment. In *Diverse bodies, diverse practices: Toward an inclusive somatics* (pp. 89–120). North Atlantic Books.

Walker, N. (2021). *Neuroqueer heresies: Notes on the neurodiversity paradigm, autistic empowerment, and postnormal possibilities*. Autonomous Press.

Ward, J. (2019). Individual differences in sensory sensitivity: A synthesizing framework and evidence from normal variation and developmental conditions. *Cognitive Neuroscience*, 10(3), 139–157. https://doi.org/10.1080/17588928.2018.1557131.

Weiner, L., & Avery-Clark, C. (2017). *Sensate focus in sex therapy: The illustrated manual*. Routledge.

Willey, A., & Subramaniam, B. (2017). Inside the social world of asocials: White nerd masculinity, science, and the politics of reverent disdain. *Feminist Studies*, 43(1), 13–41. https://doi.org/10.15767/feministstudies.43.1.0013.

Willey, A., Subramaniam, B., Hamilton, J. A., & Couperus, J. (2015). The mating life of geeks: Love, neuroscience, and the new autistic subject. *Signs: Journal of Women in Culture and Society*, 40(2), 369–391. https://doi.org/10.1086/678146.

Williams, D. J., Thomas, J. N., Prior, E. E., & Christensen, M. C. (2014). From "SSC" and "RACK" to the "4Cs": Introducing a new framework for negotiating BDSM participation. *Electronic Journal of Human Sexuality*, 17.

Wise, S. J. (2022). *The neurodivergent friendly workbook of DBT skills*. Lived Experience Educator.

Worell, J., & Remer, P. (2003). *Feminist perspectives in therapy: Empowering diverse women* (2nd ed.). Wiley.

Wright, S. (2018). De-pathologization of consensual BDSM. *Journal of Sexual Medicine*, 15(5), 622–624. https://doi.org/10.1016/j.jsxm.2018.02.018.

Yellow Bird, M. (2013). Neurodecolonization: Applying mindfulness research to decolonizing social work. In M. Gray, J. Coates, & M. Yellow Bird (Eds.), *Decolonizing social work*. Ashgate.

Zimmerman, J. M., & Coyle, V. (1996). *The way of council*. Bramble Books.

12

A CRITICAL LOOK INTO THE WORKING ALLIANCE BETWEEN GSRD AUTISTIC INDIVIDUALS AND THEIR HEALTHCARE PROVIDERS

Lydia Stetson

As a psychotherapist with an existential-humanistic orientation (Yalom, 1980), I view each individual as the expert on themselves and their experiences. Furthermore, each person constructs meaning for themselves based on their context, history, values, and motivations. How do people know what they know? How do individuals make sense and meaning in a chaotic and ever-evolving world? These are questions that are certainly beyond the scope and aim of this chapter. However, questions such as these offer a foundation for my positionality regarding gender, sexual, and relationship diverse (GSRD) Autistic individuals and healthcare providers. For instance, I construct meaning and truths from my experiences as a bisexual AuDHD (Autistic and with attention-deficit/hyperactivity disorder) cisgender woman in a functionally monogamous relationship in the United States. The way that the world makes sense to me will therefore be different than how it makes sense to a polyamorous, gay, Autistic genderfluid individual from Brazil, as we have different experiences, relationships, and interactions within the world. My experiences are no more or less valid than anyone else's. Yet, as a cisgender woman in a long-term relationship with a cisgender man, many in society view my relationship experiences as "normal," whereas they would not offer the same views toward individuals who present as GSRD more overtly. In other words, I veer away from a medicalized or neuroconventional understanding of what is normal or abnormal, healthy or unhealthy (McDermott, 2022). Instead, I view the world as nuanced and contextual, with many different truths and experiences regarding what is healthy, safe, and normal for each person. My contextual approach broadly aligns with the neurodiversity paradigm that asserts that there is no single right way to be in the world and that individuals' experiences are diverse and broad (Botha & Gillespie-Lynch, 2022).

DOI: 10.4324/9781003440154-16

Therefore, in this chapter, I aim to explore the lived experiences of GSRD Autistic individuals through my personal and professional experience and from the relevant literature, connect lived theory, and examine practical steps toward creating GSRD Autistic affirming relationships in healthcare. I will begin with a brief overview of the importance of sexuality, gender, and relationships. I will also discuss barriers to affirming healthcare and minority stress pertaining to GSRD Autistic individuals. Finally, I will explore possible courses of action healthcare providers might take to foster affirming relationships with GSRD Autistic individuals based on the literature and my and others' lived experiences.

Sexuality, gender, and relationships as aspects of the whole person

As a psychotherapist, I do not have the expertise or competence to advise individuals on the medical intricacies of birth control or fertility or on medical treatments related to sex, gender, and reproductive health. However, I often have conversations with the individuals I see in practice on these topics as they are inextricably intertwined with overall health. Additionally, I have accompanied Autistic, ADHD, and AuDHD GSRD people as they have explored their experiences in romantic and sexual relationships and with themselves as they navigate who they are and who and how they engage romantically, relationally, and sexually. For these individuals, being neurodivergent is not separable from being GSRD. In actuality, the converse is true; being neurodivergent and GSRD both inform how they make sense of themselves and how they navigate the world around them. These individuals frequently confront the daunting tasks of determining to whom they can safely disclose that they are neurodivergent, GSRD, or both and how they can communicate their needs to providers without being dismissed, rejected, or infantilized.

Additionally, I have had numerous interactions in which individuals and I process, normalize, and explore solutions regarding mood changes that coincide with contraceptive medications or menstrual cycles, thus attending to at least emotional, mental, and social domains of health. Likewise, I often have frank conversations about safe sex, including what it means to give and get consent, exploring strategies for communicating clearly and effectively with partners, options for family planning, accessing gender-affirming medical intervention, and sexually transmitted infections (STIs) prevention, thus addressing relational, financial, physical, and cultural health. I also have had the honor many times to walk with clients as they embark on journeys of discovery and empathy regarding sexuality, gender identity, and relationship orientation, thus attending to self-awareness, emotional, cultural, social, relational, and other facets of well-being. In such interactions, it is neither my goal nor my clients' to construct a specific medical plan. Instead, our goal is to foster genuine curiosity and understanding of each person's goals, values, and overall health. Throughout the remainder of this chapter, I will present the fictional case of Finn. Finn is not based on a singular person, case, or experience but is instead an amalgam of my experiences in outpatient mental healthcare as a psychotherapist with GSRD Autistic youth and in a pediatric psychology clinic nestled within a pediatric medical school clinic.

BOX 12.1 PRACTICE EXAMPLE

I meet with Finn and their parents for a psychotherapy intake session after finally scheduling Finn following several weeks that they spent on my new client waitlist. Upon sitting down, I introduce myself with my name and pronouns and ask each person what name and pronouns I can use for them. Finn is a 16-year-old non-binary individual who uses they/them pronouns. Finn lives near my office in the US Midwest, where they have lived with their biological mother, father, and younger brother for two years after moving from a neighboring state. Finn is their chosen name and does not presently match their legal name, and their gender identity on legal documentation reflects their sex assigned at birth (female), which Finn disclosed as they wished to discuss social aspects of their gender identity. Finn's parents struggle with using their chosen name and pronouns, although typically correct themselves when needed, such as by recognizing when they use the incorrect pronouns and correcting their language. Finn and their parents report that their primary concerns involve anxiety, particularly related to academic functioning, and Finn experiencing almost daily episodes of crying or "shutting down" and they wonder if they might be Autistic. After the first session, I meet individually with Finn at their request and with their parents' agreement, although I remind Finn of the limits of confidentiality regarding the risk of harm. As we discuss treatment goals, it is clear that Finn's needs, goals, and experiences are not separated into neat individual boxes. Rather, who they are is informed by, yet greater than, the multitude of different aspects of their life.

Regardless of an individual's sexual history, their desire to have children or not, experience in reproductive or sexual healthcare, or if they have a medical provider, sexuality, gender, and relationships are vital facets of the human experience. Moreover, attending to sexual and reproductive health is crucial to a person's overall health and well-being (Fennell & Grant, 2019). For instance, providing accurate sexual and reproductive health education is imperative in reducing the risk of outcomes pertaining to STIs, addressing general health concerns that affect a person's sexual health, and helping individuals engage in choices regarding sexual health and wellness (Fennell & Grant, 2019). Additionally, sexual healthcare is vital for physical and mental well-being and even lifesaving, particularly for GSRD youth who often experience external and internal stigma regarding their sexual, gender, or relationship identities (Botha & Gillespie-Lynch, 2022; McClelland et al., 2012). Furthermore, sexuality, gender, and relationship identities impact each person's experiences in not just physical health but all domains of well-being, including emotional, cognitive, social, spiritual, financial, and other areas of health (Botha & Gillespie-Lynch, 2022; Schilder et al., 2001).

Barriers to affirming Autistic sexuality, gender, and relationships in healthcare

---

BOX 12.2 PRACTICE EXAMPLE

Finn leads most sessions with me, independently choosing the topics they would like to discuss or the conflicts they have had in their life in the past weeks, which typically involve their experiences of unmasking (i.e., presenting themselves authentically and genuinely instead of how others are acting) around safe others, such as close friends. Finn also frequently discusses their thoughts and experiences related to gender and is happy to report that their friends and family are affirming and only rarely call them by the wrong name or pronouns. Finn reports that their mother even corrected Finn's grandmother when she misgendered Finn at a family dinner. As we develop rapport, Finn shares that they are asexual, panromantic, and polyamorous and that they have never told a healthcare provider this because they were unsure how they would respond. We explore Finn's fears about being rejected by providers or that providers might assume that they are asexual because they "have not found the right person yet" or are "too young to understand." At the end of the session, Finn shares that they feel relieved to talk about their sexuality and relationship ideals with someone other than their peers.

In subsequent sessions, Finn broaches the topic of talking to their medical provider about birth control or contraceptives, as they would like a tool to help manage their menstrual cycles. They ask me if taking birth control can help with heavy bleeding during menstruation and the effects of contraceptives on acne. I advise Finn that aside from practical and anecdotal experience, I have only basic knowledge of the physical aspects of birth control and wonder if they would be willing to discuss the topic with their medical provider. Finn shares that they have never talked about birth control with their providers as previous providers only asked if they were sexually active and did not ask about health and goals related to sexuality, gender, or relationships any further. Finn is also hesitant and expresses fear that their medical provider will assume that they want to start birth control to prevent pregnancy or misgender Finn due to cisnormative beliefs about reproductive system needs. We process and validate Finn's fears and examine how they can maintain safety while accomplishing their goal of obtaining medical assistance with their menstrual cycles. After researching sexual healthcare providers, Finn finds a provider that lists the provider's pronouns in their profile, although does not indicate the provider's stance toward gender-affirming care, and decides to make an appointment. Finn also schedules a follow-up therapy session the day after their appointment with their new sexual healthcare provider to debrief and process.

Attention to all aspects of health and well-being should not be the sole provenance of psychotherapists, humanistic or otherwise. Similarly, mental healthcare providers should not neglect individuals' sexual or reproductive health as the domain of medical providers (Cordes, 2022). Rather, wellness and health would benefit from empathic and affirming stances from all healthcare providers (Carpenter, 2021). Nonetheless, there are broad and pervasive barriers that individuals may face when pursuing or accessing sexual healthcare. Specifically, GSRD Autistic individuals often confront healthcare system providers who espouse cisheteronormative and neuronormative assumptions and views of health (Carpenter, 2021; Lewis et al., 2021).

Minority stress

BOX 12.3 PRACTICE EXAMPLE

Although Finn does not need to be formally identified as Autistic to make meaning in their life, not being formally identified as Autistic by a healthcare provider may prevent Finn from accessing any legal accommodations, such as accommodations covered under the Americans with Disabilities Act, they may need as they continue their education or pursue employment. Another barrier to healthcare in Finn's case was limited access to affirming mental health and medical care, as they spent several weeks waiting for an appointment to initiate therapy and struggled to find an explicitly GSRD-affirming sexual healthcare provider. Additionally, Finn's previous general health providers did not provide Finn with opportunities to discuss sexuality, gender, or relationships further than providing their name and gender identity on intake forms and asking if they were sexually active. Each of these barriers can add to Finn's experiences of stress as an individual living in a world that often prioritizes the needs of the "majority" or "typical" population.

Broadly, minority stress theory pertains to stressors marginalized individuals experience due to their membership in a minority group or multiple minority groups (Feinstein et al., 2022). Stressors are varied and diverse but can include an increased incidence of mental health concerns, such as anxiety, depression, self-harm, and suicidality. Minority stress also relates to internalized stigma and bias – that is, negative attitudes and beliefs that a person has about themselves based on discriminatory and oppressive actions and beliefs in the wider society or culture (Feinstein et al., 2022). Additionally, minority stress plays a significant role in individuals' safety with others due to concerns of others causing harm or engaging in violence toward them on the basis of their identity or identities (Heyes et al., 2016). Despite ethical imperatives common to healthcare professions to do no harm or to treat all individuals with respect and dignity, healthcare spaces often do not offer a reprieve from minority stress. Notably, minority stress significantly impacts individuals' access to safe and affirming healthcare due to stigma, harm, discrimination, or being turned away or rejected by healthcare providers on the basis of the person's identity or identities (Carpenter, 2021; Heyes et al., 2016).

GSRD experiences and disparities in healthcare

BOX 12.4 PRACTICE EXAMPLE

In our sessions, Finn shares that they understood that they are not a girl from when they were very young, although did not have the word "nonbinary" to outwardly define their gender until entering high school. Finn reports that their parents "seem to try" to understand their gender identity as nonbinary and their nonconforming gender expression, but that they seem confused when they choose stereotypically feminine clothing and accessories. Additionally, in our session following their visit with their new sexual healthcare provider, Finn expresses mixed feelings and experiences. They report that the intake paperwork had clear spaces for their chosen name and pronouns and that the medical assistant used the appropriate name in the waiting area. Additionally, the medical staff introduced themselves with their pronouns when first meeting with Finn, which they report "felt good, like they actually care and weren't just profiling me." However, Finn shares that the provider talked about menstrual cycles as part of the female reproductive system exclusively. Finally, according to Finn, the provider repeatedly asked Finn if they ever wanted to "have kids and be a mom, ugh, even though I said I didn't," which Finn expresses was frustrating although not unexpected.

Specifically, GSRD individuals frequently face significant stressors and disparities in healthcare settings. For example, GSRD individuals experience more barriers in accessing healthcare that is identity affirming than their cisgender, heterosexual counterparts (Logie et al., 2019). Moreover, many healthcare practices or organizations do not provide a GSRD-affirming stance in the physical environment or in more subtle ways. For instance, healthcare practices or buildings may use binary-gendered restrooms, provide limited or only binary options on intake forms, or refer to individuals solely on the basis of sex assigned at birth (Cordes, 2022; Heyes et al., 2016; Mark et al., 2015). Additionally, providers and practices might assume gender, sexuality, and relationship needs only fit within the bounds of cisheteronormativity and monogamy (Cordes, 2022). Likewise, healthcare providers may lack expertise in GSRD-affirming healthcare or may lack the understanding or willingness to explore their assumptions and biases (Carpenter, 2021; Streed et al., 2019).

Furthermore, although some areas of the world have enacted laws aimed at protecting GSRD individuals from harm, such as from so-called conversion therapy, these laws may not provide adequate safety, and many individuals live outside of areas where there are even meager protections from cisheteronormative violence (Río-Gonzáles et al., 2021). Additionally, in areas where affirming medical care is accessible, there are many gatekeeping barriers, such as medical providers requiring letters of support from mental healthcare providers that the GSRD individual is competent to conceptualize their identity and is not pursuing medical treatments on a whim or on the basis of psychopathology (Violeta & Langer, 2017). Gatekeeping affirming medical care is problematic for a plethora of reasons, including that it requires GSRD individuals to disclose their identities to additional individuals, increases wait times for medical care, and accrues significant additional costs. Therefore, GSRD individuals often need to be cautious when deciding to whom they are safe to disclose their gender, sexuality, and relationship identities and needs, which unduly places the burden on the individuals seeking care to ensure that their healthcare providers are safe, ethical, and competent. In cases in which the healthcare provider or system is not affirming or safe, GSRD individuals may subsequently receive inadequate or inappropriate healthcare services or even face stigma, discrimination, or threats to safety from their providers (Carpenter, 2021; Logie et al., 2019; Schilder et al., 2001).

Autistic experiences and disparities in healthcare

BOX 12.5 PRACTICE EXAMPLE

Finn's parents report that the school and Finn's doctor suggested that they may be Autistic when Finn was three or four years old due to significant reactivity to seemingly innocuous noises and their speech not developing at the same rate as their peers. However, they never pursued psychological evaluation or formal identification as their healthcare insurance has never covered psychological evaluation costs, and it would be too expensive to pay out of pocket. In our first individual session, Finn shares that they asked their parents to schedule with me due to my professional listing stating my passion for neurodiversity and sexual and gender diversity. Throughout treatment, Finn is generally open about their experiences as a self-identified Autistic individual. They note that they usually feel drained at the end of a school day and are exhausted from having to "be on" around others for the entire day. They clarify that "being on" refers to acting how their peers act and avoiding topics that they particularly enjoy due to not wanting to seem "weird." Finn is excited and willing to explore how being Autistic contributes to their meaning making and understanding of their life. Finn reports that even though their pediatrician suggested that Finn might be Autistic, they have not shared their thoughts with subsequent healthcare providers due to worry they will perceive Finn as "faking it" or "just saying they're Autistic because of social media." However, Finn decides to share their Autistic identity with their new sexual healthcare provider in hopes they can offer additional support. After their first meeting with their provider, Finn reports that their provider did not question their disclosure of being Autistic but focused on how Finn's experiences as an Autistic person impact their education.

Like GSRD individuals, Autistic individuals have also faced stigma, discrimination, and barriers to healthcare, including reproductive, gender, and sexual healthcare. Often, healthcare providers, both in the medical and mental health fields, conceptualize Autistic experiences through the lens of the medical model. In other words, healthcare professionals view Autistic individuals as disordered or deficient in comparison to allistic (i.e., non-autistic) people and aim to fix or cure Autistic individuals by changing their characteristics, needs, and traits to mirror those of allistic individuals (Rosenblatt, 2018). The medical model or pathologized view of Autistic experiences can result in Autistic individuals facing significant barriers to accessing healthcare. For instance, healthcare settings could limit access to accommodations to care, such as not providing or using augmented and alternative communication (AAC) (Light & McNaughton, 2015; Sturrock et al., 2021). Additionally, Autistic individuals may experience harmful biases regarding their sexuality, gender, and relationships related to neuronormative assumptions that Autistic individuals are disinterested or incapable of accurately conceptualizing gender or engaging in sexual activity (Dewinter et al., 2013; Hall et al., 2020; Violeta & Langer, 2017). Similarly, providers might assume that Autistic individuals invariably struggle with forming and maintaining meaningful relationships, including sexual, romantic, and platonic relationships (McClelland et al., 2012; Sala et al., 2020; Stanojevic et al., 2020).

For Autistic youth in particular, there is also a concerning possibility that providers or caregivers will see the child or adolescent as voiceless and helpless in expressing their needs, ideas, beliefs, and identities and instead overshadow the youth's voice with their own presuppositions and positions (Cheak-Zamora et al., 2019; Saunders, 2018). Furthermore, caregivers may inaccurately interpret, communicate, or advocate for the youth in their care based on biases and discomfort with the youth expressing a sexual, gender, or relationship identity (Dewinter et al., 2013). Relatedly, Autistic individuals, including youth and adults, may experience barriers in obtaining relevant healthcare services, such as obtaining autism identification from a healthcare provider, which can be a prerequisite for accessing any neurodiversity-affirming accommodations in healthcare, education, and employment (Lewis, 2017). Even if an Autistic youth or adult is able to obtain a formal autism identification by a healthcare provider, they still encounter challenges in accessing healthcare, including navigating limited insurance coverage, health costs, chronic health concerns, and connect with providers who are knowledgeable regarding neurodiversity (Casagrande & Ingersoll, 2021).

Intersecting identities

BOX 12.6 PRACTICE EXAMPLE

For Finn, being Autistic, asexual, panromantic, and polyamorous are inseparable aspects of their identity and are all interwoven throughout their experiences. In our sessions, Finn states that they often feel so different from their neurotypical, cisgender, and straight peers. Additionally, Finn sometimes laments that "when I find someone who's Autistic, they're usually straight or cis, or don't know anything about being ace. And when I find someone who is queer, they only know about being Autistic from social media, and they don't ask me about what it's like for me." For Finn, their intersecting identities frequently isolate them from others with whom they share one aspect of identity. However, Finn reports they still occasionally meet peers who are both GSRD and Autistic, and "even if they don't know my experience exactly, it's pretty close, and it feels good." Following their first visit with their healthcare provider to discuss sexual healthcare needs, Finn describes feeling disheartened that their provider did not really seem to realize how their identities intersect but do not cause one another. Specifically, Finn shared that their provider dismissed their asexuality as a "sensory thing" related to being Autistic rather than their actual sexual identity.

People are multifaceted. An individual is not defined only by their sexuality, gender identity, relationship orientation, disability, sociocultural identity, socioeconomic status, or other demographics; instead, each person is comprised of a constellation of identities and experiences that make them who they are at any given moment in time. Nevertheless, healthcare and much of research often focus on one identity at a time and exclude others. For instance, healthcare providers might engage in stigma by simplifying a GSRD Autistic individual's presenting concern as risky sexual behaviors associated with sexual, gender, or relationship diversity (Schilder et al., 2001). Similarly, providers in healthcare might assume that an Autistic person is not sexually active and therefore does not have a sexual or gender identity or might adopt a deficit-based view of Autistic health, such as the inaccurate and demeaning assumption that Autistic individuals cannot initiate or maintain relationships due to non-normative communication or sensory needs (Barnett & Maticka-Tyndale, 2015). Siloing aspects of identity does a significant disservice to individuals seeking healthcare services and can result in missing crucial information pertaining to an individual's wellness (Botha & Gillespie-Lynch, 2022; Schilder et al., 2001). Furthermore, reducing a person to one aspect of identity ignores the individual's intersectional identities, which is a significant contributor to how individuals engage with their environment. Specifically, intersectional identities refer to the lens through which individuals view the world, particularly regarding power and oppression (Botha & Gillespie-Lynch, 2022).

In light of their intersecting minority identities, GSRD Autistic individuals often face multiple forms of stigma and discrimination in healthcare systems (Botha & Gillespie-Lynch, 2022). For instance, Black, Indigenous, and People of Color (BIPOC), transgender and nonbinary people, and individuals assigned female at birth may experience difficulties or resistance from providers regarding being identified as Autistic due to the focus of the medical model of autism focusing on a stereotypically white cisgender male presentation of Autistic traits and characteristics. Lack of formal identification from a healthcare provider may, in turn, lead to individuals not having access to appropriate resources or accommodations (Botha & Gillespie-Lynch, 2022). Likewise, Autistic individuals who are also gender minorities may face barriers to gender-affirming healthcare, which is already difficult to access, due to healthcare systems or providers dismissing gender noncomformity as a symptom of the medical model's pathologized perception of autism (McClelland et al., 2012; Stanojevic et al., 2020). Moreover, the stigma and discrimination intersectional individuals experience can lead to poorer physical and mental health outcomes, including the inadequate provision of healthcare, depression, stress, and suicidality (Río-Gonzáles et al., 2021). Therefore, it is imperative that healthcare providers address and affirm GSRD Autistic individuals' intersecting identities and needs (Logie et al., 2019). Nonetheless, there is relatively little education for healthcare professionals and sparse research regarding the intersectional identities of GSRD Autistic experiences, suggesting that the imperative to improve healthcare outcomes for GSRD Autistic individuals lies within the healthcare system and society as a whole, in addition to individual healthcare providers (Bennett & Goodall, 2016; McClelland et al., 2012).

Toward an affirming working alliance

BOX 12.7 PRACTICE EXAMPLE

In the case of Finn, there are several notable barriers as well as aspects of hopefulness. Barriers to accessing healthcare for Finn include the costs associated with autism identification by a healthcare provider, even though their insurance did cover the cost of ongoing psychotherapy appointments. Finn also experienced healthcare disparities in that their provider was unreceptive to Finn's disclosures regarding their sexuality and reproductive goals and instead offered dismissive cisheteronormative and neuronormative judgments and comments on Finn's health and goals. Positively, Finn experienced relief at being able to explore their experiences of being a nonbinary, asexual, polyamorous, panromantic, Autistic person with others in and outside of the therapeutic relationship. Additionally, although Finn's sexual healthcare provider's office focused on cisheteronormative and neuronormative care, there was a small glimmer of positivity in that they made some effort to normalize gender expansiveness in marketing materials, documentation, and initial interactions.

Healthcare providers are in an excellent position to directly address and mitigate minority stress and harm from oppressive and discriminatory practices through the development and maintenance of affirming relationships with the GSRD Autistic individuals they serve. For instance, healthcare providers could take steps such as sharing their own pronouns so as to avoid othering transgender and gender nonconforming individuals and respecting others' chosen names and pronouns (Carpenter, 2021). Furthermore, healthcare providers can provide opportunities for individuals to share their needs and questions pertaining to sexual, gender, and reproductive health safely by initiating conversations about sex, gender, and relationships beyond asking if the individual is sexually active (Cordes, 2022). For example, healthcare providers who work with youth might ask what healthy sexuality, gender, and relationships mean to youth, thereby taking the burden to initiate potentially unsafe interactions off GSRD Autistic individuals who can then make a more informed decision on if they feel comfortable and safe disclosing aspects of their identities to their provider (Cordes, 2022; Logie et al., 2019).

Additionally, asking for the youth's input and perspectives acknowledges that the youth is coming from their frame of reference or context and helps inform relevant, meaningful, person-centered next steps for healthcare, education, and mental health (Brownlow et al., 2021). Relatedly, healthcare providers can foster an affirming working alliance with GSRD Autistic youth and adults by acknowledging that ability, as well as gender, sexuality, and relationship needs, are fluid and may change, thus honoring the ongoing lived experience of the individual (Lewis et al., 2021). However, although healthcare providers should respect the lived experience and disclosures of GSRD Autistic youth and adults, healthcare providers also have an ethical obligation of competency-based practice. In other words, it is imperative that healthcare providers actively address biases, assumptions, and beliefs they hold regarding GSRD and Autistic individuals and seek out education or consultation on best practices for GSRD Autistic affirming healthcare (Carpenter, 2021; Hall et al., 2020).

Future directions for GSRD Autistic affirming healthcare spaces

BOX 12.8 PRACTICE EXAMPLE

Overall, Finn's case presents a possible model with which to view GSRD Autistic youth's experiences navigating sexual healthcare. Nonetheless, it is my hope that this fictional case highlights how healthcare disparities can seem commonplace and subtle while having a significant, detrimental impact on GSRD Autistic experiences and that it will prompt considerations of systemic and individual change in healthcare spaces.

Prior to 1973, the American Psychiatric Association characterized homosexuality as a pathological disorder in the *Diagnostic and Statistical Manual* (DSM) based on deviation from what society conserved to be normal sexuality (i.e., heteronormativity) based on a rigid gender binary (Drescher, 2015). Likewise, gender expansiveness and nonconformity have been a matter of debate in academic and clinical domains, with some arguing that individuals who do not identify or present with the gender stereotypes corresponding with their sex assigned at birth were disordered, such as in the case of gender identity disorder (Río-González et al., 2021). Furthermore, a widely held assumption in many societies and in research literature has been that committed and monogamous relationships are inherently better, safer, and more satisfying than casual and nonmonogamous relationships (Mark et al., 2015). However, societal attitudes and clinical or research focus on sexuality, gender, and relationships have begun to move toward challenging such rigid binary thinking in favor of more expansive and affirming beliefs, albeit slowly (Blanc, 2023; Mark et al., 2015).

Similarly, in stark contrast to the medical model, the neurodiversity movement or paradigm, as well as the contextual model, emphasizes lived experience and seeks an empathic understanding of the differences between Autistic and allistic experiences without unnecessarily pathologizing experiences and meaning making (Saunders, 2018). Furthermore, the neurodiversity movement highlights the concept that being Autistic is a way of functioning in the world cognitively, socially, and psychologically that frequently diverges from neuronormative functioning, not a deficit or pathology. Resultingly, the predominantly neuronormative society disables or restricts Autistic individuals' access to many environments or contexts (Botha & Gillespie-Lynch, 2022). Thus, like societal attitudes and beliefs toward gender, sexuality, and relationships, attitudes pertaining to neurodiversity are also showing very slight movement toward a more affirming approach.

Changes in societal attitudes toward GSRD Autistic individuals are positive. Nonetheless, it is imperative that research and healthcare institutions, including medical and mental or psychological healthcare systems, strive to create safe, inclusive, and affirming spaces. Future research should continue to explore the lived experiences and intersectional identities of GSRD Autistic individuals and inform best practices in healthcare (Bennett & Goodall, 2016; Rosenblatt, 2018; Saunders, 2018). Additionally, healthcare institutions can improve by enacting systemic and environmental changes, such as offering open-ended responses regarding sexuality, gender, and relationships in documentation systems. Likewise, institutions may utilize nongendered facilities (i.e., unisex restrooms) or services (i.e., sexual health clinics might provide dental dams alongside condoms or not refer to obstetrics and gynecology as women's health) and promote accessibility by considering the use of AAC as needed and providing clear information regarding healthcare needs and appointments (Light & McNaughton, 2015; Logie et al., 2019; Sturrock et al., 2021). Finally, healthcare institutions may improve the provision of services by providing ongoing professional development regarding implicit bias and cultural humility to healthcare providers (Fennell & Grant, 2019; Schilder et al., 2001).

References

Barnett, J. P., & Maticka-Tyndale, E. (2015). Qualitative exploration of sexual experiences among adults on the autism spectrum: Implications for sex education. *Perspectives on Sexual and Reproductive Health*, 47(4), 171–179. https://doi.org/10.1363/47e5715.

Bennett, M., & Goodall, E. (2016). Towards an agenda for research for lesbian, gay, bisexual, transgendered and/or intersexed people with an autism spectrum diagnosis. *Journal of Autism and Developmental Disorders*, 46(9), 3190–3192. https://doi.org/10.1007/s10803-016-2844-z.

Blanc, A. (2023). Attitudes toward sexual behaviors: Relationship with gender and sexual orientation. *Current Psychology*. https://doi.org/10.1007/s12144-023-04398-3.

Botha, M., & Gillespie-Lynch, K. (2022). Come as you are: Examining autistic identity development and the neurodiversity movement through an intersectional lens. *Human Development*, 66(2), 93–112. https://doi.org/10.1159/000524123.

Brownlow, C., Lawson, W., Pillay, Y., Mahony, J., & Abawi, D. (2021). "Just ask me": The importance of respectful relationships within schools. *Frontiers in Psychology*, 12, 678264. https://doi.org/10.3389/fpsyg.2021.678264.

Carpenter, E. (2021). "The health system just wasn't built for us": Queer cisgender women and gender expansive individuals' strategies for navigating reproductive health care. *Women's Health Issues*, 31(5), 478–484. https://doi.org/10.1016/j.whi.2021.06.004.

Casagrande, K., & Ingersoll, B. R. (2021). Improving service access in ASD: A systematic review of family empowerment interventions for children with special healthcare needs. *Review Journal of Autism and Developmental Disorders*, 8(2), 170–185. https://doi.org/10.1007/s40489-020-00208-9.

Cheak-Zamora, N. C., Teti, M., Maurer-Batjer, A., O'Connor, K. V., & Randolph, J. K. (2019). Sexual and relationship interest, knowledge, and experiences among adolescents and young adults with autism spectrum disorder. *Archives of Sexual Behavior*, 48(8), 2605–2615. https://doi.org/10.1007/s10508-019-1445-2.

Cordes, C. C. (2022). Just ask: Promoting inclusive and holistic sexual health in primary care. *Families, Systems, & Health*, 40(2), 300–303. https://doi.org/10.1037/fsh0000706.

Dewinter, J., Vermeiren, R., Vanwesenbeeck, I., & van Nieuwenhuizen, C. (2013). Autism and normative sexual development: A narrative review. *Journal of Clinical Nursing*, 22(23–24),3467–3483. https://doi.org/10.1111/jocn.12397.

Drescher, J. (2015). Out of DSM: Depathologizing homosexuality. *Behavioral Sciences*, 5 (4), 565–575. https://doi.org/10.3390/bs5040565.

Feinstein, B. A., Dyar, C., Poon, J. A., Goodman, F. R., & Davila, J. (2022). The affective consequences of minority stress among bisexual, pansexual, and queer (bi+) adults: A daily diary study. *Behavior Therapy*, 53(4), 571–584. https://doi.org/10.1016/j.beth.2022.01.013.

Fennell, R., & Grant, B. (2019). Discussing sexuality in health care: A systematic review. *Journal of Clinical Nursing*, 28(17–18),3065–3076. https://doi.org/10.1111/jocn.14900.

Hall, J. P., Batza, K., Streed, C. G., Boyd, B. A., & Kurth, N. K. (2020). Health disparities among sexual and gender minorities with autism spectrum disorder. *Journal of Autism and Developmental Disorders*, 50(8), 3071–3077. https://doi.org/10.1007/s10803-020-04399-2.

Heyes, C., Dean, M., & Goldberg, L. (2016). Queer phenomenology, sexual orientation, and health care spaces: Learning from the narratives of queer women and nurses in primary health care. *Journal of Homosexuality*, 63(2), 141–155. https://doi.org/10.1080/00918369.2015.1083775.

Lewis, L. F. (2017). A mixed methods study of barriers to formal diagnosis of autism spectrum disorder in adults. *Journal of Autism and Developmental Disorders*, 47(8), 2410–2424. https://doi.org/10.1007/s10803-017-3168-3.

Lewis, L. F., Ward, C., Jarvis, N., & Cawley, E. (2021). "Straight sex is complicated enough!": The lived experiences of autistics who are gay, lesbian, bisexual, asexual, or other sexual orientations. *Journal of Autism and Developmental Disorders*, 51(7), 2324–2337. https://doi.org/10.1007/s10803-020-04696-w.

Light, J., & McNaughton, D. (2015). Designing AAC research and intervention to improve outcomes for individuals with complex communication needs. *Augmentative and Alternative Communication*, 31(2), 85–96. https://doi.org/10.3109/07434618.2015.1036458.

Logie, C. H., Lys, C. L., Dias, L., Schott, N., Zouboules, M. R., MacNeill, N., & Mackay, K. (2019). "Automatic assumption of your gender, sexuality and sexual practices is also discrimination": Exploring sexual healthcare experiences and recommendations among sexually and gender diverse persons in Arctic Canada. *Health & Social Care in the Community*, 27(5), 1204–1213. https://doi.org/10.1111/hsc.12757.

Mark, K. P., Garcia, J. R., & Fisher, H. E. (2015). Perceived emotional and sexual satisfaction across sexual relationship contexts: Gender and sexual orientation differences and similarities. *Canadian Journal of Human Sexuality*, 24(2), 120–130.

McClelland, A., Flicker, S., Nepveux, D., Nixon, S., Vo, T., Wilson, C., Marshall, Z., Travers, R., & Proudfoot, D. (2012). Seeking safer sexual spaces: Queer and trans young people labeled with intellectual disabilities and the paradoxical risks of restriction. *Journal of Homosexuality*, 59(6), 808–819. https://doi.org/10.1080/00918369.2012.694760.

McDermott, C. 2022. Theorising the neurotypical gaze: Autistic love and relationships in The Bridge (Bron/Broen 2011–2018). *Medical Humanities*, 48, 51–62.

Río-González, A. M., Zea, M. C., Flórez-Donado, J., Torres-Salazar, P., Abello-Luque, D., García-Montaño, E. A., García-Roncallo, P. A., & Meyer, I. H. (2021). Sexual orientation and gender identity change efforts and suicide morbidity among sexual and gender minority adults in Colombia. *LGBT Health*, 8(7), 463–472. https://doi.org/10.1089/lgbt.2020.0490.

Rosenblatt, A. (2018). Autism, advocacy organizations, and past injustice. *Disability Studies Quarterly*, 38(4). https://dsq-sds.org/article/view/6222/5137.

Sala, G., Hooley, M., & Stokes, M. A. (2020). Romantic intimacy in autism: A qualitative analysis. *Journal of Autism and Developmental Disorders*, 50(11), 4133–4147. https://doi.org/10.1007/s10803-020-04377-8.

Saunders, P. (2018). Neurodivergent rhetorics: Examining competing discourses of autism advocacy in the public sphere. *Journal of Literary & Cultural Disability Studies*, 12(1), 1–17. https://doi.org/10.3828/jlcds.2018.1.

Schilder, A. J., Kennedy, C., Goldstone, I. L., Ogden, R. D., Hogg, R. S., & O'Shaughnessy, M. V. (2001). "Being dealt with as a whole person." Care seeking and adherence: The benefits of culturally competent care. *Social Science & Medicine*, 52(11), 1643–1659. https://doi.org/10.1016/S0277-9536(00)00274-4.

Stanojevic, C., Neimeyer, T., & Piatt, J. (2020). The complexities of sexual health among adolescents living with autism spectrum disorder. *Sexuality and Disability*, 39, 345–356. https://doi.org/10.1007/s11195-020-09651-2.

Streed, C. G., Hedian, H. F., Bertram, A., & Sisson, S. D. (2019). Assessment of internal medicine resident preparedness to care for lesbian, gay, bisexual, transgender, and queer/questioning patients. *Journal of General Internal Medicine*, 34(6), 893–898. https://doi.org/10.1007/s11606-019-04855-5.

Sturrock, A., Chilton, H., Foy, K., Freed, J., & Adams, C. (2021). In their own words: The impact of subtle language and communication difficulties as described by autistic girls and boys without intellectual disability. *Autism*, 26(2), 332–345. https://doi.org/10.1177/13623613211002047.

Violeta, K. J., & Langer, S. J. (2017). Integration of desire, sexual orientation, and female embodiment of a transgender woman previously diagnosed with autism spectrum disorder: A case report. *Journal of Gay & Lesbian Mental Health*, 21(4), 352–370. https://doi.org/10.1080/19359705.2017.1354794.

Yalom, I. D. (1980). *Existential psychotherapy*. Basic Books.

CONCLUSION

13

LOOKING FROM A DOUBLE RAINBOW

Proposing New Ways of Looking at Autistic Sexualities, Relationality, and Genders

Hanna Bertilsdotter Rosqvist, Anna Day and Meaghan Krazinski

> What we call the beginning is often the end. And to make an end is to make a beginning. The end is where we start from.
>
> *(T. S. Eliot, 1943)*

T. S. Eliot reminds us that beginnings and endings are intertwined: we end this text hoping that it inspires our readers to continue their explorations of Autistic gender identity, sexuality, and relationality through a different lens than perhaps they started with. We end as we began, celebrating the beauty and variance within light that rainbows show, while acknowledging that rainbows emerge only from a combination of light and stormy weather. We celebrate Autistic gender identity, sexuality, and relationality while giving space for difficult experiences feelings that may arise as we give "name to the nameless so it can be thought" (Lorde, 2017, p. 8, cited in Czyzselska, 2022). Writing this book has provided space for us to explore our own becomings, sexualities, bodies, and genders and for our understandings of these to shift during its creation. We hope that this book shows that Autistic and "queer people excel at relationship resilience, at strong connections, at these world-changing and world-shaping relationships" (Middleton, 2022, p. 111). We are aware in writing this ending chapter of the pull to revisit our beginning chapter – exploration and becoming never ends but ever circles. But end we must, but let our words continue their journey through our readers and as we continue our own work.

In the following, we present reflections on each chapter as we draw together the overall gestalt of what we have learned, unlearned, or perhaps relearned as we have worked on the text. All the chapters have shown us both that "there is always so much more to learn" (Czyzselska, 2022, p. xvii), be that about Autistic sexuality, the meaning and connection created through BDSM/kink, or giving ways of naming and communicating areas not previously ventured into.

DOI: 10.4324/9781003440154-18

We end with a final section in which we look forward, proposing new ways of looking at Autistic sexualities, genders, and relationality.

Evolving understandings: Naming the nameless so it can be thought

In the introduction, we emphasised that although this book is about exploring and celebrating Autistic sexualities, genders, and relationalities, we also wished to recognise that exploring sexuality may involve revisiting experiences and realising, or now being able to acknowledge to ourselves, that they were not consensual. We again remind you that **all responsibility for sexual violence lies solely with the perpetrator.** The writing of the text has simultaneously been joyful and painful,[1] allowing us to name to ourselves that which was previously unidentifiable. Stern (2019) writes that

> until the situation is right for meaning to become *more itself* in the special way that language allows, it remains unformulated. The act of formulation, that is, takes place only when meaning is "ready" to become more than it has been; and to be ready it must percolate for as long as it takes.
>
> (*p. 7, emphasis original*)

Eliot (1943) wrote eloquently about the challenge of conveying ideas through words, leaving "one still with the intolerable wrestle with words and meanings". In their chapter, Hagerlid describes as a wish for "developing a terminology that better mirrors my autiqueer experience", contrasted with the experience of "feel[ing] the gap between markers often used when referring to BDSM practices and their own embodied experiences of BDSM". The wish for such a terminology is, as Hagerlid points out, linked to desiring authentic connection with "someone else with whom I can share and explore these desires". Hagerlid reminds us to question what terminology means, in what context, and to whom and calls for others to continue work on a method to develop our own terminology. Day and Krazinski similarly explore how limiting language to words can entrap us within our masks and prohibit exploration of queerness. They question how we can connect with others if we do not have words to describe our internal experiences to ourselves, let alone others. We wonder how collectively we have been constrained by trying to write about experiences that by their very nature often *do not have words*, and by the heteronormative and neuronormative scripts with which society presents us. Intimate connection (be it emotional, sensorial, or sexual) is often speaking about a nonverbal meaning, whereby the "medium I must use limits me: I have no choice but to use words to describe a kind of experience that is defined precisely by the fact that there is often not words for it" (Stern, 2019, p. 99).

The chapters by Hagerlid, and Day and Krazinski lead us to question what "terminology", or naming, means: does this need to be through words, or can this be through a shared embodied language?[2] We draw here on Merleau-Ponty (1945/1962),[3] who proposed that knowing or experiencing is created by the body and the relationship between the body subject and the world. Is there terminology to express sexuality or intimacy where bodyminds are irrevocably intertwined (perhaps particularly for those involved in BDSM/kink): "Just as the words we choose are so often part and parcel of the meanings they convey, so too are gestures, prosody, facial expression and styles of movement often inseparable from the meanings *they* convey" (Stern, 2019, p. 142, emphasis original).

Unlearning and becoming

Dominant forms of sex education commonly focus on making neurotypical information accessible for Autistic people but at the same time typically do not incorporate common Autistic experiences such as hyper- or hyposensitivity (and fluctuations therein), stimming, processing time variability, and meltdowns/shutdowns in sexual situations. Unlike these approaches, Delilah and Bertilsdotter Rosqvist introduce different community-developed concepts and put them to good use to form a checklist to guide further sexual self-exploration. This provides support for exploration of bodily pleasures and frames seeking them out as being in a "sensory amusement park" or a "sensory playground, while also acknowledging the hard task of exploring desires that we have been taught to hide. Stimming is a central theme in their chapter as they prompt readers to "let it out, connect with your stimming ability". To nurture and develop stims is important given many of us have been taught to hide or even stop them. Part of the "unknowing" (Jackson-Perry, 2020) or "unlearning" is relearning how to stim and to connect with our stimming abilities. Informed by community theorist Thomas Henley, Delilah and Bertilsdotter Rosqvist suggest us to create and explore our own "Stimming Communication Profiles".[4]

Themes of "unlearning" and "becoming" are explored by contributors in several ways throughout the book. Exploration of "unlearning" includes questioning "(hetero)normative policing and expectations", which Jackson-Perry posits as a balancing between "a sometimes-hyperconsciousness of social rules . . . alongside the notion that Autistic people are less susceptible than non-autistic peers *to* those rules". "Unlearning" requires redefining (or in Bertilsdotter Rosqvist and Nygren's words, "rereading") experiences of Autistic sexualities, relationality, and genders based on theorising "drawn at least in part from internal observations" (Murray, 2019) rather than "external manifestations" such as social and cognitive expressions (Murray et al., 2023). This requires mindful attention to positionality in knowledge production, critiquing notions of neuronormativity, and decentering neurotypical epistemic standpoints (Bertilsdotter Rosqvist et al., 2020). Throughout the book, authors play with the idea of shifting the imagined audience away from the neurotypical gaze (McDermott, 2021) to members of the Autistic community instead, hoping the chapters serve primarily the members of the Autistic communities. Through a diversity of writing styles, authors engage language creatively and non-normatively to more closely express the contours of their inner experiences.

Jackson-Perry notes that "social intervention hampers participants' intimate lives, while their Autistic subjectivities mitigate challenges and offer solutions". The social intervention discourse that informs common (neurotypical-led) sexual education aimed at Autistic people (where neurotypicals show autistic people "how to do it") works in tandem as "two systems supporting each other" with what Jackson-Perry refers to as "autism is the problem with Autistic sexuality" discourse. Several of the authors in our book, among them Jackson-Perry, emphasise the importance of grounding, following, and exploring Autistic intimate lives in Autistic bodyminds (including our intense interests; Jackson-Perry), and finding community with others by sharing experiences. Pliskin et al.'s participants also highlighted the value of finding community and connection discussing topics about which they previously felt alone.

As De Veen (2022) writes, the "idea of emergence or becoming is important, it's about honouring process, an unfolding that allows time to review, deconstruct, reconstruct, change your mind and your direction" (p. 271). As we "unlearn", we can increasingly "become". Writing, editing, and reflecting on the book content has allowed us to find "a new space . . . a destination" (Roche, 2019, p. 255), a of way of being "that is beautifully cut adrift from the endless layers of performativity that have weighed me down my whole life" (Roche, 2019, p. 11). We link this idea of "becoming" to what Bollas (1987, 2018) describes as the "unthought known", those experiences we have when we have a sense of knowing something, yet remain unable to articulate or identify what that is. Like Manning (2020), we suggest may in part be because Autistic people attend to inventions of embodied becomings more steadfastly. Many of the authors indicate that unmasking means acknowledging the level to which we are beholden to the becomings of the body and sensory world, and therefore we know how to *become with* another in infinite degrees of invention. For this reason, kink in its explicit constraints allows paradoxical emergence of sensate freedom, a theme that runs throughout the book. A more detailed discussion of becoming is explored by Day and Krazinski, but we find this notion interwoven within many of the book's chapters.

Becoming is an "invitation to emerge into something we know that has been lost somewhere along the way but also to explore openly the not yet known. We are not fixed, imprisoned entities, but rather full of potential, possibility" (De Veen, 2022, p. 271). Many of the chapters extend this invitation in various guises, from exploration of gender identity and (un)masking (Day & Krazinski), connecting with our authentic selves (Hagerlid; Jackson-Perry), finding safer spaces in which to "be" (Delilah & Bertilsdotter Rosqvist), and discovery of identity in therapeutic spaces (Stetson; Pliskin et al.). Throughout the book, we find multiple accounts of "elation at being seen, seeing themselves or expressing themselves in a way which aligns with their felt sense of self" (Johnson, 2022, p. 41)

Ways of being and locating ourselves

Many chapters explore different ways of being and how it is that we come to orient ourselves within a heteronormative, neuronormative world, examining how "cis normativity . . . is a baseline flaw which obscures the complexity, wonder, and brilliance of the human experience" (Johnson, 2022, p. 37). The "template of heteronormativity wrongfoots us in our attempt to understand how we relate to each other" (Middleton, 2022, p. 109). We hope this book contributes to conversations that interrupt positionings of sexual orientations in relation to cisheteronomativity as the default and therefore positions anything outside of it in relation to it. We hope to instead offer space to relationalities that have yet to be named and even might not need to be. Jackson-Perry explains the way cisheteronormativity is seen by many of his participants as oppressive and compulsory.[5] Hagerlid explains the way in which neuro-conventional sex produces an alienation from self and from core values that are necessary to their self-expression. Centering heteronormative vanilla sex is an epistemic suppression that can produce a type of dysphoria. Dysphoria typically refers to one's gender presentation within a particular context, but Hagerlid's text implies that some Autistic people may experience distress-connected *acts, modes*, and *types of expression* as much (if not more) than a particular gender presentation. Likewise, Jackon-Perry demonstrates that being Autistic opens up curiosity about feeling authenticity by questioning not what a neurodivergent body is, but what a neurodivergent body can do (cf Bertilsdotter Rosqvist et al., in press).

Hagerlid describes how the personal and applied realms connect to larger research paradigms as they reflect on the process of wading through theories and research accounts of Autistic sexualities, relationality, and genders. They explore these alongside their own lived experiences as data, tethered to affect and emotion. Hagerlid speaks with both a sense of saddening and hurt, and excitement and affirmation. This has implications for some of the most pressing conversations in research and practitioner circles around higher rates of sexual violence for Autistic people, particularly those assigned female at birth.

Rocha and Benedetto take up the call for doing research differently by uti-lising community-driven methodology to explore Autistic sexuality, focusing on sensory differences, navigating between hyper- and hyposensitivity, sensory pleasures and risks of overload. They also explore how these may impact on consent and the ability to communicate withdrawal of consent, with several participants reporting sexual assaults. If we seek to create curriculums and spaces that affirm various types of sexual expression, we must first consider the role of curriculum in making assumptions about the types of sex one wants to engage in. If Autistic people are taught to "feel crammed into an excruciatingly narrow set of arbitrary conventions", normativity may contribute to a sense of alienation from the self that may normalize sex acts that do actually not feel most natural. Instead, we should affirm one's right to embody that expression in ways that feel most natural and interrogate the definitions of natural that are linked to neuronormativity. This means nursing and nurturing a loving curiosity about what our bodies *can do* (and not what our bodies *can't do*).

Unmasking Autistic pleasures in safer spaces[6]

Connected to finding a shared terminology is also the need to locate safer spaces in which to share and explore our desires. Hagerlid shows how "BDSM provided them with a space where they could be genuinely authentic and accepted for who they were at their most vulnerable" (cf Pearson & Hodgetts, 2023). Similarly, Delilah and Bertilsdotter Rosqvist stress the importance of safer spaces for exploring our desires, ourselves, and sense of community with others, calling on us to find these spaces, unmask, and in the words of a participant, "what we are taught to hide may instead be hot to let out".

Exploring *what our bodies can do* runs through multiple chapters (e.g., Hagerlid; Day & Krazinski; Delilah & Bertilsdotter Rosqvist). During this exploration, new names and meanings appear (e.g., Nygren & Bertilsdotter Rosqvist). We "reauthor" our bodies (Yergeau, 2018) such that body is not just a body but a becoming (cf Johnson, 2022, p. 33). Kink is a way to explore our bodies and pleasures within our own ways of communicating and processing. It allows for nonspeaking communication, clear communication, safety protocols, and sociality based on interests. Within kink contexts, Autistic ways of being may feel "at home", less exceptional. For example, a meltdown in a BDSM context may be referred to in the BDSM community as a "drop"[7] and is something that may happen to all regardless of neurotypes. The kink community holds shared values around care (including aftercare), preparation, and support in the case of a drop, which also creates group norms around routine check-ins for the post-session well-being of a partner. Hagerlid, and Delilah and Bertilsdotter Rosqvist nuance the meanings of a meltdown as something that may not be a bad thing: sometimes there are what Thomas Henley refers to as happy meltdowns.[8] It may be that edging close to a meltdown, in the knowledge that this might mean going over the edge and experiencing the change from high and pleasure, to meltdown and displeasure that recontextualises a meltdown into a sensual experience. This edging and exploration is part of getting to know oneself and one's body and loving curiosity about what our bodies *can do* (and what our bodies can't do). Within a BDSM/kink context, *the difference is in safety*, "where the control is given over [by a submissive] in a controlled way" to a person (the Dominant) of one's own choice.

Embodiment is also explored by Day and Krazinski in their discussion of unmasking, becoming, and queer identity. They explore the meaning of the body and what we can do with it, relating embodiment to sensory experiences – for example, with both kink and getting inked as receiving interoceptive input from the "inside" and proprioceptive input from the "outside". They reflect that "we are always in the process of manifesting ourselves" (Stern, 2019, p. 148), be that through shifting our external appearance to align with nonbinary gender identity or through self-expression through ink.

Fusing Autistic bodies

Embodiment may be explored through sensory pleasures (among them sex), aligning our physical body to match our gender identity, choosing to express embodiment through kink or ink, stimming, or fusing. All are forms of seeking connection and relationality with ourselves or others. Autistic fusing is invoked by several of the authors. Hagerlid reflects on their different experiences of Autistic fusing and connects this to monotropic flow states, including a collective monotropic flow, referring to BDSM as "collectively engaging in an activity while being in autistic hyperfocus" (Hagerlid; see also Ambler et al., 2017). When we must navigate a neurotypical world in a "meat suit", fusing can come as a great relief and allows us to feel connected to our authentic selves and crave to experience more often. We note here that the portal to fusing can be sexual, but it can also be relational in other ways, through giving oneself over fully to a monotropic wave of a fascination or interest.

Connecting monotropic flow states to stimming, Hagerlid notes that "BDSM is part of how I stim and self-regulate, and my need for engaging in BDSM tends to be higher under periods of high stress". Based on their own experiences rooted in their own Autistic sensory processing style, they suggest *sensory relief* and *sensory direction*. Hagerlid builds on Pearson and Hodgetts (2023) in discussion of *sensory joy*, which they explain as "a feeling that simultaneously encompasses bliss, satisfaction, arousal, and calm." We also see reference to fusing in Jackson-Perry's chapter – with their description of the ways in which intense interests are also a form of relating functioning as a portal to a shared space of the most intimate nature.

Sharing experiences with each other

Speaking back to previous research based on parental or professional accounts of Autistic sexualities and where neurotypical people show Autistic people "how to do it", Bertilsdotter Rosqvist and Nygren point out "I don't want you to show me" and further develop what it may mean to share experiences with each other, including fusing as a sharing of sensory experiences. Informed by the film *In My Language* (2007) by Mel Baggs and the novel *A Room Called Earth* by Madeleine Ryan (2020), where the sharing of sensory experiences rather than explaining sensory experiences is central (as opposed to showing how it is to be done or defining our embodied experiences), Bertilsdotter Rosqvist and Nygren stress the importance of sharing experiences with each other, which sometimes involves fusing with the text as we read. This fusion is an invitation to a reading experience aimed at making us feel loved and desired.

This theme of connection runs through other chapters, be it in connecting with our own bodies or with others. Chapters discussing kink emphasise connection, which Goerlich (2021) highlights as an ultimate goal of BDSM/kink, by the give and take of power, authority, and sensation to achieve connection. Sensory play can result in increased bonding and connectivity.

Communicating, interconnecting our authentic bodies

Day and Krazinski discuss queering of the body and connection through ink, and ink as stories, as "connection and expression to myself". Connection and relationality do not need to be sexual, and not all kink/BDSM practices involve sexual intimacy. What is important, however, is the connection that is offered by whatever means by which the person chooses to explore their physicality (e. g., through ink or kink), perhaps particularly important in a world where Autistic people are so often misunderstood.[9] Aside from communication over kinks prior to a scene, a normalized part of aftercare within the broader BDSM culture is sharing introspection and self-reflection with regard to the contents of a scene. Aftercare opens doors for the practice of marking acts and experiences from a place of embodied knowledge outside of the reach of the neuroconventional and heteronormative narrator. Thereby, aftercare and post-scene reflection can be an empowering way to create autiqueer counternarratives of sexuality and sexual practice and form part of connection making.

Central in "connection and expression to myself" is authenticity. Johnson (2022) suggests that rather than seeking to find one authentic self that gives no space for the fluidity of becoming, the goal is to find expression that "feels better, easier, more peaceful and more aligned with other parts of the self, expression that is constantly constructed, not something pure and final" (Johnson, 2022, p. 26). This further follows the call of Jackson-Perry to "move toward the goal of a 'flourishing intimate Autistic life', with the possibilities for pleasure, safety, authenticity, and interconnectivity that this implies".

Pearson and Rose (2021) speculate that Autistic people may favor a model of identity that is more centered on core values and desires lower levels of external self-monitoring since our identities are derived from "the intersections of their values, interests, and experiences" (cf Vance, 2021). Jackson-Perry points out that this disposition by which self-expression must be in greater integrity with one's core, authentic self may inform why Autistic people are more likely to be gender nonconforming as they may be more capable in bypassing norms that do not suit them (Walsh & Jackson-Perry, 2021). This favoring of identities less aligned to neurotypical norms also can permit more constant connection to monotropic flow states (Pearson & Rose, 2021). We extrapolate this to Hagerlid's descriptions of BDSM experiences and note that access to these experiences of identity characterized by low self-monitoring and monotropic flow may be fundamentally critical to a positive sense of sexual identity for some Autistic people.

In line with this, Pliskin et al. stress the importance of bearing witness to your surroundings through mindfulness practices and how these connect to accessing pleasure and transcendent sensory states that many Autistic people describe as core aspects of their sense of self and well-being. However, Pliskin et al. note that these practices may need adaptation from ubiquitous understandings to integrate neurologies that have hyper- and hyposensitivity as part of their unique makeup. They point to the generativity produced by linking reflection on stimming and sensory experiences to mindfulness practices and further linked to the importance of bearing witness to yourself. In relation to this, Pliskin et al. discuss interoceptive differences and how for many Autistic people these become hindered via trauma and epistemic injustice. Practices for reconnection to one's body can help with enabling a very personal journey to unmasking, which can be especially scary when one has been "coerced into neurotypical standards". Likewise, they actively encourage participants to discard pieces that do not work for them, encouraging agency and understanding that impacts sexual and relational well-being.

Let's communicate: Consenting talking bodies

Hagerlid explores BDSM as a space for consent practice that aligns with Autistic communication, contrasting this to what they refer to as norms of "mute sexualities" – from which "the agreement that a sexual encounter was going to take place and what that sexual encounter would entail was to take place in a kind of idealized silent and telepathic consensus". In contrast to this, Hagerlid stresses their wish and need for "explicit communication from my partners". They experience "BDSM to be a *collaborative power play*", a "temporally constructed role play that alters normal power dynamics". Hagerlid describes a feeling of delight and affirmation in the level of communication that must take place for consent. This runs counter to many neurotypical framings and assumptions about excessive communication and negotiation before engagement "killing the mood". This narrative of delight in negotiation runs counter to much of how Autistic people are figured in cultural imagination. Often Autistic people's communication is portrayed as cumbersome (too little or too muchness) and out of step with the often-centered neurotypical person. Hagerlid's account speaks to the way communication is not at odds with sexual arousal and may, in fact, function oppositely for many Autistic people. Likewise, Jackson-Perry's participants described how direct and honest communication around sexuality, natural to many Autistic people, was often snuffed out or outright ignored in more formal settings. We ask, who benefits when Autistic people are uncritically figured as vulnerable in neurotypical imagination and instead wonder how affirming non-normative rhythms, modes, and lengths of communication might make consent (and its withdrawal or refusal) more accessible and give agency where access to consent is denied through emphasis on speech and language as the only mode of refusal, emphasizing negotiation and how given the way sensory interplay and BDSM are common interests of Autistic people? Pliskin et al. emphasize how frameworks for consent need to involve much beyond just heteronormative penetrative sex. Autistic people need tools and models for communication that are more robust, varied, and multiplicitous than the neurotypical standard. This means that contrary to the way Autistic people are often figured as needing "simplification" of sexual education, we must not draw false equivalences between need for clarity versus generalizations and simplification. Instead, to meet the needs of Autistic people, we must normalize developing more robust understandings of consent with a variety of needs, profiles acts, and settings.

"Walking with" Autistic clients

In contrast to how predominantly neuronormative society disables or restricts Autistic individuals' access to many environments or contexts, among them healthcare spaces, Stetson offers a model of an GSRD Autistic affirming healthcare space and practical steps toward creating GSRD Autistic affirming healthcare relationships through her imagined client "Finn". Stetson illustrates the importance of the clinician "walking with" their clients "as they embark on journeys of discovery and empathy regarding sexuality, gender identity, and relationship orientation, thus attending to self-awareness, emotional, cultural, social, relational, and other facets of well-being". This includes fostering "genuine curiosity and understanding of each person's goals, values, and overall health". Importantly, Stetson stresses that Autistic clients' levels of disclosure may depend on their perception of how neuroaffirming the provider is. This indicates the ways neuroaffirming and gender-/sexuality-/relationship-affirming care must go hand-in-hand in order for providers to gain a holistic sense of a client's needs.

Similarly, Pliskin et al. suggest several practices through which a neuroaffirmative sexual educator can support Autistic people. This includes bearing witness to the social system and bearing witness to learning contexts. Pliskin et al. discuss the ways in which having tools for understanding one's Autistic identity as socially positioned in conjunction with other social location can be an antidote to epistemic injustice. They describe unpacking these understandings along media representations of autism and coming to greater insights into how we understand ourselves against the larger cultural contexts that represent neurodivergence, sexuality, and gender. Pliskin et al. suggest that some of the most common mental health approaches such as cognitive behavioral therapy may be blunt instruments that assume neurotypicality, causing more harm than good. Using the double empathy problem as a lens reveals that these tools may promote masking behaviors. Pliskin et al. recontextualize the focus of emotional regulation as an "individual problem" (with an individual solution) by understandings rooted in the social model of disability. Instead of dysregulation being a medicalized problem rooted in the individual, dysregulation is a product of a dynamic environment that does not offer the accommodations Autistic people need to access states of well-being. Pliskin et al. describe the importance of building group norms that decenter neurotypicality and cultivate conditions for emotional co-regulation based on the input of the participants themselves and decoupling group norms from cultural trappings of neurotypical normalcy.

Doing things differently: Implications for practice

Several chapters discuss the important of "doing things differently" – for example, changing approaches in research and understanding gender diversity and supporting access to healthcare (Stetson; Munday). Contributors provide recommendations for practice and moving forward, whether it be in clinical practice or for research, and explore how we might find safe spaces in which to tell our stories, be that in research or clinical spaces. Pliskin et al. describe how group members reported feeling connected around topics regarding that they always felt alone, feeling more comfortable being themselves without fear of being rejected, and loosening the need to "fix" themselves. Participants found a safe space to connect with others, and we see links here to Day and Krazinski's discussion on finding connection and unmasking. Munday discusses how medical approaches both pathologise gender diversity and also creates a hierarchy of "proving" trans identity by medical transition. We see links here to Day and Krazinski's discussion of shifting embodiment as part of becoming – that is, transition from an insider view (we choose how we present our embodiment according to our own preferences) versus an outsider view (societal expectation that shifting embodiment requires medical transition). Munday also asks how we can neuroqueer research, and to center Autistic and gender-diverse voices and increasing representation and inclusion within research. Rocha and Benedetto echo Munday's call for doing research differently, suggesting community-driven approaches to understand Autistic sexuality and providing support for Autistic individuals to comprehend their bodies, needs, and boundaries and affirm them when necessary. Similarly, Toft, from his study on LGBT+ Autistic youth, stresses the importance of focusing on LGBT+ Autistic youth's own constructs of sexuality and gender. This is particularly important for LGBT+ Autistic youth who may neither conform to expectations of queerness nor expectations of ways of being Autistic. This includes ways (such as autigender and autisexual) that refer to how being Autistic can influence how gender or sexuality are experienced. Stetson highlights the impact of systemic assumptions of cisheteronormativity and neuronormativity on access and engagement with healthcare for Autistic people who have GSRD identities, both on accessing affirming care as well as practical aspects of service delivery (e.g., forms with only binary choices, binary-gendered restrooms). She stresses that we each engage with the world differently according to our own positionality, and this impacts on our interactions with it as to how we frame "healthy, safe, and normal" for each person. Stetson's chapter invites us (and healthcare providers) to question how our personal constructions and experiences will impact on our service delivery and so forth and provides practical suggestions for service providers to improve affirming care.

Looking further

Reflections on the chapters lead us to the following key points:

1. Developing a terminology that better mirror our embodied experiences.
2. The acknowledgment of the emotional and collective work it means to explore and redefine our embodied experiences.
3. The importance of politics of citation.
4. Rather than show, share experiences, explore what our bodies can do aiming at a "flourishing intimate Autistic life".

As we wrote, we reflected on how meaning is constructed in terms of our gender, our Autistic identity, our sensory sexual encounters, the meanings ascribed to our bodies, and the meaning of consent. We loop back to the "becoming" and "unlearning" as described at the start of this chapter – we continuously create and make sense of meaning. It is an unending process. Sometimes we cannot quite form the meaning, whether it be how we express our embodiment or understand our sensory sexuality, because we "cannot quite yet be the person who would be expressed through that meaning" (Stern, 2019, p. 114). What does exist, however, is the *possibility* of a meaning" (Stern, 2019, p. 114), and it is this possibility that gives us hope that will inspire further reflection in theorising, research methods, and understandings of Autistic sexualities, genders, and relationality.

Notes

1 "Gender can be fun! It can be neutral, boring, painful but also freeing, exciting, dangerous" (Johnson, 2022, p. 40).
2 "My embodiment is flamingly autistic. If you know how to recognise it, you can see it in the movements of my hands, the rhythmic rocking of my body. . . . For those who do not know how to recognise Autistic embodiment, I suppose I just come across as weird" (Walker, 2021, p. 115).
3 "It is through my body that I understand people" (Merleau-Ponty, 1945/1962, p. 186).
4 thomashenleyuk, *Stimming communication (2023)*, https://www.instagram.com/p/Cq_AeORsP_F/?img_index=1.
5 Even for those who may identify as such, the category proves to be oppressive and narrow for many Autistic people.
6 Roestone Collective (2014) points out that despite the phrase "safe space" originating with the facilitation of protective spaces for free expression among women's and LGBTQ+ groups, overuse of the term can obscure that the cultivation of such a space is "deeply relational" work in which the messiness of naming problems and harms is essential to creating safer spaces and possibilities for future ones. "Safer spaces"

signifies a commitment to a praxis that acknowledges the labor with maintaining these spaces as they evolve.

7 https://bdsmwiki.info/Drop

8 thomashenleyu (2022), *Happy meltdowns*, https://www.instagram.com/p/Cfcnixp NdXp/. Here, we seek to emphasize the need for destigmatizing meltdowns. We emphasize that we are not arguing that most meltdowns are happy meltdowns but that only the person experiencing the meltdown should identify whether it is "good" or "bad", or welcome or painful. We also present this evidence to point the reader back to always giving agency to the person to describe their own subjective experience, especially since we commonly see the other end of emotional displays misread for Autistic people, wherein there are systematic dismissals of Autistic personal accounts of suffering simply because the person appears docile or does not display distress in normative ways.

9 "When I meet someone whose body speaks my language
We notice, we click, we communicate
And in the moment that we understand each other
It feels more like dialect than deficit" (Alex, 2022).

References

Alex. (2022). Double empathy, empathy. In J. Booth, K. Fox, R. Steventon, & P. Neads (Eds.), *NeurodiVERSE* (pp. 101–103). Flapjack Press.

Ambler, J. K., Lee, E .M., Klement, K. R., Loewald, T., Comber, E. M., Hanson, S. A., Cutler, B., Cutler Tempe, N. C., & Sagarin, B. J. (2017). Consensual BDSM facilitates role specific altered states of consciousness: A preliminary study. *Psychology of Consciousness: Theory, Research, and Practice*, 4(1), 75–91. doi:10.1037/cns0000097.

Bollas, C. (1987). *The shadow of the object: Psychoanalysis of the unthought known*. Free Association Press.

Bollas, C. (2018). *The shadow of the object: Psychoanalysis of the unthought known (30th anniversary edition)*. Routledge.

Bertilsdotter Rosqvist, H., Chevalier, C., & Nygren, A. (In press). Authoring bodies: doing collective somatic knowing as a neuroqueer feminist phenomenology method. In H. Bertilsdotter Rosqvist & D. Jackson-Perry (Eds.), *The Palgrave handbook of research methods and ethics in neurodiversity studies*. Palgrave.

Bertilsdotter Rosqvist, H., Stenning, A., & Chown, N. (2020). Introduction. In H., Chown, N. Bertilsdotter Rosqvist and A. Stenning (Eds.), *Neurodiversity studies: A new critical paradigm*. Routledge.

Czyzselska, J. C. (Ed.) (2022). *Queering psychotherapy*. Karnac.

De Veen, B. (2022). Emotional diaspora. In J. C. Czyzselska (Ed.), *Queering psychotherapy* (pp. 255–272). Karnac.

Eliot, T. S. (1943). *Little Gidding in four quartets*. Harcourt, Brace.

Goerlich, S. (2021). *The leather couch: Clinical practice with kinky clients*. Routledge.

Jackson-Perry, D. (2020). The autistic art of failure? Unknowing imperfect systems of sexuality and gender. *Scandinavian Journal of Disability Research*, 22(1), 221–229. https://doi.org/10.16993/sjdr.634.

Johnson, E. J. (2022). On working with trans and gender-expansive clients. In J. C. Czyzselska (Ed.), *Queering psychotherapy* (pp. 25–42). Karnac.

Lorde, A. (2017). Poetry is not a luxury. In *Your Silence Will Not Protect You* (pp. 7–11). Silver Press.

Manning, E. (2020). *For a pragmatics of the useless*. Duke University Press.

McDermott, C. (2021). Theorising the neurotypical gaze: Autistic love and relationships in The Bridge (Bron/Broen 2011–2018). *Medical Humanities*, 48(1), 51–62. doi:10.1136/medhum-2020-011906.

Merleau-Ponty, M. (1945/1962). *The phenomenology of perception* (C. Smith, Trans.). Routledge.

Middleton, A. (2022). Queer sex and relationships. In J. C. Czyzselska (Ed.), *Queering psychotherapy* (pp. 109–126). Karnac.

Murray, D., Milton, D., Green, J., & Bervoets, J. (2023). The human spectrum: A phenomenological enquiry within neurodiversity. *Psychopathology*, 56(3), 220–230. doi:10.1159/000526213.

Murray, F. (2019). Me and monotropism: A unified theory of Autism. *Psychologist*, 32, 44–49.

Pearson, A., & Hodgetts, S. (2023). "Comforting, reassuring, and . . . hot": A qualitative exploration of engaging in bondage, discipline, domination, submission, sadism and (sado) masochism and kink from the perspective of autistic adults. *Autism in Adulthood*. Ahead of print. http://doi.org/10.1089/aut.2022.0103.

Pearson, A., & Rose, K. (2021). A conceptual analysis of autistic masking: Understanding the narrative of stigma and the illusion of choice. *Autism in Adulthood*, 3(1), 52–60. doi:10.1089/aut.2020.0043.

Roche, J. (2019). *Trans power: Own your gender*. Jessica Kinglsey.

Roestone Collective. (2014). Safe space: Towards a reconceptualization. *Antipode*, 46(5), 1346–1365. https://doi.org/10.1111/anti.12089.

Stern, D. B. (2019). *The infinity of the unsaid: Unformulated experience, language and the nonverbal*. Routledge.

Vance, T. (2021). The identity theory of autism: How autistic identity is experienced differently. October 17, 2021. http://neuroclastic.com/the-identity-theory-of-autism-how-autistic-identity-is-experienced-differently/.

Walker, N. (2021). *Neuroqueer heresies: Notes on the neurodiversity paradigm, autistic empowerment, and postnormal possibilities*. Autonomous Press.

Walsh, R., & Jackson-Perry, D. (2021). Autistic cognition and gender identity: Real struggles and imaginary deficits. In M. Kourti (Ed.), *Working with autistic transgender and non-binary people: Research, practice and experience* (pp. 49–70). Jessica Kingsley.

Yergeau, M. (2018). *Authoring autism: On rhetoric and neurological queerness*. Duke University Press.

INDEX